The Ideas
and Techniques
That Will
Make You
a Better Cook

20
RUHLMAN'S
TWENTY

MICHAEL RUHLMAN

Photographs by Donna Turner Ruhlman

CHRONICLE BOOKS
SAN FRANCISCO

Library of Congress Cataloging-in-Publication
Data available.

ISBN 978-0-8118-7643-8

Manufactured in China

Designed by **Vanessa Dina**

Food styling by **Donna Turner Ruhlman**

Typesetting by **DC Typography**

10 9 8 7 6 5 4 3 2 1

Chronicle Books LLC
680 Second Street
San Francisco, CA 94107
www.chroniclebooks.com

ACKNOWLEDGMENTS

This book is dedicated to Marlene Newell, of Oakville, Ontario, whose invaluable thoughts, organization, and apparently ceaseless, always intelligent work in the kitchen made this book possible in the short time I had to write it. I am a compulsive writer—I'm compelled to write in the way sharks are compelled to swim. Marlene runs a cooking site called CooksKorner (www.cookskorner.com) and is a compulsive cook, a good one, self-taught. What defines her is that elusive descriptor whose ultimate source is rarely known: passion. Marlene is a passionate cook. Ask any chef what they look for in a new young cook, and the answer is never a good education, pedigree, résumé, intelligence, good hands, speed. It's almost always passion. Passion cannot be taught. Everything else can.

Throughout the writing of this book, Marlene took on the responsibility of testing, retesting, commenting, and revising recipes. In more than one instance, she took a recipe that was simply not working and figured out how to fix it. She tracked every change we made in the kitchen to ensure it actually made it into the revised manuscript. When all the recipes were ready to be sent out into the world, she enlisted a small core of cooks to further test and comment, and to address issues we were uncertain about. If any of the recipes here don't work, *we know who to blame.* (Kidding, Marlene! I bow to you with deep gratitude. You've done an amazing job. I couldn't have done it without you.)

Marlene's testers, to whom I am also indebted: Barbara Laidlaw, Matthew Kayahara, Dana Noffsinger, and Kim Shook. Thank you all.

Thank you, Bill LeBlond, the editor at Chronicle Books who said, in a flash of inspiration, "Now that's a book I could really get behind," before I could blink (Wait a minute, what did I say?!).

I'm enormously grateful to Vanessa Dina, who has brought such an elegant presentation to the black-and-white paragraphs I delivered.

Judith Dunham, this book's copy editor, brought clarity where there was confusion, and accuracy to the recipes and instructions where there were faults and inconsistenies, always invisibly, leaving me to take the credit. Thank you, Judith.

I leaned on many chefs when I had questions or needed feedback on ideas in this book. I am very lucky to be able to call on them and very grateful for their friendship: Michael Pardus, Bob DelGrosso, Dave Cruz, Shuna Fish Lydon, Cory Barrett, Michael Symon, Doug Katz, and Eric Ripert.

I've learned so much from Thomas Keller—everything from details (curing salmon with citrus) to technique (cooking, puréeing, and straining vegetables for soups and sauces) to kitchen philosophy (finesse)—I scarcely know in my mind where he ends and I begin.

And last, boundless thanks to my wife, Donna Turner, for the photography that fills this book. Donna spent many years working as a newspaper and magazine photographer, with side interests in fine art but not food. She was instead forced by the circumstance of her marriage into the world of food photography and, to my delight and pride, covers it like a journalist, understanding that my interest in food photography is in conveying information, and in showing food the way it really should look in a home kitchen. I was your biggest liability, Donna, and you never let it show. For that, for everything, thank you.

INTRODUCTION

This is a book about fundamental techniques for today's kitchen. It is also a book with recipes. Foremost, it is a book about thinking about food. All cooking rests on a set of fundamental techniques. If you know those fundamentals, there's very little you won't be able to do in the kitchen. Happily, there aren't a thousand of them. There aren't even a hundred. I've created a list of the twenty basics you need to know in order to do all the rest.

The goals of *Twenty* are straightforward. 1) To identify and describe the fundamental techniques that all cooks, regardless of their skill or station, need and use. 2) To describe the techniques with the intent of getting at their nuances, how the techniques work, why they matter, the mechanisms that make them so pervasive and useful. 3) To photograph the techniques in a way that furthers an understanding of what they are and how and why they work. 4) To create recipes that showcase and provide practical applications for these far-reaching fundamentals.

When you look at the list of my techniques, you'll notice that some appear to be ingredients rather than techniques. While they are ingredients, they are also tools, and the best tools have multiple uses. Using these tools—salt, water, acid, onion, egg, butter, flour, sugar—is technique. Each of these entities has multiple uses. Understanding all the uses of a single ingredient is like pumping steroids into your cooking muscles.

Other sections are about working with fluid flavors: sauces and soups and flavorful elixirs.

The finale of the book is defined by heat: applying heat to food, knowing what kind of heat to apply to what kind of food, for how long, and then, often, removing that heat.

These twenty are my attempt to organize and describe the fundamentals of cooking for the contemporary home kitchen. They begin where cooking begins, with thinking.

THINK:
Where Cooking Begins

THINKING IN THE KITCHEN.

It's underrated. If you have a recipe, do you have to think? When you open a book that says, "Combine A and B, add C, stir, and bake for 20 minutes at 350°F/180°C," do you simply follow the instructions?

Cooking doesn't work that way. Cooking is an infinitely nuanced series of actions, the outcome of which is dependent on countless variables. What's the simplest dish you can think of? Let's say buttered toast. Can you write a perfect recipe for it? There is no exact way to convey how to make buttered toast and account for all variables. The temperature of the butter has a huge impact on the final result, as does the type of bread, how thick it's cut, and how hot your toaster gets. Because all the variables in cooking can never be accounted for, whether you're cooking from a book or cooking by instinct, it stands to reason that the most important first step in the kitchen is simply to *think*, even if all you're making is buttered toast.

Thinking in the kitchen is underrated. Thinking.

Before you begin. Stand still. Think.

It's an incredibly powerful tool—perhaps your most important tool and technique in the kitchen—but I don't hear chefs or TV cooking shows talking about it explicitly. Think about thinking for a moment. Can you prove that falling objects accelerate rather than fall at a constant speed simply by thinking about it? This took people thousands of years to realize before Galileo proved it, but we can answer the question by performing a simple thought experiment.

In your mind, hold a brick slightly above a bucket full of water and drop it. Imagine the splash. Now, in your mind, hold the brick as high as you can over the bucket. You know what's going to happen and why—you're jumping back before that brick hits the water. Why will the splash be bigger? Because the brick held from high up is traveling much faster than the brick held low. You've just suggested that falling objects accelerate rather than travel at a uniform rate, a critical rule of physics, just by thinking about it.

When you're cooking, imagine what is about to happen. Imagine what you expect something to look like. A piece of meat in a sauté pan— how seared should it look? What should the oil look like before you put the meat in the pan? If it doesn't match up with the image in your head, ask yourself why. You're told to reduce the cream by half. Imagine what the bubbles will look like when that cream has lost half its water. Think about it. If that cream boils over, as cream often does, what does that mean? Does it mean you have a mess on your stove? Yes. But more important, it means you have less cream in the pot than you may need, now that half of it is smoking on the burner. Think about what you're cooking. Stay ahead of it.

Organize and prepare. These are the two critical acts in a kitchen, and they happen by thinking first. Begin any task with these two acts— organize and prepare—and you're on your way. Ignore them and you've put yourself at risk even before you've begun. Ninety-five percent of kitchen failures can be traced back to a failure to organize and prepare at the outset.

Restaurant kitchens have a French term for organization and preparation—and it's every bit as useful in a home kitchen—*Mise en place.*

Mise en place (MEEZ ohn plahs) translates literally to "put in place," but what it really means is "organize and prepare." It means everything in its place, on your countertop, beside your stove, on your stove, and, most critically, *in your mind.*

Mise en place is a restaurant description of a cook's station and all the sixth and ninth pans filled with minced shallot and roasted peppers and green beans that have been cooked off and shocked, the trays in the lowboy cooler with the portioned beef, lamb, and pork, the bain-marie insert filled with spatula, sauce spoon, and ladle. It's a setup designed to make successful the improbable ability to cook and serve dozens and dozens of different dinners, many simultaneously, in a very short time, day after day after day. It works.

There's no reason it won't work for you in your kitchen at home. All you have to do is decide to do it. Stop and think before you begin.

The importance of *mise en place* cannot be overstated. It doesn't mean simply putting all your ingredients in ramekins on your cutting board or next to your stove (let alone, if you're following a recipe, to have read the recipe all the way through). It's ultimately about *thinking*. Organizing your *mise en place* forces you to think through your actions, to plan in your mind the course of your actions.

The second mandate in the ethos of *mise en place*, one that is rarely made explicit, is to recognize not only what you need in front of you, but also what does not belong, what should *not* be on your board, beside the stove, in your brain.

One of the keys to successful cooking is to *remove obstacles that may be in your path*. Clear your way. If cooking is an unbroken series of actions, one motion leading to another leading to another, then it should be obvious that any obstacles that might trip up those actions ought to be removed before you begin. Clear your path, and you are less likely to stumble. This means having all your ingredients before you and having the mixing bowl out so that you don't have to interrupt your cooking to hunt for it. It also means removing anything extraneous from your work area. Get rid of the shopping list, empty glass of milk, and car keys on your counter. Even if the objects are out of your way but still in your vision, remove them.

Here is a moment I will never forget. I was working the grill station in the American Bounty Restaurant—the final restaurant in the curriculum at the Culinary Institute of America—for my book *The Making of a Chef.* Chen, a fellow student, was working sauté, perhaps the busiest station on the line. And he was a mess. Onion peelings, scraps of brown towel that had been used to light burners, spilled salt and pepper, and encrusted sauce covered his work surfaces. Chen was doing 360s trying to keep up with the pace, deep in the weeds, when the chef instructor, Dan Turgeon, stepped in and stopped him. He forced Chen to stop.

"When you're in the weeds," he said to Chen, "this clutter starts to build up." He surveyed the mess on Chen's station. "If they cut you open, this is what your brain would look like."

I laughed because Turgeon stated exactly what weeds are like. When you are working hard and fast, you are thinking about what you're cooking, and you are imagining what you're cooking should look like. What happens in this busy-ness of cooking is that what you are imagining and what your eyes are actually seeing merge. When clutter is in your field of vision, it can trip up your thoughts, and you stumble mentally, slow down, and have to recover.

Chen stopped, wiped down his station, and returned to the work of cooking.

There are all kinds of home cooks—people who cook to unwind; people who cook as a hobby; people who cook because they want to feed their family healthful, tasty, economical meals; and people who cook because it's the least objectionable option in fulfilling a daily need. Regardless of what kind of cook you are, the most basic rules apply. First and foremost is that cooking is easier, faster, more efficient, more successful, and more fun when you think first, when you prepare and organize, when you set up your *mise en place*.

This is not an additional step—it's simply doing all that you would do throughout the cooking anyway. You're just doing it ahead of time, spending less time between cupboard and counter, refrigerator and stove. Be sure your counter or work area is completely clear. Go to the refrigerator, pull everything you're going to need, and set it out. Go to the cupboard, and pull everything there you'll need. Gather your tools beside your cutting board, set the pans you'll need on the stove, and get the oven hot if you're using it. Think about the sequence of your actions. And *then* begin to work, and as you work, while you're doing one thing, think about what you'll be doing next and next after that.

Clear your way. Always be thinking.

SALT:
Your Most Important Tool

I'VE SHARED THIS STORY BEFORE, BUT it bears repeating since the truth of it feels so obvious to me now. Yet it arrived like a rap on the skull with a cop's nightstick. It was winter of 1998, and I'd just begun working with Thomas Keller on *The French Laundry Cookbook*. We were talking a lot about food and cooking, and I asked what would seem to be an obvious question but is one I don't often see chefs asked: "What's the most important thing for a cook to know?"

He didn't pause long before saying, "Seasoning."

"Seasoning, meaning what?" I asked.

"Salt and pepper," he said. Then he narrowed it further. "Salt, really. How to use salt."

"How to use salt?"

"Yeah," he said. "It's the first thing we teach new cooks. How to season the food."

I'd been to culinary school, where learning to season food was talked about continually. It was one of the first things I'd learned in my first kitchen, when we were making basic soups. We were taught to taste a soup, then taste it with a little more salt to see the difference. We were also told to do the same thing with vinegar. We were taught that if you tasted the salt, it was too salty. But I was never told that using salt was the most important act in the kitchen. I'd interviewed scores of chefs, and no one had ever said the most important thing to know how to do in the kitchen is how to salt your food. And yet it's true.

I would go on eventually to write books about charcuterie and *salumi*, the craft of preserving meats, which relies heavily on salt. Salt is a fundamental ingredient in understanding the history of civilization precisely because it enabled us to preserve food, thousands of years before refrigeration and transportation made food so accessible. It allowed food to travel long distances, either as goods to trade or as sustenance for long voyages in world exploration. Salt was once more valuable than precious metals; men were paid with it. Salt is, I'm not the first to point out, the only rock we eat.

All this I would come to know, but when Keller said what he did, I felt an immediate jolt and revelation: *of course*. It made so much sense. It was always in the air, the notion of seasoning. It was the most common directive from chef to cook. When something was wrong with a dish, the most common reason was too little or too much salt. There was even a hand gesture that most people in restaurants pick up through osmosis, the gesture for seasoning: pinching all the fingers together and rotating the hand as if sprinkling salt. If you're at a restaurant that only offers salt on the table by request, catch a waiter's eye and make this gesture, and he or she will simply nod and bring you salt. How to salt food is the most important thing to know in the kitchen. And it's partly why people often find restaurant food salty. Because chefs know how important salting is and want to get the seasoning exactly right, they sometimes push it a little too far. Salt is so powerful that when you do take it too far, it can ruin the food.

Because our bodies need salt to survive, our palates have become highly attuned to salt. We like it, but we also sense when there's too much. Too much can hurt us. Now that our contemporary diet relies to such an extent on processed food, where sodium hides out in many forms, often unnoticed by our tongues, the side effects of consuming too much salt, namely hypertension, can lead to a number of serious problems and have become a national concern. There are many reasons to avoid eating processed foods—food in cans and brightly colored bags and sealed in microwave-ready plastic—and their high sodium content is one. If you don't have a pre-existing problem with high blood pressure and if you eat natural foods—foods that aren't heavily processed—you can salt your food to whatever level tastes good to you without worrying about health concerns.

The Default Salt: Coarse Kosher

Of the many different kinds of salt, the one I recommend for everyday use is coarse kosher salt, preferably Diamond Crystal, or, if that's not available, Morton's, which has an anti-caking agent.

The primary reason for using a coarse salt is that salt is best measured with your fingers and eyes, not with measuring spoons. Coarse salt is easier to hold and easier to control than fine salt. Salting is an inexact skill, meaning there is no way to describe in words how much salt to use in any given dish. Instead, it is up to the cook, a matter of taste. Also, people's salt preferences differ, given one's experience and expectations of saltiness. So always salt to taste. When a recipe for a sauce or a stew includes a precise measure of salt, a teaspoon, say, this is only a general reference, or an order of magnitude—a teaspoon, not a tablespoon. You may need to add more. How do you know? Taste the food.

Because you should salt your food throughout the cooking, it only makes practical sense that you measure with your fingers. If you have to use measuring spoons every time you add salt, you'd drive yourself crazy. And since salting is an inexact skill, it doesn't make sense in most cooking to use measuring spoons.

Learn to season by feel and by sight. It will make cooking easier. If you pay attention, you will soon learn how much a teaspoon of salt is by looking at it. Measure out a teaspoon of coarse salt, hold it in your palm, and get to know what a loose teaspoonful looks like. Try picking up as much salt as you can between four fingers and your thumb. Measure it. Pick up as much salt

between three fingers and your thumb. Measure it. Now you know how much salt you're adding and don't have to dig around for measuring spoons. As I've said before, my favorite kitchen gadgets are at the end of my arms.

It's important to use the same brand of salt; otherwise you won't be able to teach yourself how to season consistently. Diamond Crystal is flakier than Morton's. Morton's is denser, so that the same volume is saltier than Diamond Crystal; a tablespoon of Morton's weighs more. If you're used to seasoning with Diamond Crystal and you start using Morton's, you may well oversalt your food.

Again, the reason to use coarse salt is that it's easy to control. But if you feel more comfortable using-fine grain salt, there's no reason you shouldn't. I met one chef who preferred it because it dissolved more quickly in liquids than coarse salt. There are many good fine-grain salts, usually sea salts, to choose from. Fine sea salt is my preference for salting fish. Here again, use your senses. A tablespoon of fine sea salt can weigh twice as much as coarse kosher salt. That means if a recipe calls for a tablespoon of kosher salt and you use a tablespoon of fine sea salt, you will have added twice the amount of salt called for in the recipe.

Do not use iodized salt. It has a chemical taste that's not good for your food. Salt companies began adding potassium iodide to salts in the 1920s to prevent iodine deficiencies, which could lead to serious thyroid problems. This is no longer a concern in developed countries. If you eat a relatively balanced diet, you shouldn't need to worry about your thyroid, and you certainly don't want the unpleasant flavor in your food. Don't use regular, granulated table salt, for the same reason; it has additives that don't taste good.

An important note about salt in these recipes: All recipes use Morton's coarse kosher salt so that volume and weight are the same— that is, 1 tablespoon of salt is ½ ounce/15 grams.

Other Kinds of Salt

In addition to ordinary sea salt, which may contain trace mineral elements, numerous "finishing" salts are now widely available, such as *fleur de sel* (harvested in France) and Maldon salt (harvested in England), Himalayan pink salt (not to be confused with tinted curing salt), black salt from India, smoked salts, and salts infused with flavors (plum, truffle, saffron, vanilla, mushrooms). My favorites are *fleur de sel* and Maldon, which have a fresh, clean flavor and a lovely delicate crunch; they add flavor, visual appeal, and textural pleasure to foods. They tend to be expensive, so you wouldn't want to use them in cooking, only as a finishing garnish. These are a matter of taste; if you're into specialty salts, there are plenty to explore (see Sources, page 351). But garnishing salts and kosher salt for cooking should be thought of as two different entities entirely.

How To Use Salt

SALT THROUGHOUT THE COOKING PROCESS

First and foremost is salt's use in general cooking. It heightens flavors across the board, morning, noon, and night, from savory to sweet. It should be the first thing you think about once you're organized and begin cooking. I begin salting immediately. When the first onions go into the pan to sweat, I follow them with a little salt, which both seasons them and helps begin to draw out moisture and get them cooking. When the main ingredient goes into the pan, tomatoes for a sauce, say, so does a little more salt. Not too

much, but in an hour, when I taste that sauce, it's going to have a little more depth and flavor than had I not seasoned it. Sure, I could season all at once, right at the end, but the flavor will be a little different. The sauce will lack depth and balance, and may even taste salty.

Stocks, soups, sauces, and stews all benefit from early salting rather than salting at the end, which gives the salt no opportunity to distribute itself throughout the ingredients. You've got to give salt a little time to work its magic.

SALTING MEATS

One of the most powerful uses of salt is on meat. When to salt may be the most influential factor in salt's overall impact on the meat. In most cases, you can't salt meat too early. I recommend you salt your meat as soon as you bring it home from the store and then wrap it up. The salt will dissolve and penetrate the muscle so that the meat is uniformly seasoned inside and out. The old-school French guys will tell you not to salt early because doing so sucks out the juices. This is not a valid point. It's mainly water that's being drawn out, thus concentrating the meat flavor, not vitiating it. Salting early has an additional health and flavor benefit in that it inhibits spoilage bacteria. If you brought home some fresh pork chops and you salted one immediately but did not salt the other, and left them in the refrigerator for a week, the unsalted pork chop will likely have begun to develop off odors and will feel faintly slimy. The salted pork chop will escape those fates because it has, in a sense, been mildly cured, or preserved.

The thicker the cut, the earlier you need to salt it. If you're planning a very large cut, such as a rib roast, it's best to salt it a few days before cooking (and leave it uncovered in the refrigerator to dry a little and concentrate the flavors).

The only time I don't salt meat well in advance is when I want the salt to remain on the surface and help form a kind of crust. One example is a chicken to be roasted. If you salt a chicken well in advance of cooking, or if you brine a chicken, the salt will dehydrate the skin, and the skin, when roasted, will be a smooth, shiny golden brown. This is fine if that's how you like it. But I like a salty, crusty skin on a roasted bird, so I salt a chicken aggressively, using about a tablespoon of salt, just before it goes into a very hot oven.

But as a rule, you can't salt meat too early.

SALTING FISH

Fish is so delicate that big grains of coarse salt can actually "burn" the flesh. It's best to use fine sea salt for fish and to apply it just before cooking. If it's a big or whole piece, you can season it a little after it comes out of the heat. If you're poaching fish, season the poaching liquid (see pages 274–275).

SALTING VEGETABLES AND FRUITS

Salt has a powerful osmotic effect on organic material. Salt provides the mechanism for our cells to exchange nourishment, and this is how salt can penetrate to the center of a brined pork loin. The presence of salt draws water across a cell's membrane in an attempt to equalize the concentration of salt on either side of that cell. Because vegetables have such a high proportion of water, salt's impact on both flavor and texture is substantial and rapid.

Salt slices of eggplant/aubergine for a good example of salt's ability to leach water from a vegetable. This collapses the cells and reduces the eggplant's ability to absorb cooking oil, resulting in a leaner finished dish. Or transform the texture of zucchini/courgettes for a delectable bite and flavor.

To understand salt's impact on flavor, try comparing a tomato slice that has been salted for ten minutes and one that has not been salted. The difference is so powerful that you will always remember to salt tomatoes well before serving them. Also keep in mind that the juices drawn out are very flavorful and can be added to a vinaigrette or blended with butter for a sauce.

Because of salt's power over these water-heavy foods, it's important not to salt them too early or they can turn to mush. Too much water flooding from their cells will cause the vegetables to collapse and give them an unpleasant texture. They can actually become more difficult to chew than fully hydrated vegetables.

Salting fruits heightens both their flavor and their sweetness. Salting watermelon is a perfect example. Sprinkle a little salt on a slice of watermelon and taste—it's delicious. This is why melon works so well with salty ingredients such as feta cheese or prosciutto.

SALTING WATER

Consider the many recipes that say, "Bring a pot of salted water to a boil." What exactly does that mean? It's like a recipe that reads, "Get a piece of meat and give it flavor."

Here is the truth about salted water. There are two kinds: 1) water you use to cook pasta, grains, and legumes, and 2) water you use to cook green vegetables.

There was a time in my life, ages ten through thirty-three, when I would put a pinch of salt into a big pot of pasta water, believing it would actually do something. What was I *thinking*? *Was* I thinking?

It wasn't until I was in culinary skills class, having cooked pasta, oh, about a million times, that someone told me to *taste* the pasta water. It should taste nicely seasoned, my chef instructor said, and we should evaluate it as we had evaluated a clear soup's seasoning. That way, your pasta will be nicely seasoned, too.

For a big pot of water, this requires more than a pinch. I add about 2 tablespoons of salt for every 1 gallon/4 liters of water, or, to be precise, ½ ounce for every 50 fluid ounces of water, or 40 grams for 1 liter, a 1-percent salt solution. The result, whether you're cooking pasta or rice or any other grain, will be perfectly seasoned. So taste your cooking water. However salty it is, that's how salty your pasta or grain will be.

Although cooking green vegetables in mildly salty water is perfectly fine—especially for vegetables with a lot of surface area, such as broccoli, that you plan to eat straight from the pot—cooking them in heavily salted, brine-strength water results in a nicely seasoned, vividly colored vegetable. This is especially so when precooking vegetables. Most green vegetables can be cooked through, then plunged into ice water, a process called "shocking," so that they can be gently reheated later. In this case, cooking them in heavily salted water is best.

Heavily salted means roughly a scant 1 cup of salt per 1 gallon of water, or to be precise, 50 grams per 1 liter. This also happens to be a good level of salinity for brines.

SALTING FAT- OR OIL-BASED SAUCES

Salt doesn't dissolve in oil or fat. But all fat- or oil-based sauces—mayonnaise, vinaigrette, hollandaise—begin with water, so use it to dissolve the salt. When making a vinaigrette, for instance, season the vinegar first. This way the salt has a chance to dissolve. Then add the oil. This way your fat- or oil-based sauce will be uniformly seasoned.

USING SALTY INGREDIENTS

One way to salt food is to use ingredients that are very salty. This is a form of seasoning. A great example is a Caesar dressing, which is seasoned with anchovy. The anchovy adds more than salt, but it does add salt, which enhances the flavors of the dressing.

COOKING TIP: Fish Sauce Isn't Just for Thai Curries!

My first chef and now good friend, Michael Pardus, changed my seasoning life when he said, "I season macaroni and cheese with fish sauce."

It shouldn't have surprised me, but it did, and it's a good example of how we're conditioned to think inside the box. Fish sauce is Asian, so we use it in Asian preparations, not in Western cooking. The thing is, it's a really powerful seasoning device across the board, just like that anchovy in the Caesar salad. It delivers salt and the umami effect of fermented fish, which is what it's made from—one whiff and there's no doubt about that. Umami, sometimes referred to as a "fifth taste" and described as "savoriness," is achieved through a number of ingredients: salt, Parmigiano-Reggiano, mushrooms, and maybe nothing more so than fish sauce. How can something that smells nasty have such a powerfully good effect on foods? Umami. You would never want to sip this stuff straight. (Though find yourself drinking with Pardus at three A.M. and you may do a straight fish-sauce tasting of varying qualities; since quality differs, buy good-quality fish sauce at Asian markets.) But added to mac and cheese, to a salad dressing, to chicken soup, fish sauce can make all the difference.

This is something to keep in mind when you're composing dishes. If a salad or a soup or stew needs a little something, instead of reaching for the ramekin of kosher salt, think about adding something salty—nuts, olives, salty cheese such as feta or Parmigiano-Reggiano, fish sauce (often called by the Thai and Vietnamese names, *nam pla* and *nuoc nam*), or bacon.

SALTING SWEETS: BREADS, PASTRIES, AND DESSERTS

Most sweet preparations, and all flour-based ones, can be enhanced with a judicious addition of kosher salt. Salt is used pervasively in the baking and pastry kitchen, but much more judiciously. Bread without salt is insipid. Salt in a pie crust enhances the crust's flavor. Use salt to enhance flavors in cakes, cookies, custards, and creams. In sweets, you should be less aware of the salt than in a savory preparation, unless it's part of the contrast to sweetness. Some sauces, such as caramel and butterscotch, move from good to great when you get the salt level exactly right. Do taste tests and evaluate the salt level of sweet things in the same way you'd evaluate a soup or sauce.

Intensely sweet things, caramels and complex chocolates, benefit from a light garnish of salt, preferably a finishing salt such as *fleur de sel*, but coarse kosher salt works here, too. It sounds counterintuitive, but it's not when you consider the pervasiveness of putting nuts on a chocolate sundae or in brownies. These provide a nutty salty counterpoint to the sweetness.

Using Brines—Liquefied Salt

A brine is one of the most powerful tools in the kitchen. It seasons meat, inside and out; it delivers aromatic flavors (try a rosemary brine with chicken, page 307, if you doubt the power of this); and it alters the cells of the meat in a way that allows them to hold more water, resulting in a juicier finished dish.

> ### COOKING TIP:
> **To prevent salmon from extruding that unappealing white albumen as the flesh cooks, put the fish in a 5-percent brine for 10 minutes before cooking.**

Although brine is a powerful tool, it can be abused. Make the brine too strong or leave the meat in too long, and you may have an inedible piece of protein on your hands.

For an all-purpose, strong but forgiving brine, I recommend a 5-percent brine: 1 ounce of salt per 20 ounces of water, or 50 grams of salt per 1 liter of water (or, if you don't have a scale, 2 tablespoons Morton's kosher salt per 2½ cups of water). In order to dissolve this much salt, you need to heat the water. If you want to flavor your brine with aromatics, such as herbs, spices, or citrus, add them to the water before you bring it to a simmer.

It's important to let the brine cool completely before you add the meat so that you don't cook the meat. One way to shorten the cooling time is to add all the salt and aromatics to half of the water and bring it to a simmer to dissolve the salt; measure out the rest of the water cold (if you have a scale, weigh the remaining half of the water in the form of ice for brine you can use immediately). Remember that the aromatics need time, a good 30 minutes in hot water, to get their full infusion into the liquid.

The brine basics are these: Always brine meat in the refrigerator. Never reuse brine—it won't have the correct salt level and will have drawn out blood and other impurities from the meat. When possible, it's best to let meat rest after removal from the brine to allow the salt concentration to equalize.

Preserving with Salt

Historically, the most important function of salt had nothing to do with flavor. It was most important as a preservative. And in that, salt still works as it did thousands of years ago. Salting food immobilizes the bacteria that cause food to spoil and also reduces the water activity in meat that encourages the growth of bacteria. We no longer need to preserve food with salt, but we still do it because it gives us some of our most cherished foods: bacon, ham, cured salmon, for instance. And it's so easy to do. See pages 35 and 39 for recipes.

Oops! What To Do if You Go Overboard with Salt

Even if you're salting correctly, every now and then, it's going to happen. You're going to add too much and render the food unpleasant to eat, if not inedible. Regrettably, there's no quick fix, but there are ways to avoid wasting food you've oversalted. Removing salt from food you've cooked, say, a soup, sauce, or stew, is impossible, but you can add to the dish.

If you have time and ingredients, the best solution is to make a second batch of whatever you've oversalted and combine the two. If this isn't an option, adding big starchy ingredients—potatoes, rice, pasta, bread—that need a lot of salt for flavor and adding fats such as cream can dilute the salt concentration.

Above all, there's no reason to throw food away. Even if you don't have time to make a second batch, refrigerate the food until you do.

Another instance where oversalting is not uncommon is in using brines or other salt-heavy dry cures. This can be easily fixed. If you fear you've left your meat too long in the brine or in the salt, soak the meat in fresh water for as long as you overbrined it. The salt will be drawn out into the water.

If you've oversalted something that has been brined or dry cured and then cooked (bacon or ham, for instance), simmer the meat in water, then discard the water and finish cooking.

To reiterate: Salting is not something that should be done at the table, after the cooking is finished, but at the outset and then throughout the cooking. Learning how to salt—done only by teaching yourself, by thinking and tasting and comparing, and tasting some more—will do more than any other single skill to improve your cooking. Most recipes in this book call for some salt, so pay attention to how it's used. Here, I've created recipes to showcase all the powerful ways that salt works, from seasoning to preserving to altering texture.

RAW ZUCCHINI SALAD/SERVES 4

Zucchini/courgette undergoes a radical transformation when it's salted, from stiff and bland to flexible and flavorful. I learned this from my friend Michael Symon, who learned it from Jonathan Waxman, a ground-breaking American chef. Most vegetables go through changes when salted, but salting squash is one of the fastest and most visually distinctive alterations. Here, it's dressed simply with lemon juice in which shallots and garlic have been macerated, along with olive oil. For enhanced crunch, toasted nuts can be added, and for more fresh flavors, fresh soft herbs such as basil, chives, tarragon, or dill. But the vegetable is the focus: it's light and refreshing but also satisfying, making this a great vegetarian side dish, perfect for late summer and early fall when the squash are abundant.

2 zucchini/courgettes (1½ pounds/680 grams), preferably 1 green and 1 yellow, cut on the bias into slices ⅛ inch/3 mm thick, or julienned

Kosher salt

1 tablespoon minced shallot

1 garlic clove, minced

1 tablespoon lemon juice

2 tablespoons olive oil

Freshly ground black pepper

¼ cup/40 grams toasted slivered almonds or toasted roughly chopped walnuts (optional)

¼ cup/30 grams fresh soft herbs such as parsley, basil, or chives, cut into chiffonade (optional)

Put the zucchini/courgettes in a colander and sprinkle evenly with 1 teaspoon salt. Toss and sprinkle evenly with another 1 teaspoon salt (you're looking for good distribution of salt). Let stand for 10 to 20 minutes (the squash should be limp but still have some bite to them).

In a small bowl, combine the shallot, garlic, and lemon juice.

Shake the moisture off the vegetables. Taste them. If too much salt remains, rinse the squash briefly under cold water and pat dry. In a medium bowl, toss the zucchini/courgettes with the olive oil. Spoon the lemon shallot mixture over and toss some more. Season with pepper—and more salt and lemon juice if you think it needs it. Garnish with nuts and fresh herbs, if using.

SAGE-GARLIC-BRINED PORK CHOPS/SERVES 4

Pork is one of the best meats to brine because brine helps pork stay juicy. Overcooking pork is perhaps the main way people err when they prepare it; brining allows a little leeway when cooking the pork. It's also a way to infuse the meat with flavors—here shallot, lemon, pepper, and sage.

The following brine can be increased or decreased if you want to brine more or fewer chops. Just make sure that the salt level remains at 5 percent (see page 23 for the correct proportions). This brine will also work for a boneless pork loin; increase the brining time to 16 to 24 hours. To brine a tenderloin, leave the loin in the brine for about 8 hours.

BRINE

1.5 ounces kosher salt in 30 ounces of water, or 50 grams kosher salt in 1 liter of water, or 1½ tablespoons Morton's kosher salt in 3¾ cups water

1 large shallot, sliced

10 cloves garlic, smashed with the flat side of a knife

1 lemon, halved

1 packed tablespoon fresh sage leaves

2 bay leaves

1 tablespoon black peppercorns, cracked in a mortar with a pestle or on a cutting board with the bottom of a heavy pan

4 bone-in pork chops, each about 8 ounces/ 225 grams

TO MAKE THE BRINE: In a medium saucepan over high heat, combine the salt water, shallot, garlic, lemon, sage, bay leaves, and peppercorns and bring to a simmer. Remove from the heat and allow the brine to come to room temperature. Refrigerate the brine uncovered until cold.

Submerge the pork chops in the brine and refrigerate for 6 to 8 hours.

Remove the chops from the brine, discarding the brine. Rinse the chops and pat dry with paper towels/absorbent paper. Let them sit at room temperature for about 1 hour before you cook them. They can be sautéed, breaded and panfried, pan-roasted, or grilled/barbecued. I think they're best panfried. See page 305 for the panfrying technique.

Preparation photographs begin on the next page.

1/Brine *mise en place*: salt, pepper,
garlic, lemon, and sage and bay leaves

2/Pork chops submerged in the brine.

3/Standard breading procedure: flour, then egg, then bread crumbs

4/Hold the breaded chops on a rack so that the bread crumbs on
the bottom don't have a chance to become soggy.

5/To gauge if your oil is hot enough, insert a chopstick. If it bubbles immediately, the oil is ready.

6/You should have just enough oil so that it rises at least halfway up the sides of the chops when they're all in the pan.

7/Turn them carefully with a slotted spatula or fork, careful not to crack the crusty exterior.

8/Cook the chops until they're medium rare to medium (they'll continue to cook once they're out of the oil).

9/Make the butter-caper sauce while your chops rest.

10/Serve the sauce over the rested pork chop.

LEMON CONFIT/MAKES 5 CURED LEMONS

Lemon confit (kohn-FEE)—the peel of preserved lemons—is one of the most beguiling seasoning devices I've encountered. It's the kind of flavor that, if you add it to a chicken jus or gravy or a vinaigrette, people exclaim, "What is that flavor?" They can't place it, but they love it. The flavor is hard to describe—it's definitely lemony, but there's more complexity to it in addition to the lack of acidity. It's a bit of an eccentric riff on the fruit, the hipster version of lemon.

Common in North African cuisines, preserved lemons can be found at specialty stores, but they're so easy to make at home that it seems silly to spend a lot of money on them (unless you need them that day!). Lemons take about three months in salt before the transformation is complete. Lemon confit is a fantastic complement to many foods; any time that lemon juice works, confit flavors will work, too. The confit is great with fish, chicken, and veal, but also with richer meats such as pork, duck, and lamb (see Braised Lamb Shanks with Lemon Confit, page 263). It is delicious on salads, elevates most stews, and is a superb garnish for braised dishes. No matter how you use lemon confit, it can take a dish from delicious to extraordinary.

Traditionally, the lemons are packed in salt, though I add sugar to balance the salinity. When the lemons have cured, remove them from the salt, cut away the flesh as well as the pith, which will be mushy, leaving just the peel. It can be minced, chopped, sliced, or left in large pieces. If you're using the peel straight, you should give it a brief soak in water to eliminate some of the saltiness. Taste and evaluate. If you're cooking with the peel, the salt will leach into the cooking liquid.

Some cultures use the juice of preserved lemons and limes as a beverage, mixed with soda water and served over ice (in this case they're preserved whole, not halved).

Preserved lemons will keep in your pantry indefinitely, though you'll see various levels of oxidation or browning as they age. The only thing you need to be concerned about is mold; if for any reason your lemon is in contact with the air, mold can grow. I hope it's needless to say that you shouldn't eat this mold. Cut it away and discard.

Scale the following recipe up or down as needed. The only critical requirement is that the lemons remain completely submerged and that you use a nonreactive vessel in which to cure them.

2 pounds/910 grams kosher salt

1 pound/455 grams sugar

5 lemons, halved vertically

1 cup/240 milliliters water

In a large bowl, combine the salt and sugar and stir with a spoon or whisk to distribute the sugar in the salt. Put the lemons in a 2-quart/2-liter nonmetal container and pour the salt mixture over them. Jiggle and rap the container to make sure the mixture falls into all the crevices. Add the water (the moisture will help the salt stay in contact with the lemons). Cover the container and store in a cupboard or in the refrigerator for 3 months (it's a good idea to date the container or mark your calendar when they will be cured). The lemons will keep indefinitely.

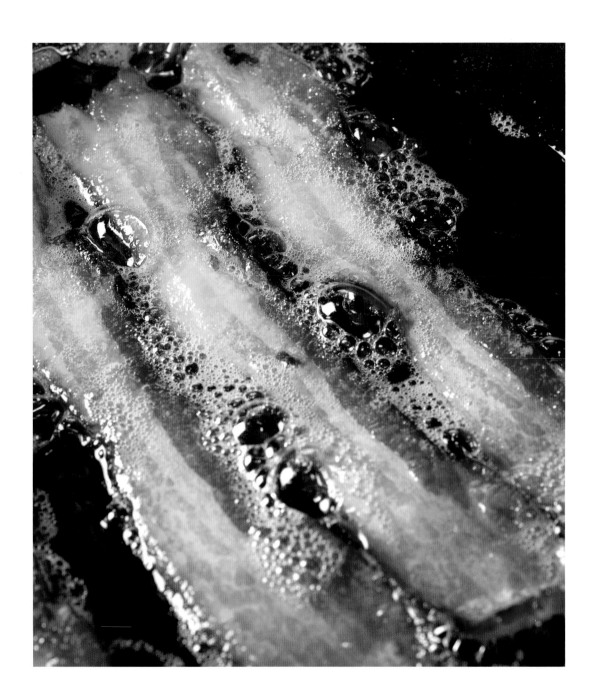

BACON AT HOME/SERVES 12 TO 16

Making your own bacon is as easy as marinating a steak. When you do, you'll find out what true bacon is all about, as opposed to the brine-pumped, water-logged versions available at the supermarket. It's about the power of salt. American bacon is traditionally smoked. If you have a conventional smoker or a stove-top smoker, by all means use this instead of your oven. In Italy, most bacon, pancetta, is not smoked, though it's often dried. But smoke is by no means the critical part of the preparation.

With most salt-cured items, it's important to balance the salt with sugar or some kind of sweetener. I like to use brown sugar, just enough for balance, not sweetness. Bacon that will be smoked benefits from sweetness, but here you want the savory notes of the garlic and herbs to come though.

Traditional bacon has a curing agent, sodium nitrite. Sodium nitrite is not a chemical additive; it's an antimicrobial agent that prevents the growth of harmful bacteria, keeps the meat rosy, and gives bacon its distinctive flavor. The vast majority of nitrite in our bodies comes from vegetables, which pick it up from the soil. In the preparation here, the sodium nitrite is optional; be forewarned, though, that if you don't use it, your bacon will be the color of a cooked pork chop, and it will have a much more porky flavor to it, more like spareribs than bacon. (For a source for sodium nitrite, see page 352.)

Pork belly takes about a week to cure and requires a two-part cooking process. First, it's slow roasted or smoked to cook it through. Then it is typically cooled, sliced and sautéed to render the fat and crisp it up.

Below are two excellent cures: one savory, more in the style of Italian pancetta, and a sweeter honey-mustard cure. I find the sweet cures to go well with traditional smoked bacon, so if you intend to smoke the bacon, use the sweet cure. Otherwise, I would use the savory cure. Both work beautifully however you want to finish your bacon.

SAVORY PEPPER BACON CURE

3 tablespoons kosher salt

1 teaspoon sodium nitrite (optional)

2 tablespoons dark brown sugar

4 garlic cloves, smashed with the flat side of a knife

1 tablespoon coarsely ground black pepper

4 bay leaves, crumbled

2 teaspoons red pepper flakes

HONEY-MUSTARD-GARLIC BACON CURE

3 tablespoons kosher salt

1 teaspoon sodium nitrite (optional)

2 tablespoons dark brown sugar

¼ cup/60 milliliters Dijon mustard

¼ cup/60 milliliters honey

8 to 10 garlic cloves, smashed with the flat side of a knife and then finely chopped

4 or 5 sprigs fresh thyme (optional)

5-pound/2.3-kilogram slab pork belly

Continued on the next page.

TO MAKE THE CURE: In a bowl, combine all the ingredients for your chosen cure.

Place the pork belly in a large resealable plastic bag, about 2½ gallons/9.5 liters, or in a nonreactive container of the same capacity. Rub the cure all over the pork. Seal the bag or cover the container and refrigerate for 7 days, occasionally rubbing the meat to redistribute the seasonings and turning the bag or the belly every other day.

Remove the meat from the cure, rinse well, and pat dry with paper towels/absorbent paper. Discard the cure. The belly can be refrigerated in a fresh plastic bag for several days until you are ready to cook it.

If roasting the pork, preheat oven to 200°F/95°C. Place the meat on a rack on a baking sheet/tray. Roast until the internal temperature reaches 150°F/65°C, about 2 hours. Begin checking the temperature after 1 hour. (If you have cured a belly that still has the skin on, slice off the skin now while the fat is hot; save it for stocks and stews such as the Winter Vegetable Garbure on page 79.)

If you have a smoker, smoke the belly with the wood of your choice at 200°F/95°C until it reaches an internal temperature of 150°F/65°C.

Let the bacon cool to room temperature. Wrap it well in plastic wrap/cling film and refrigerate until chilled. The bacon can be kept in the refrigerator for up to 2 weeks or cut into slices or chunks, wrapped well, and frozen for up to 3 months.

When ready to use the bacon, cut it into ⅛-inch/3-millimeter slices or ½-inch/12-millimeter lardons and sauté (see page 241) slowly until the fat is rendered and the bacon is crisp.

1/Give the bacon a dry rub of kosher salt, pink curing salt, sugar, and aromatics.

2/It's easiest to cure in a large resealable bag.

3/Sodium nitrite contributes bright red color and piquant flavor.

4/The top piece, with a yellow-orange cast, was smoked; the second one was roasted.

5/After roasting and cooling, slice the bacon.

CITRUS-CURED SALMON

MAKES 2 TO 2½ POUNDS/1 TO 1.25 KILOGRAMS CURED SALMON

I'm not a big fan of cooked salmon, but I adore cured salmon for its deep flavor and dense texture. It's easier to make than bacon, and salmon is easier to find than fresh pork belly! I like the freshness that citrus zest brings to the salmon, but once you've got a sense of how curing salmon works, you can add different flavors, such as fennel or dill, and change the sugar to brown sugar or honey.

Cured salmon is best sliced so thinly that it's translucent. If you find this difficult, it can be diced or finely chopped.

One side of salmon will be enough to create hors d'oeuvres for 15 to 20 people, or an appetizer or first course for 8 to 10. For an easy canapé, mix some minced red onion or Macerated Shallots (page 84) into crème fraîche, spread it on a crouton, top it with a slice of salmon, and garnish with chives or a little grated lemon zest. Of course, it's also awesome on a bagel with cream cheese.

1 cup/225 grams kosher salt

½ cup/100 grams sugar

1 tablespoon grated orange zest

1 tablespoon grated grapefruit zest

1 teaspoon grated lemon zest

1 teaspoon lime zest

One 2- to 3-pound/1- to 1.5-kilogram skin-on salmon fillet, pin bones removed and very thin pieces of flesh trimmed

In a small bowl, combine the salt and sugar and stir to distribute the sugar throughout the salt. In another small bowl, combine the citrus zests.

On a work surface, lay a sheet of aluminum foil large enough to extend beyond the length of the salmon. Spread a third of the salt mixture in the center of the foil to serve as a bed for the salmon. Place the salmon skin-side down on the salt. Distribute the citrus zest evenly across the salmon. Pour the remaining salt mixture over the salmon. It should be covered. Fold the foil up to contain the salt. Place another sheet of foil over the salmon and crimp the sheets together firmly. The idea is to have a tight package in which the salt mixture is in contact with all surfaces of the salmon.

Set the foil package on a baking sheet/tray. Set a pan or dish on top of the salmon and weight it down with a brick or a few cans. This will help press the water out of the salmon as it cures. Refrigerate the salmon for 24 hours.

Unwrap the salmon and remove it from the cure, discarding the foil and the cure. Rinse the salmon and pat dry with paper towels/absorbent paper. To remove the skin, place the salmon skin-side down on a cutting board. Holding a sharp, thin, flexible knife at about a 30-degree angle, cut between the flesh and the skin. When you can get a grip on the skin, pull it back and forth against the knife to separate it from the flesh. Set the salmon on a rack or on paper towels/absorbent paper on a tray and refrigerate for 8 to 24 hours, to allow the salt concentration to equalize and to dry the salmon further. Wrap the salmon in parchment/baking paper and store in the refrigerator for up to 2 weeks.

Preparation photographs begin on the next page.

1/A whole side of salmon, skin on, pin bones removed, will be cured with nothing more than salt, sugar, and citrus zest.

2/First, trim any very thin pieces of flesh.

3/Rest the salmon skin-side down on some of the salt-sugar mixture and cover it with citrus zest.

4/Try to disperse the zest uniformly and plentifully across the salmon.

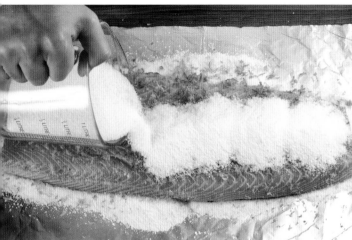

5/Pour the remaining salt-sugar mixture over the top.

6/Wrap it up in foil.

7/The salmon will release a lot of liquid, so I like to double-wrap it.

8/Tighten the foil so that the dissolved salt and sugar form a brine surrounding the salmon.

Continued on the next page.

9/Cover the salmon with a second tray and add weights, such as foil-wrapped bricks or heavy cans, to help extract water from the flesh.

10/After 24 hours, the salmon will have released plenty of liquid and will be fully cured.

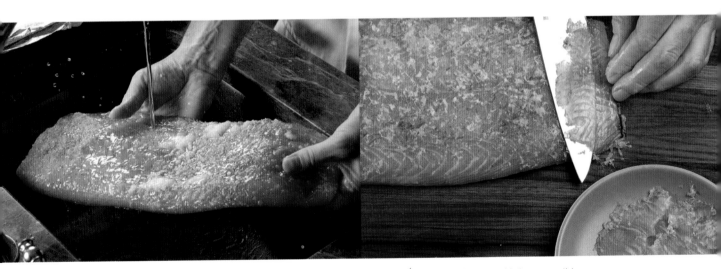

11/Rinse the salmon under cold running water to remove the cure.

12/Slice the salmon as thinly as possible.

CARAMEL SUNDAE WITH EXTRA-COARSE SALT/SERVES 4

Salt and caramel are one of those perfect pairings that are not quite intuitive. Tell a child you want to put salt on her caramel sundae, and she'll look at you as if you're either cruel or crazy. You might just as well have offered spinach. But try it, and you'll get a sense of what a powerful finishing device salt can be, offering sharp flavor and textural contrasts to the intense nutty sweetness of caramel. Salt is a critical ingredient in an excellent butterscotch and can also be added to the caramel sauce. It's also good on caramel candies or caramel chews. I like to use a coarse sea salt so that you actually get some crunch from it.

Ice cream (see page 332 if you want to make your own)

Caramel Sauce (page 180)

½ teaspoon coarse sea salt such as *fleur de sel* or Maldon salt

Divide the ice cream among 4 dishes. Pour about ¼ cup/60 milliliters of the sauce over each serving. Sprinkle with about ⅛ teaspoon salt and serve.

3

WATER:
The Unrecognized Miracle in the Kitchen

WATER IS SO UBIQUITOUS, SO PREVALENT in cooking, that many books, magazines, and newspapers don't even include it as an ingredient in recipes—"on the assumption that our readers have a ready supply," according to the *New York Times* editor Nick Fox. This assumption implies that if you didn't have unlimited water, you would be fatally handicapped in your cooking—an accurate implication. What I like about the *Times*'s assumption is that it both calls attention to and obscures the fact that water is one of the most important ingredients in the kitchen.

In its omnipresence, its seemingly unlimited nature, we tend to overlook it for what it is: a miracle ingredient we use every day. Water, like salt, is essential to the maintenance of life, and in the kitchen it is equally important as both ingredient and tool.

H_2O behaves in radically different ways from other molecules. When it freezes, for instance, it doesn't grow more compact, but becomes less so; it opens up so that it floats in liquid water. Frozen water can skip the liquid phase and move straight into the gaseous phase (this is how wet clothes hung on a line in freezing temperatures dry). You can change water's shape, but not its volume, which has a consistent weight. Water's density, its compactness—the strength of the two hydrogen atoms bonded to an oxygen atom and the intense attraction of one H_2O molecule for another—makes it an exceptionally efficient cooking medium. Water holds an extraordinary amount of thermal energy and conveys its temperature very quickly to food. You'd have to leave your hand in a 200°F/95°C oven for a long time before it became uncomfortable. Sticking your hand in the same temperature water would scald your skin in seconds.

The density of water is the reason that it is relatively slow to heat up, contains so much energy, and is also slow to cool down. This density allows fat to rise to the surface of a soup or stock and be skimmed from the top. One of water's most important attributes is that it boils at 212°F/100°C. It can exist simultaneously as liquid and solid at 32°F/0°C, which is how cold you want an ice bath, the water and ice. Add salt to such an ice-water mixture, and you lower its freezing point, making it colder and thereby allowing you to chill food very fast or to transform a custard into ice cream. When ice melts, it absorbs energy; plunge hot food into an ice bath, and that energy speeds out of the food and into the water. (Imagine plunging something hot into freezing-cold oil; it wouldn't get cold nearly as fast as if you were to plunge it into water of the same temperature.) When water turns to vapor, it takes energy with it and so cools our bodies when we sweat and cools liquids held in a porous vessel. When water condenses on a cold surface, it gives up that heat.

When water gathers enough energy, it will not be able to maintain its volume, and it jumps into vapor, which can contain even more energy than water in liquid form. Therefore, vapor, or steam, can be hotter than 212°F/100°C and make for an efficient cooking tool.

When you understand the behavior of water, you can begin to have more control over it, and having control over a ubiquitous ingredient and tool makes you a more efficient cook. To understand cooking, develop an intuitive sense of the properties of water, and identify and learn its main uses.

Three properties make water a powerhouse ingredient in the kitchen: water is extremely dense; its chemical composition—those strong hydrogen bonds—makes it good at pulling other molecules apart; as a liquid, it cannot rise above 212°F/100°C.

We use water as a cooking tool in five distinct ways:

1/As a direct cooking medium (boiling, steaming, poaching)

2/As an indirect cooking medium (water bath)

3/For cooling and freezing

4/In the form of a brine

5/As a tool for extracting flavor from food and serving as the medium for flavor

Direct Cooking

As a direct cooking medium, water has a variety of applications. We *boil* two things, green vegetables and pasta. Yes, we can and sometimes do boil lots of things, but these two categories of food require the fastest, moistest cooking. If you were to poach pasta or green vegetables, the outside would become overcooked long before the inside was done. Vegetables can be roasted, but because air is much less dense than water, roasting takes longer; it's also hotter and so has browning effects. The fast cooking of green vegetables helps you take advantage of their deep green color, which is part of their appeal.

Boiling does not involve a lot of technique, but it does involve *some* technique. The most common error people make when they boil food is using too little water. When you're in a hurry, or have a lot going on in the kitchen and are *not thinking*, it's easy to choose the wrong pot or to put too little water in it. Boiling in abundant water is the key to good boiling. The energy that water can contain, not the volume of water, is what matters. The more energy you've built up, the faster you can cook what you're boiling, and the faster it cooks, the better it is. If you put in more food than the water has energy to give it, the food poaches in water that must now gather up more energy to give to the food. Ideally, you should have so much water relative to the amount food that the water doesn't lose its boil when you put the food in it.

Thomas Keller is such a fierce advocate of this kind of boiling for green vegetables that he has instructed cooks at his French Laundry restaurant to recook an entire batch of fava/broad beans added to water that lost its boil. He wants the water to be heavily salted and at a vigorous boil (salted water can get even hotter than unsalted water). This is something to keep in mind when boiling green vegetables. If you don't have big enough pots, try to get the water temperature back up as fast as possible by covering the pot. (Be sure to remove the cover as soon as the water returns to a boil. If you don't, you can easily overcook and discolor the vegetables.)

Pasta, too, should be cooked in abundant water as quickly as possible.

We can also steam green vegetables above boiling water. Although steam can be hotter than boiling water, it is less dense; therefore, steaming can be less predictable than boiling, which is always, and infallibly, at 212°F/100°C. Steamed green vegetables and boiled green vegetables are nearly identical, but I find boiling more consistent than steaming. Doughs and some other grain preparations benefit from steam, as the intense moist heat doesn't completely saturate the product. Chinese buns and dumplings, for instance, are excellent steamed, and couscous is traditionally steamed over the stew it will accompany.

We *poach* food that benefits from moisture but does not benefit from speedy cooking or is so delicate that the high temperature or agitation of boiling water, or both, would damage the food. We poach fish, eggs, delicate mixtures of ground meat or seafood, root vegetables, and legumes. Poaching is such an important and distinctive use of water that I devote a whole chapter to it (pages 272–287).

Indirect Cooking

When we use water as an indirect cooking device, there is a barrier between the water and the food, most often some kind of vessel set into hot water. A water bath is simply a roasting pan/tray or other pan partly filled with hot water. Using a water bath takes advantage of water's capacity for gentle heating to set custards and to cook other egg-based dishes and other preparations such as a *pâté en terrine* (pah-TAY ohn teh-REEN), meat loaf in a terrine mold. Set ovenproof dishes in this water bath and their contents will cook at a temperature of 180° to 200°F/83° to 95°C. Part of the advantage of a water bath is that it is continuously evaporating; as the water becomes vapor, it takes heat away with it. So even as the water bath is heated by the oven, it is cooled by evaporation, ensuring that very moderate heat surrounds whatever you're cooking. Proof of the power of the gentleness of water-bath cooking is that a cheesecake baked in an oven typically cracks as it cools; a cheesecake cooked in a water bath in the oven typically will not.

Cooling and Freezing

The capacity of water to absorb thermal energy makes it an effective cooling device. One of the main things a cook does is control temperature, and water is a great temperature controller. Not only does it heat food to a specific temperature. It also can drop a food's temperature rapidly. We frequently need to cool food (technique #20), usually to halt its cooking. When we remove food from the heat, the latent heat within the food keeps cooking it. That's why a thermometer inserted into a roast beef or leg of lamb may initially read 130° to 140°F/54° to 60°C but will continue to rise for ten minutes or so after the meat is removed from the oven. This is also true for green beans, custards, cakes, anything that you heat.

Sometimes we want to control the heat by taking food to a certain temperature, then stopping the cooking *fast*. When green beans are exactly right—bright, bright green and completely tender—we can plunge them into ice water, which sets the color and tender texture. When we whisk a mixture of eggs, sugar, and cream over heat until it thickens to the perfect

SOUS VIDE: A New Cooking Technique

A cooking technique in its infancy (relative to other, ancient ones) uses another form of indirect water heating. *Sous vide* (soo VEED), French for "under vacuum," refers to vacuum-sealed food cooked in water held at a precise temperature. A vacuum-sealed steak can be cooked at exactly 130°F/54°C, to a perfect medium-rare, removed from the bag, and quickly seared in a pan. This method removes the guesswork from cooking. It also achieves textures that are otherwise impossible. Beef short ribs contain connective tissue that makes them tough, so they need to be cooked for a long time in a moist environment until they are so well-done they're falling-apart tender. With *sous vide*, short ribs can be cooked below 140°F/60°C for many hours, until the connective tissue has softened, and yet they remain medium-rare. Many vegetables can be cooked this way with remarkable accuracy. About the only foods that can't be cooked *sous vide* are green vegetables, which will turn an unappealing color when enclosed in a hot bag.

Sous vide cooking has always had a limited role in the kitchen, largely because the equipment—immersion circulators and high-quality vacuum sealers—has been very expensive. With the availability of affordable appliances, *sous vide* cooking may become an increasingly valuable technique in the home kitchen.

KEY TERMS

WATER BATH: To prepare a water bath, a roasting pan/tray or baking pan or even a large pot is filled with enough water to come at least two-thirds up the sides of the cooking vessel placed in the water bath. You can place the empty cooking vessel in the pan and add hot tap water until it comes two-thirds up the sides, then remove the vessel and slide the water bath into the oven to heat until you're ready to cook your food. Or you can put the filled cooking vessel into the pan, add very hot tap water, and slide the pan into a hot oven. If you are using a large roasting pan, you may have trouble moving it from counter to oven without sloshing water all over the place. If this is a concern, put the pan in the oven first, then use a pitcher or saucepan to fill the roasting pan.

ICE BATH: An ice bath is a mixture of ice and water—ice for the freezing temperature, water to ensure that whatever is put in the bath is surrounded by the uniformly freezing temperature. So that the water is as cold as possible, it's important to have the right amount of ice. An ice bath needs to contain about 50 percent water and 50 percent ice to be effective.

You can lower the temperature of an ice bath considerably by adding salt, just as you add salt to ice when making ice cream. This will make your water bath extra efficient. It is also a great way to chill a bottle of wine fast!

---

consistency, we strain the mixture into a bowl set in an ice bath to preserve the texture and prevent the eggs from cooking further.

Water is also used to freeze food. When salt is added to ice and water, the freezing point of water is lowered. Without the presence of salt, water and ice will remain at around 32°F/0°C; add abundant salt, and the temperature can drop many degrees below that. Salt (or anything dissolved in the water) inhibits the formation of ice. The salt makes it harder for the water molecules to attach to the ice because it gets in the way. Therefore, the water has to be even colder than the 32°F/0°C it needs to attach itself to the ice when there's no salt getting in its way. This is how we freeze custards into ice cream, and flavored waters and juices into sorbets and ices.

Brine

Water is an excellent carrier of salt. When water contains enough salt, it becomes a brine. A brine not only seasons food to its center; it can also make food juicier. Salt changes the cell structure, allowing the cells to take in more water. Brine also flavors food. Aromatic seasonings in a brine get carried into the meat as the salt works its osmotic wonders.

Finally, and perhaps most important of all, brine preserves food by disabling bacteria that cause spoilage. I say "most important" because brines were fundamental to the advancement of civilization, allowing explorers to travel long distances. Pork, held in a strong salt solution, would keep indefinitely. Beef could be preserved by corning it—that is, by brining it. We continue to make corned beef and pastrami, not because our survival depends on it, but because they are so delicious.

Brines are really about the salt, not about the water; the water facilitates the salt. So the brining technique is on page 23.

Flavor Extraction

Perhaps the most important and least appreciated—or least examined—way we use water is to pull flavor from other ingredients and to hold that flavor and give it shape.

When most foods are heated in water, the water takes on the flavor of the food. It's remarkable when you think about it. The same thing doesn't work with oil, or with any other non-water-based fluid. What gives water this power are those hydrogen atoms, which are so muscular in their efforts to bond, to pull things apart, to dissolve other compounds. If you pour some water over sliced onion and carrot, and heat the water, you're going to have water that's sweet and delicious from these very sweet root vegetables. Caramelize the onions deeply, pour water over them, heat the water for about 20 minutes, season with salt and pepper and a splash of sherry, and you've got a delicious onion soup. Put some onions in a pan used to roast a chicken, add scraps from the roasted chicken such as the wing tips, cook the onions a little, pour water over them, cook the water until it's gone, and then add a little more water (see page 195 for specifics), and you'll have a flavorful sauce to serve with your chicken.

Pour ingredients that are heavily water-based over food, and the flavors merge. Empty a can of whole peeled tomatoes over sautéed beef chuck, add some onion and garlic, simmer for a few hours, and you'll have an easy beef stew for serving over a thick, hearty pasta. Sauté some bacon, then sauté some chicken pieces in the bacon fat, add sliced onion and garlic, and pour half wine and half water over the ingredients and cook them! You'll have an easy coq au vin in less than an hour—thanks to water.

I've long urged people to refuse to buy manufactured broths and stocks. Home cooks do more damage to their food than good when they reach for the canned product. Granted, for some preparations, primarily soups, you need some sort of flavorful liquid. A few quarts/liters of water won't make a fulfilling chicken soup. But more often than not, you can use water along with some common vegetables, and your finished dish will be cleaner and more satisfying than if you'd reached for a can of broth. None of the main course recipes in this chapter requires homemade stock, though I give a technique for easy stock at the end of the chapter if you want to have your own on hand.

WEEKDAY COQ AU VIN/SERVES 4

Coq au vin (koke o VAHN), chicken cooked in wine, sounds like a fancy French dish but is rustic fare. Originally made with a tough old rooster, it is a dish perfectly adapted to the contemporary kitchen. This great one-pot meal uses common ingredients, and no stock is required—just water and wine.

The method for cooking this French classic varies, but I've tried to make it as efficient as possible, requiring little time at the stove. There's no reason this version can't be a staple weekday meal. The coq au vin can be prepared in an hour, but for much of that time, the chicken is in the oven. It's also a dish that can be prepared up to three days ahead, refrigerated, and finished in about five minutes. Coq au vin is nourishing and delicious on its own. It can be followed by a simple salad, and I also like to serve it with wide egg noodles or pappardelle, or roasted potatoes.

4 chicken legs

4 ounces/155 grams bacon strips, cut into ½-inch/12-millimeter pieces, or 4 ounces/ 155 grams slab bacon, cut into lardons

1 medium onion, finely diced

4 garlic cloves, smashed with the flat side of a knife

Kosher salt

3 tablespoons all-purpose/plain flour

1 carrot

8 shallots, peeled, or 8 Roasted Shallots (page 82)

2 bay leaves

½ pound/225 grams white mushrooms, quartered

1½ cups/360 milliliters red wine

2 tablespoons honey

Freshly ground black pepper

Optional garnish: chopped fresh parsley, julienned Lemon Confit (page 33), grated lemon zest, Gremolata (page 270)

Preheat the oven to 425°F/220°C/gas 7.

Place the chicken legs on a large baking sheet/tray and roast for 20 minutes. Remove from the oven and reduce the oven temperature to 325°F/165°C/gas 3.

While the chicken is roasting, put the bacon, onion, and garlic in a large ovenproof frying pan, Dutch oven, or other heavy ovenproof pot (my choice is a large cast-iron pan if you have one). The cooking vessel should be large enough to hold the chicken legs snugly in one layer. Add two three-finger pinches of salt and enough water just to cover the ingredients. Cook over high heat until the water has cooked off, about 5 minutes. Reduce the heat to medium-low and cook, stirring, until the onion has begun to caramelize, about 5 minutes more. Sprinkle the flour over the onion and bacon and stir to distribute it.

Nestle the chicken skin-side down into the onion mixture in one layer. Tuck the carrot into the pan, followed by the shallots (if using roasted shallots, reserve them until the end) and bay leaves, and then the mushrooms. (The mushrooms can rest on top if there's not enough room in the pan; they'll cook down.) Add the wine and honey and season with pepper. Add enough water to reach three-fourths of the way up the chicken. Bring to a full simmer over high heat. Slide the pan, uncovered, into the oven.

Cook the chicken for 20 minutes. Remove the pan from the oven, turn the chicken pieces skin-side up, and stir the ingredients to make sure that they cook evenly. Taste the sauce; add salt if it needs more. Continue to cook until the chicken is tender, about 20 minutes longer. Remove the pan from the oven. Just the skin side of the chicken should be above the liquid. (If using roasted shallots, add them to the pan.) If serving the chicken immediately, turn on the broiler/grill. Broil/grill

Continued on page 53.

the chicken until the skin is crisp, 3 to 4 minutes. Remove and discard the carrot and bay leaves. Serve the chicken and sauce in pasta bowls and garnish as desired.

If the chicken is not being served immediately, it can be kept on the stove top for hours, or it can be refrigerated for up to 3 days. You may want to take the opportunity to degrease the sauce. Spoon off the fat that rises to the surface, or refrigerate the chicken and remove the congealed fat before reheating the sauce. To serve it, reheat it in a 325°F/165°C/gas 3 oven for 30 minutes and broil/grill to crisp the skin.

Preparation photographs begin on the next page.

1/Buy slab bacon, or cure your own, so you can determine how to cut it.

2/Cut lardons into ½-inch/12-millimeter pieces.

3/Large lardons add heft to most meat braises and stews.

4/Moist heat renders fat and tenderizes the bacon.

5/Water helps break down the onions so they caramelize more quickly.

6/The deeper brown the onions are, the more complex the flavor of the stew.

7/Add flour to the onion mixture and cook off the raw taste.

Continued on the next page.

8/Nestle the partially roasted chicken legs into the pan in one layer.

9/Add wine, water, and aromatics.

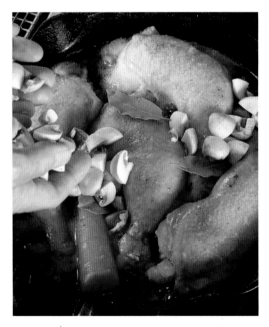

10/Bring the water and wine to a simmer, before finishing in the oven.

PAN-STEAMED SNAP PEAS/SERVES 4

Pan steaming is a kind of subtechnique of water, a unique way to cook tender vegetables. It means simply putting the vegetables and a small amount of water into a very hot pan and covering it tightly so that the pressurized steam cooks the vegetables very quickly. It should only take a minute or so.

1 pound/455 grams snap peas, stems and tough veins removed

2 tablespoons butter

Kosher salt

Put a large sauté pan or other shallow pan with a lid over high heat. Combine the peas and ½ cup/ 120 milliliters water in a bowl. When the pan is so hot that water beads on the surface, pour the peas and water into the pan. Cover it immediately and, holding the lid down tightly, shake the pan as the water steams violently. After the peas have steamed for 1 minute, reduce the heat to medium-low and remove the lid, add the butter, and season with salt. Serve immediately.

ROTISSERIE CHICKEN AND LEEK SOUP/SERVES 4

Chefs know this instinctively but have been hesitant to share it with home cooks: if you don't have homemade stock, use water rather than open a can of broth. The best chefs would never even think of using canned broth. You shouldn't either. When you cook with good ingredients, you don't need to rely on store-bought support liquids. Instead, you build the backbone of a recipe throughout the cooking. Here's a great example, using a Scottish cock-a-leekie-style soup to demonstrate water's supremacy and power.

I've been known to make a stink about how easy it is to roast a chicken. If you think ahead enough to roast a chicken (page 249), you can use that instead of the store-bought rotisserie chicken here, and your soup will be better for it. But I wanted this no-stock soup to be as easy as possible for those who might think that making stock is out of their realm or too difficult.

Cock-a-leekie soup often includes barley. Some starch can be added if you wish—barley, orzo, rice, diced potato—or, for body *and* texture, croutons or chopped toasted bread. But the soup is delicious clean and lean as is, packed with chicken and leeks. Accompany with a crusty baguette for a nourishing and satisfying meal.

1 large onion, sliced

2 carrots, sliced

4 garlic cloves, smashed with the flat side of a knife

2 bay leaves

1 tablespoon tomato paste/purée

One 3- to 4-pound/1.4- to 1.8-kilogram rotisserie chicken, meat shredded, bones and skin reserved

6 cups/1.4 liters water

Kosher salt

3 or 4 leeks

2 tablespoons butter

Freshly ground black pepper

2 tablespoons white wine vinegar, plus more as needed

Optional garnishes: grated lemon zest, chopped fresh parsley, slivers of Lemon Confit (page 33), extra-virgin olive oil, croutons

In a soup pot, combine the onion, carrots, garlic, bay leaves, and tomato paste/purée. Add the reserved chicken bones and skin and the water, which should cover the ingredients. Bring to a simmer over high heat, then reduce the heat to maintain a very low simmer. Add two three-finger pinches of salt and cook uncovered for 45 minutes to 1 hour.

Meanwhile, cut the root ends from each leek and trim the ragged ends of the leaves. Halve the leeks lengthwise and wash thoroughly under cold water, checking for dirt between the layers of leaves. Cut the leeks off where the pale green turns to dark green and add the dark green parts to the simmering pot. Cut the white and pale green parts crosswise into ½-inch/12-millimeter pieces and reserve.

In a 5-quart/4.7-liter Dutch oven or other heavy pot over medium heat, melt the butter. Add the leek pieces and cook, stirring, until heated through, about 2 minutes. Reduce the heat to low.

Strain the stock directly into the pot holding the leeks. Discard the contents of the strainer. Taste and season with salt and pepper as needed. Add the white wine vinegar; you're looking for a clean, bright, well-seasoned flavor, but you shouldn't taste the vinegar. Add the chicken meat, bring the soup to a simmer, and cook, stirring, until piping hot, 3 to 4 minutes. Garnish, if desired, and serve.

PERFECT MEAT LOAF WITH CHIPOTLE KETCHUP

SERVES 4, WITH LEFTOVERS

The French have a dish they call *pâté en terrine*—meat that is ground/minced, pressed into a terrine mold, cooked in a water bath, chilled, and then sliced and served cold. It sounds fancy but all it really is, is meat loaf. The reason it's cooked in a water bath is to ensure that the meat and fat stay uniformly suspended and that the fat doesn't separate out and float on top of what would be a dry, rubbery pâté. The same gentle cooking will result in the very best meat loaf possible: thoroughly cooked but still moist and succulent.

The meat here can be any kind, though I like the traditional mix of beef and pork. I always recommend grinding your own—you control the meat and fat and are more likely to have a safer mixture from a bacterial standpoint. But I also know that a middle-of-the-week meat loaf should be easy to make, so call your grocery store in advance and ask for the cuts I recommend here (the preground/preminced meats are almost always too lean for a juicy meat loaf).

This recipe uses the water bath method stolen from the French pâté, along with other techniques to build flavor in the meat, such as sweating onions (see page 69) and deglazing with wine. It also uses what's called a *panade* (pah-NAHD), bread soaked in milk, which adds moisture and keeps the texture from becoming too dense.

The mixture can be made up to four days ahead, wrapped, and refrigerated (the salt acts as a mild preservative). The meat loaf can be finished an hour before you need it and kept warm until you're ready to finish it. It's also delicious cold—I love meat loaf sandwiches.

If you're grinding your own meat, it's important to keep the meat very cold up until packing it in the mold. I season it ahead and chill it in the refrigerator or freezer. The meat is best if it's just on the edge of being frozen before grinding.

You'll need a terrine mold for this preparation or an 8½-by-4-inch/21.5-by-10-centimeter loaf pan.

Because you won't get any caramelization using a water bath, I like to finish a meat loaf by coating the top with the spicy ketchup and browning it under a broiler/grill. If you don't have time to make the ketchup, you can use the traditional bottled standby (it's what my kids prefer, sigh).

1 teaspoon vegetable oil

1 medium onion, finely diced

Kosher salt

¼ cup/60 milliliters Madeira wine, sherry, or red wine

2 large eggs

⅓ cup/75 milliliters milk

2 to 4 thick slices baguette or other good bread, toasted and roughly chopped

2 pounds/910 grams well-marbled beef chuck roast, diced and well chilled

½ pound/225 grams well-marbled pork shoulder, diced and well chilled

2 large garlic cloves, minced

1 teaspoon freshly ground black pepper

1½ tablespoons chopped fresh marjoram

1 tablespoon fresh thyme leaves

½ cup/120 milliliters ice-cold red wine

2 tablespoons Worcestershire sauce

Chipotle Ketchup (page 61)

Continued on the next page.

Heat a sauté pan over medium heat. Add the oil. When the oil is hot, add the onion and stir to coat with oil. Sprinkle with a three-finger pinch of salt and sauté the onion until transparent and tender, 3 to 5 minutes (reduce the heat if it appears to be burning). Raise the heat to high and add the Madeira. Let most of the wine cook off, then transfer the onion mixture to a plate and refrigerate uncovered until thoroughly chilled (or slip in the freezer if you're in a hurry).

In a medium bowl, beat the eggs with the milk. Add the bread and let it soak until thoroughly saturated and soft. (If you're not grinding your own meat, the toasted bread should be very well chopped or even pulverized in a food processor.)

If you're grinding your own meat, put both meats in a bowl and add 1 tablespoon salt and the garlic, pepper, marjoram, thyme, and saturated bread. Pass the mixture through a meat grinder fitted with a medium or small die into a large bowl (the bowl of a stand mixer works well). Add the onion mixture, red wine, and Worcestershire sauce. Using a wooden or metal spoon, mix thoroughly until the ingredients are uniformly distributed (or mix it in a stand mixer with the paddle attachment just long enough to combine all the ingredients).

Fill a terrine mold or 8½-by-4-inch/21.5-by-10-centimeter loaf pan with the meat mixture and cover with aluminum foil. If you're concerned about scratching the inside of the mold when cutting the finished meat loaf, line it with foil before filling it. The meat can be refrigerated for up to 4 days at this point.

To cook the meat loaf, preheat the oven to 300°F/150°C/gas 2.

Place the mold in a roasting pan/tray and fill the pan with enough hot tap water to come two-thirds to three-fourths up the sides of the mold. Remove the mold and place the pan in the oven. When the water bath is hot (it should be about 180°F/82°C—you can heat it quickly on the stove top if you wish), cover the mold with foil and place it in the roasting pan. Cook until an instant-read thermometer inserted into the center of the loaf reads 150°F/65°C, about 1½ hours. Remove the water bath from the oven and the mold from the water bath.

Turn on the broiler/grill. Remove the foil and coat the top with the ketchup. Broil/grill just to give the top some color. Cut into slices and serve. There will be abundant juices in the pan; spoon the juices over the meat loaf, or mix them with some of the extra ketchup to make a sauce.

Chipotle Ketchup/MAKES 2½ CUPS/600 MILLILITERS KETCHUP

2 teaspoons vegetable oil

1 large onion, thinly sliced

Kosher salt

One 28-ounce/800-gram can whole peeled tomatoes, juice reserved

5 garlic cloves

2 teaspoons ground cumin

3 chipotle chiles in adobo sauce, seeded

2 tablespoons brown sugar

2 tablespoons red wine, sherry, or cider vinegar

1 tablespoon fish sauce (see page 22)

Heat a sauté pan over medium-high heat. Add the oil. When the oil is hot, add the onion and stir to coat with oil. Sprinkle with a three-finger pinch of salt and cook, stirring occasionally, until the onion is tender and translucent, 3 to 5 minutes.

Transfer the onion to a blender and add the tomatoes and juice, garlic, cumin, chiles, brown sugar, wine, and fish sauce. Process on high speed until the mixture is smooth and uniform. Transfer to a medium saucepan. Cook the ketchup over medium-low to low heat, uncovered, stirring occasionally, until it is reduced by two-thirds and is thick and spreadable, about 3 hours. Leftover ketchup can be refrigerated for up to 1 week or frozen for up to 1 month.

PASTRAMI SHORT RIBS/SERVES 4

This preparation uses water in two ways: as a salt and flavor delivery device (brine) and as a heat delivery device (steaming). Short ribs are a great cut to use because they tend to be less expensive than the more tender cuts of beef, but with long, slow cooking, they become exquisitely tender. Moist heat is needed to turn the tough connective tissue into gelatin. Braising is the customary technique for accomplishing this. Here, the ribs are steamed.

Pastrami is typically made with the beef brisket, which is brined, given a coating of black pepper and coriander, and smoked for flavor, then steamed. The same method works beautifully with short ribs. In this preparation, the ribs are grilled to pick up that smoky flavor. If you have a stove-top smoker, that will work as well.

Like traditional bacon and corned beef, pastrami cure calls for pink salt, or sodium nitrite, a curing salt that keeps the meat a vivid red and gives it a distinctively piquant flavor (Himalayan pink salt is a different salt entirely). See page 352 for more about sodium nitrite. It's not strictly required in this preparation, but the cooked meat will have a little different flavor and will look like well-done beef, grayish rather than red.

The pastrami ribs are excellent with sautéed cabbage, sauerkraut, or roasted potatoes. You could also slice the meat and serve it with rye bread and coleslaw for a new version of the Rachel sandwich (a Reuben made with pastrami in place of corned beef).

This recipe uses bone-in short ribs but will work just as well with boneless short ribs if those are what's available to you. And it will work with a brisket if you prefer that!

BRINE
7½ cups/1.8 liters water

6 tablespoons/90 grams kosher salt

1 teaspoon pink salt (sodium nitrite)

2 tablespoons brown sugar

5 garlic cloves, smashed with the flat side of a knife

2 teaspoons black peppercorns

2 teaspoons mustard seeds

1 tablespoon coriander seeds

1 tablespoon red chile flakes

2 teaspoons allspice berries or ½ teaspoon ground allspice

1 teaspoon ground nutmeg

Two 2-inch/5-centimeter cinnamon sticks, broken into pieces, or 1 teaspoon ground cinnamon

6 bay leaves, crumbled

1 teaspoon whole cloves or ½ teaspoon ground cloves

2 teaspoons ground ginger

8 meaty bone-in short ribs

¼ cup/30 grams black peppercorns

¼ cup/20 grams coriander seeds

TO MAKE THE BRINE: Combine all the brine ingredients in a medium saucepan and bring to a simmer. Remove from the heat, allow the brine to cool to room temperature, then refrigerate until chilled.

Place the short ribs in a resealable plastic bag. Pour the brine over the ribs and seal the bag. Place the bag in a bowl and refrigerate for 5 to 7 days, lifting the bag and moving the ribs around every other day so that all are in contact with the brine.

When you're ready to cook the ribs, remove them from the brine, rinse, and pat dry with paper towels/absorbent paper. Prepare a medium-hot fire in a grill/barbecue (see technique #18, Grill). You're after the smoke here, so if you wish, have some wood chips soaking to add to the coals.

In a frying pan over medium-high heat, toast the peppercorns until fragrant, 3 to 4 minutes. Grind the peppercorns in a coffee grinder or spice mill. Repeat the process with the coriander seeds. You want a very coarse grind, not a powder. Combine the pepper and coriander and dredge the short ribs in the spices.

Ready the coals, adding wood chips if using. Arrange the short ribs on the grill rack directly over the coals, cover the grill, and cook the ribs on all sides until they have picked up plenty of smoky flavor, 20 to 30 minutes total. Remove the ribs from the grill.

The ribs can be refrigerated for up to 5 days before being steamed. If cooking them immediately, preheat the oven to 225°C/110°C/gas ¼. Put the ribs in an ovenproof pan or pot with a lid; the pan should be large enough to accommodate the ribs in a single layer. Add enough water to come 1 inch/2.5 centimeters up the sides of the ribs. Bring the water to a vigorous simmer, cover the pan, and put it in the oven. Cook until the ribs are fork tender, about 4 hours, turning them once midway through the cooking. Serve immediately.

SUBTECHNIQUE: STOCK

The purest form of using water to extract flavor from food is stock making. Pour water over meat and bones and vegetables, heat the mixture, and eventually all the flavor from the meat and vegetables and all the protein from the bones and cartilage will wind up in the water. It's simple and easy, and is probably the single most important difference between restaurant cooking and home cooking. This is often the first technique taught at culinary schools.

If it's such a game changer, why isn't it one of the main techniques here?

A few reasons. Most people don't make stocks at home and no amount of encouraging will change that. It's simpler to build the stock making right into the process of cooking. Flavor extraction is what's happening whether the chicken bones are in a big stockpot or a small braising pan. Mainly, I wanted stock making to be a subtechnique, rather than an imposing main technique, because every time we're using a water-based liquid, we're making stock. Recognizing this fact is the real game changer.

Generally, making stock gets a bad rap. People tend to talk about it with the same enthusiasm as, say, cleaning the gutters. That's wrong.

Where did we get the notion that stock making requires giant pots and huge amounts of time? It *can* be like that, and it's a great way to put a lot of stock away in the freezer to have on hand, but there's no reason you can't make small amounts of stock. The carcass of a roasted chicken makes about 4 cups/960 milliliters of an amazing stock. You don't even have to use a whole carcass, just parts. Let the water do its magic on a single piece of chicken if you want. It's beautiful.

Want to make a really good soup? In the morning, put a medium onion, a carrot, and a chicken leg in a pot, cover it with water, and put it on a back burner on low. That night, when you're making soup, just strain the liquid into your soup pot. The soup will be infinitely better than if you'd used store-bought broth.

I can't abide people who like to cook but claim they can't be bothered with making stock because it's too hard or too much of a bother. They're probably making stock all the time without realizing it.

Here are all the stock basics you need to know. Water will pull out the deliciousness of whatever you cook in it. If you put a grilled/

Continued on the next page.

barbecued steak in water, the water would eventually taste like that grilled steak. Pouring 6 cups/1.4 liters water over the carcass of a roasted chicken will give you a wonderful, versatile roasted chicken stock. Adding onion and carrot gives the stock sweetness. So does tomato paste/purée, which also deepens the color. Garlic adds more sweetness and flavor. Cracked peppercorns contribute a gentle spiciness; bay leaf adds savory depth. Parsley and thyme add floral notes. Do you have to add all this stuff? No. The chicken carcass alone would give the stock a good light flavor. Onion is an important ingredient in a stock, so at minimum, I'd use some chicken and an onion. Other than that, nothing is absolutely essential.

The time it takes for water to do its extracting depends on what you're heating. Vegetables require only an hour in the water, so it's a good idea to add them at the end of a long-cooked meat stock. Bones give up their connective tissue, which becomes gelatin, the protein that gives a stock body; this takes a lot more time. Light, porous poultry bones can be done in a few hours, whereas heavier beef and veal bones benefit from eight or more hours to ensure you've captured as much gelatin as possible.

The other critical factor is how much heat you bring to the stock. If a stock is hot enough to simmer, fat will emulsify into the water, and the stock will be cloudy and have a cloudy flavor. In addition, the agitation of the water will break apart the vegetables. They'll fragment, and you'll lose the stock that these fragments have absorbed when you strain them out. The best stock results when the water is below simmering but still hot, 170° to 180°F/77° to 82°C. My favorite way to cook stock is to put the uncovered pot into a low oven (180° to 200°F/82° to 95°C). It stays hot, but the cooling effect of evaporation prevents the stock from getting too hot. The stock also stays out of the way.

When the stock is done, strain it and use it right away or put it in the refrigerator. I like to strain stock through cloth to remove all the fine particles. Skim the fat off the top of the stock, or chill it and remove the congealed fat. (You can use cheesecloth/muslin for straining the stock, but I keep four or five All-Strain cloths, which are better and less expensive; see Sources, page 352.)

Here's how easy stock can be if ease is what you're looking for. Put a chicken carcass and an onion in a pot, cover it with about 1 inch/2.5 centimeters of water, and cook in a low oven for 3 to 12 hours. Actual work time? Three minutes. So I simply don't believe people who say they don't have time to make stock.

STOCK BASICS

- Meat gives stock flavor.
- Bones and cartilage provide body.
- Vegetables add sweetness.
- Various other ingredients (garlic, tomato, herbs, peppercorns) contribute good flavors, adding to the stock's complexity.
- Red meats and bones are best blanched or roasted before using them to make stock.
- Skim any froth or foam that rises to the surface when you first bring the water up to heat.
- Cook meat and bones in hot but not visibly simmering water, about 180°F/82°C, for hours. (The surface of the water should be still, but the pot should be too hot to hold your hand to.)
- Add vegetables and herbs at the end (they need to be in the water for only an hour or so).
- Strain the stock through a kitchen cloth for the cleanest finished stock.
- Chill the stock, then remove the congealed fat from the surface.

EASY CHICKEN STOCK/MAKES ABOUT **4 CUPS/960 MILLILITERS** STOCK

Rather than make the stock with the carcass of a roasted chicken, you can follow this same method using a whole cooked chicken or roasted whole pieces. But the most efficient and economical way to make a small quantity of stock is to use left-overs from another meal. If you roast a chicken, your main ingredient is already prepared. Just add an onion, get water hot for a couple hours, and you've got delicious stock.

1 roasted chicken carcass (and any leftover pieces or bones that have not been dispatched)

1 large onion

2 carrots

2 bay leaves

1 teaspoon black peppercorns

1 tablespoon tomato paste/purée

Optional additions: a few garlic cloves, sprigs of fresh parsley and thyme

Break the chicken carcass into pieces. Put the chicken and any leftovers in a 3-quart/2.8-liter ovenproof saucepan and add water to cover. You will need about 6 cups/1.4 liters.

If cooking the stock on the stove top, put the pan, uncovered, on a back burner on low for a few hours. The surface of the water should be still, but the pot should be too hot to hold your hand to.

If cooking the stock in the oven, put the pan, uncovered, in an oven preheated to 180° to 200°F/82° to 95°C and cook for at least 4 hours or as long as 12 hours. (I simply put the pan in the oven and cook the stock overnight.)

Add the remaining ingredients, bring the stock back to temperature over high heat, then reduce the heat to low or return the pan to the oven. Cook for 1 hour longer.

Strain the stock through a fine-mesh strainer or, better still, through cheesecloth/muslin or a kitchen cloth. Store in the refrigerator for up to 1 week or in the freezer for up to 3 months.

ONION:
The Chef's Secret Weapon

IF ONIONS WERE AS RARE AS TRUFFLES, chefs would pay dearly for them. The onion is among the most powerful flavoring devices in the kitchen and works in numerous ways. But because onions are abundant and cheap, they, like salt and water, tend to be overlooked for what they are: a miracle ingredient that transforms food in many ways, in nearly every style of cuisine around the globe. I buy onions every time I'm in the grocery store, not because I need them, but because I fear not having an onion when I do need it. Not having an onion in the kitchen is like working with a missing limb.

To harness the power of the onion, the first thing to recognize is that onions are not a one-note ingredient like, say, lemon juice. Lemon juice is lemon juice. Add more, or add less, and it's always lemon juice. Onion has a volume knob controlled by how much heat you bring to it, and for how long, before you add the other ingredients it will support. Used raw, onions have one effect on a soup or sauce or stock; lightly cooked but not browned, another effect; cooked for a long time but still without color, still another effect; taken further and browned, still another. Poach onions, and they're different again. Roast them, and they're a unique preparation. Macerate onions in vinegar, and you have yet another effect.

Onions add both sweetness and savoriness—that meaty umami effect that we recognize as a satisfying depth of flavor—in varying degrees depending on how you heat them.

Yes, as an ingredient, the onion is a star. I love a stew with large chunks of onion, or whole small onions cooked until tender. Onion rings are one of my very favorite things to eat, period. A grilled/barbecued onion is fantastic on a burger or steak. But onions are even more valuable when used as a tool, the unseen mechanism that makes so many dishes satisfying. The name derives from the Latin *unio*: "one, oneness, unity." The impact of onions on food is unlikely the reason for the name, but they do seem to have a unifying effect on a dish, serving as a kind of net that connects and unifies the many flavors in a finished preparation.

In terms of onion as tool/technique, there are three main subjects to recognize: the workhorse onion itself, sweating, and caramelizing.

The Onion Itself

The basic white and yellow storage onion is your workhorse onion, the onion you should always have on hand. When you shop, you should look at the quality of the onion rather than seek out a specific type. Spanish onions, yellow onions, white onions, and even red onions all work the same. Look for firm bulbs with a tight dry skin. I prefer them big, so I usually choose Spanish. Big onions are more efficient—I spend less time peeling. If I need half an onion, the other half can be wrapped and stored in the refrigerator.

Onions are harsh because they pick up sulfur from the soil and store it. In nature this serves as a protective device, and this is what's responsible for the sting in your eyes when you're cutting a lot of onions. The sulfur compounds break down into hydrogen sulfide, sulfur dioxide, and sulfuric acid. Happily, the sulfur products are volatile and dissipate quickly in heat or acid before they reach our mouths. (When serving onions raw, it's a good idea to rinse or even soak them.)

The so-called sweet onions are grown in soil that doesn't have a lot of sulfur and so are less harsh. You can cook with these onions, but once they're heated, they behave exactly like regular onions, so it doesn't make sense to cook with them if they're more expensive than white or Spanish onions.

Sweating

This is such an important technique in the kitchen that it almost deserves its own chapter, but because onions are what cooks typically sweat, by themselves or with other ingredients, sweating is a subtechnique of the onion.

Sweating means to gently heat the onion (or any vegetable) in a small amount of oil or butter without browning it. It's called sweating because that's what the onion appears to be doing; the heat forces water to the surface of the onion in little beads. As the onion loses water, its flavors begin to concentrate, and the heat transforms the sugars into increasingly complex and delicious compounds. If you want to taste the difference, simmer some raw onion in a small amount of water for ten minutes, and do the same with some onion that has been sweated first. The water with the sweated onions will be distinctly sweeter. Sometimes you want that raw effect. I prefer raw onions in most stocks, rather than cooked onions, because the finished stock can become too sweet, especially if you reduce it and concentrate the sugars. For the vast majority of preparations, we want to heat the onions first, and sweating is the most common of these steps.

There are a few critical things to understand about sweating. By far the most important is that the longer you sweat onions, the sweeter and more complex their flavor becomes. This is the volume knob effect. Sweat them for a few minutes, just until they're translucent and softened, and they have one flavor. Sweated for two hours, without color, they are deeper, richer, and sweeter. The "without color" part is important. Once they've lost enough water and get hot enough to begin to brown, the flavor becomes radically different from that of sweated onions. This entirely different preparation is called caramelizing.

Mediterranean cuisines have their own cooking term for sweating. In Italy, it's called *soffrito* (soh-FREE-toh), literally "sub- or under-frying." It's often done in conjunction with other ingredients—pancetta, garlic, carrots, tomato—and is often taken to the point that the onion becomes golden or caramelized, depending on the dish. Creating the *soffrito* is considered the mandatory first step for most soups, sauces, and risottos. This is because gentle gradual heating, primarily of onions, has such a powerful impact on a finished dish.

Any home cook can elevate his or her cooking by a giant leap simply by cooking the onions a little more softly for a little more time. See especially the Winter Vegetable Garbure (page 79), which cooks the onions this way below a sheet of bacon rind. This flavors the stew and keeps the onion moist so that it doesn't brown. I picked up this excellent technique from Dave Cruz, chef de cuisine of Ad Hoc in Yountville, California.

Again, sweating onion for hours is not necessarily what you want to do all the time. But it's important to recognize the impact sweating has and to evaluate what effect you're looking for. Perhaps it's onion gently sweated for a stock or a meat loaf so that it retains some bite, or long-sweated onion as the base for a vegetable stew. Think about it. Make a plan based on what you want. And use the onion to help you get there.

Caramelizing

When we increase the heat and cook most of the water out of the onions, they will brown. We call this caramelizing. The heat causes the proteins to release amino acids, which react with the sugars to create a flavor at once sweet, savory, and nutty. This is one of the most extraordinary reactions in the kitchen, so much so that a well-known dish features caramelizing: French onion soup.

Continued on page 72.

1/To slice onions, first knock out the core.

2/If you don't remove the core, your onions will remain attached at the root end. Leave the root when dicing an onion.

3/Cut from the outside, angling toward the center.

4/Your onions should be sliced into a similar size and shape so they caramelize evenly.

5/Onions caramelize nicely in an
enameled, cast-iron pot.

6/Onions are 95 percent water and will
release liquid as they cook.

7/Onions can't brown until their water
cooks off.

8/Do not rush onions after browning
has begun.

If you heed the lesson of caramelized onions in no-stock onion soup, you realize their power to transform all kinds of soups and stews. In the easy coq au vin (see page 51), the chicken is not cooking only in water. You're making caramelized onion and chicken stock. Caramelizing onions before you add the water to any soup or stock will contribute that intense sweetness.

The key to caramelization is time. You can't caramelize onions quickly. Breaking down the components that make the onion so remarkable takes time. The onions need to cook in stages, and if you try to use too much heat, some of the onions will burn before the other onions are even brown. However, you can hurry them along by covering the pot when you first begin to cook the onions so that they steam and get hot all the way through more quickly than they would in an uncovered pot. You can also cover the onions in water with a little added butter and boil them until the water cooks off. This quickly extracts sugars and begins breaking down the onions. But in the end, onions need time to caramelize properly.

Happily, onions can cook for a long time, completely neglected, if the temperature is low enough, and you can take them off the heat and finish them later. It's simply a matter of planning ahead. You can caramelize small batches of onions fairly quickly if you pay attention to the pan, but larger batches need time to caramelize evenly.

A heavy-gauge pot or pan—one that holds and distributes heat evenly—is a big asset. My favorite type of pan for caramelizing onions is an enameled cast-iron pan. It is heavy, and foods resist sticking so that the caramelization remains on the onions rather than on the surface of the pan.

To caramelize onions, peel and slice them as thinly as possible. Heat a little butter or canola oil in a heavy pot or pan, add the onions, and cook slowly over low heat, stirring occasionally.

First they will sweat, then they will drop a lot of water so that they're virtually stewing in onion water. The water will eventually cook off, and the onions will continue to break down and become brown. Onions are about 95 percent water, so a big pot of onions will cook down to very little, but they will be highly concentrated, and that's a good thing.

While there are infinite gradations of caramelization, practically speaking, the gradations break down into two types: lightly caramelized—when the onions are browned but still retain some of their shape—and heavily caramelized—when a big batch of onions is reduced to what appears to be nearly a darkish brown paste. How much you caramelize your onions depends how you want your finished dish to taste. Think about it.

The Amazing Shallot

There are many other kinds of onions beyond the storage onion. Most are grown for their bulbs. Some, like the leek, one of my favorite ingredients, grow leaves rather than bulbs. I also like onions that are cooked and served whole, such as shallots and pearl onions, as well as chives, ramps, and other onions that grow wild. All are wonderful ingredients, but one—the shallot—deserves special attention for its versatility and power in the kitchen.

The shallot is by far the most valuable and useful onion after the storage onion. It's the kind of ingredient that can bring the home cook to a new level of achievement. The shallot concentrates the best qualities of the onion, without the harshness. Raw shallots are sharp, but they are quickly and easily tamed.

The shallot works just like the storage onion but has a sharper flavor when raw and a greater oniony sweetness and flavor after it has been cooked or macerated in acid. Shallots give you double the benefits of the storage onion. Minced and mixed with some vinegar or lemon juice, they make an extraordinary garnish in vinaigrettes and mayonnaise or can be sprinkled on cooked vegetables. They can be sweated and added to the same preparations. Sweated, they are a great way to begin almost any kind of savory sauce. Add them raw to mushrooms you're sautéing and they will light up those mushrooms. Caramelized, they add intense flavors to sauces, soups, and stews. Used whole, they are a great component in stews. I like to caramelize them whole by roasting them. Then I add them to braised dishes at the end (such as the Coq au Vin).

TRADITIONAL FRENCH ONION SOUP/SERVES 4 TO 6

The power of water joins the power of onion in what may be one of the best soups in the Western canon. The soup deserves this high praise not only because it's delicious and satisfying, but because it was borne out of economy. This is a peasant soup, made from onions, a scrap of old bread, some grated cheese, and water. Season with salt and whatever wine is on hand or some vinegar. Do not be tempted to use stock! Even if it's really good homemade stock, it will detract from the economy of the dish, which can easily become too heavy and cloying. (And please don't add the canned stuff. How many onion soups have been trashed by adding store-bought broth? A fair share in my kitchen until I learned how to use water.)

I've never seen a recipe for onion soup that didn't use stock or broth, and yet this changes the soup completely—it becomes beef-onion soup or chicken-onion soup. I could not find a historical basis for my conviction until I began researching a specific style of bistro in Lyon, France, called a *bouchon* (boo-SHOHN). There are only about twenty of these restaurants in Lyon, and they serve a very distinct, country-style, family-meal menu. At some, you sit at communal tables, and platters are passed from table to table. What I like about *bouchons* is that they serve elemental, efficient food. It had to be, as a husband and wife usually worked the place. I spoke with a journalist in Lyon, an expert on the subject of *la vrai bouchon*, "the true bouchon," who confirmed what I'd always suspected. At a *bouchon*, and indeed at most peasant households, a time-consuming and costly stock would not be used for onion soup. Onions and a splash of wine for seasoning and a crust of bread with some cheese melted on it— that is all you need to make a very fine soup with a pure caramelized onion flavor.

Plan ahead when making the soup because the onions take a long time to cook down, from a few hours to as many as five if you keep the heat very low, though you need to pay attention only at the beginning and the end. Before the onions caramelize, they'll release copious amounts of water (be sure to taste this liquid!), which must cook off first. You can simmer the onions hard if you want to reduce the cooking time; be sure to tend the pot and stir often, or the onions can stick and burn. You can also caramelize the onions a day or two in advance, and refrigerate them until needed. If you do this, the final soup can be finished in the time it takes to heat the water and melt the cheese on top.

1 tablespoon butter

7 or 8 Spanish onions (7 to 8 pounds/3.2 to 3.6 kilograms), thinly sliced

Kosher salt

Freshly ground black pepper

6 to 12 slices of baguette or any country-style bread (it's best if they cover the width of your serving bowls)

⅓ cup/75 milliliters sherry

Red or white wine vinegar (optional)

Red wine (optional)

½ to ¾ pound/225 to 340 grams Gruyère or Emmenthaler cheese, grated

Continued on next page.

Use a large pot, with a capacity of about 7½ quarts/7.1 liters, that will hold all the onions. An enameled cast-iron pot will provide the best surface. Place the pot over medium heat and melt the butter. Add the onions, sprinkle with 2 teaspoons salt, cover, and cook until the onions have heated through and started to steam. Uncover, reduce the heat to low, and cook, stirring occasionally (you should be able to leave the onions alone for an hour at a stretch once they've released their water). Season with several grinds of pepper.

Preheat the oven to 200°F/95°C. Place the bread slices in the oven and let dry completely (you can leave the slices in the oven indefinitely, as the heat is not high enough to burn them).

When the onions have completely cooked down, the water has cooked off, and the onions have turned amber—this will take several hours—add 6 cups/1.4 liters of water. Raise the heat to high and bring the soup to a simmer, then reduce the heat to low. Add the sherry. Taste and season with salt and pepper as needed. If the soup is too sweet, add some vinegar. If you would like a little more depth, add a splash of red wine. I like the onion-to-liquid ratio with 6 cups of water. But if you'd prefer a little more delicate soup, add 1 cup/240 milliliters water.

Preheat the broiler/grill. Portion the soup into ovenproof bowls, float the bread on top, cover with the cheese, and broil/grill until the cheese is melted and nicely browned. Serve immediately.

1/Properly browned onions should be uniformly brown.

2/Once your onions are brown, add water to extract the flavor.

3/Cheese will cover the bowls uniformly if grated, not sliced.

4/Ladle hot soup into bowls before covering with bread and cheese.

5/Onion soup should be so thick with onions that the croutons rest on top.

6/Serving in small bowls covered with cheese makes for a nice presentation.

WINTER VEGETABLE GARBURE/SERVES 6

Garbure (gar-BYR) is a soup packed with ingredients so that it's almost a stew. It typically includes cabbage, bacon, and some form of preserved goose. The version here uses only winter vegetables. The hearty soup gets its seasoning and great body from bacon rind and its depth of flavor from sweating the garlic and onions beneath the rind.

2 leeks

2 tablespoons butter

1 large onion, cut into medium dice

2 to 4 shallots, sliced

4 to 6 garlic cloves, roughly chopped

Kosher salt

1 piece bacon rind large enough to cover the bottom of the pan (about 8 inches/ 20 centimeters across)

8 cups/2 liters water

4 celery stalks; 2 whole, 2 cut into bite-size pieces

4 carrots; 2 whole, 2 peeled and cut into bite-size pieces

2 bay leaves

2 tablespoons tomato paste/purée

2 potatoes (about 1 pound/455 grams), peeled and cut into bite-size pieces

⅛ teaspoon cayenne pepper

1 pound/455 grams white cabbage, cut into bite-size pieces

1 teaspoon fish sauce (optional but advised)

About 1½ tablespoons red wine vinegar or sherry vinegar

2 tablespoons finely sliced fresh chives

Cut the root end from each leek and trim the ragged ends of the leaves. Halve the leeks lengthwise and wash thoroughly under cold water, checking for dirt between the layers of leaves. Cut the leeks off where the pale green turns to dark green. Cut the white and pale green parts crosswise into ½-inch/12-millimeter slices. Tie the green leaves together with butcher's twine.

In a Dutch oven or other heavy pot over medium heat, melt the butter. Add the sliced leeks, onion, shallots, and garlic, and cook, stirring occasionally, until softened, about 5 minutes. As the vegetables cook, season them with a couple of three-finger pinches of salt (1 teaspoon). Reduce the heat to low or medium-low, lay the bacon rind over the vegetables, and continue to cook for about 1 hour. Lift the bacon rind about midway through and stir the vegetables. After 1 hour, the vegetables should be very soft but still pale in color, not browned.

Add the water and bound leek tops, whole celery stalks, whole carrots, bay leaves, and tomato paste/purée. Raise the heat to high and bring to a gentle simmer, then reduce the heat to low and cook for about 1 hour.

Remove the leek tops, celery, carrots, and bay leaves from the pot and discard. Remove the bacon rind (it can be scraped of excess fat and reserved, then cut into strips and fried as cracklings). Taste the broth and season with salt as needed. Add the potatoes, raise the heat to medium and simmer for 10 minutes. Stir in the cayenne. Add the cut celery, cut carrots, and cabbage, return the soup to a simmer, and cook until the vegetables are cooked through, about 10 minutes longer. Season with the fish sauce (if using) and the vinegar. Stir the soup, taste, and adjust the seasoning. Serve garnished with the chives.

GREEN BEAN, CORN, AND ONION SALAD WITH ROASTED SHALLOT VINAIGRETTE/SERVES 4

I like salads of cold, cooked vegetables with a tasty vinaigrette—they're satisfying and nourishing and can act as a main course or a side. Here, green beans are the base to showcase other, sweeter vegetables. The sweetness of the onion, its sharpness tempered by blanching, holds all the flavors together. You almost can't go wrong with any combination of sweet vegetables offset by a simple vinaigrette. The salad shows how the plain onion can be handled in different ways, blanching for the salad and roasting for the vinaigrette. Understanding how the onion works gives you great versatility in the kitchen.

The salad is seasoned with Espellete (es-pe-LETTE), a red chile pepper named for the French commune in the southwestern tip of France, near the Spanish border, where the pepper is grown. Like cayenne pepper, it's dried and ground to a powder and used as a seasoning. It's not as hot as cayenne and has a fruitier flavor. Espellete is available in specialty stores, but if you can't find it, you can substitute cayenne pepper.

Kosher salt

1 large onion, thinly sliced

1 pound/455 grams green beans, stem ends picked off

2 Roasted Shallots (page 82)

2 ears of corn

¼ cup/60 milliliters good red wine vinegar or sherry vinegar, or as needed

Freshly ground black pepper

½ cup/120 milliliters canola oil, or as needed

Espellete powder or cayenne pepper (optional)

Lemon Confit (page 33), julienned (optional)

Bring a large pot of water, salted for green vegetables (see page 21), to a boil. (You'll boil the onions first, the green beans second, and then the corn, all in the same pot of water, so you'll need a strainer or spider to remove the onion.)

Boil the onion for 1 minute. Using the strainer, transfer the onion slices to an ice bath (see page 49) and chill for about 2 minutes. Remove the onion slices to a paper towel–/absorbent paper–lined bowl. Boil the green beans until tender, about 5 minutes. Transfer them to the ice bath and chill for 3 to 4 minutes. Remove the beans to a paper-lined bowl. Boil the corn for 2 minutes, then immerse the ears in the ice bath until completely chilled, about 5 minutes. Add more ice cubes to the ice bath as needed.

In a blender, combine the shallots, the ¼ cup vinegar, a three-finger pinch of salt, and several grinds of black pepper. Process briefly, then, with the motor running, add the ½ cup oil in a thin stream. Taste the vinaigrette. If it is too sharp, blend in a little more oil. If it's too sweet, add a little more vinegar.

Cut the corn off the cob, cutting deeply enough against the cob so that the corn comes off in planks.

Remove the paper from the bowl of the green beans. Toss the green beans with half of the vinaigrette. Taste and season with salt and pepper if desired. Arrange the green beans on a serving platter or on individual plates, scatter the onions over the beans, and drizzle with the remaining vinaigrette. Top with the planks of corn and scatter any remaining kernels around the periphery of the salad. Season with Espellete or Lemon Confit, if desired, and/or black pepper.

ROASTED SHALLOTS/MAKES 1 ROASTED SHALLOT PER SHALLOT

Roasting shallots makes them very soft and very sweet. They make a fantastic garnish and ingredient. Add them to soups, stews, or sauces, or purée them in vinaigrettes. Serve them whole alongside roast beef, pork, or chicken, or chop them to a paste and heat them with a little water and butter, seasoned with vinegar, for a quick pan sauce. They couldn't be easier to prepare.

Shallots, unpeeled, roots cut off

Butter or canola or olive oil

Kosher salt

Freshly ground black pepper

Preheat the oven to 400°F/200°C/gas 6.

Put the shallots on a piece of aluminum foil large enough to enclose them or in a cast-iron pan. For each shallot, add about 1 teaspoon of butter. Sprinkle with salt and a few grinds of pepper. If using foil fold it around the shallots and seal tightly.

Roast until the shallots are completely soft and a knife can be inserted without resistance, about 1 hour. When the shallots are cool enough to handle, remove the skins. Store in the refrigerator for up to 3 days.

1/Shallots can be roasted enclosed in foil or rubbed with oil and placed in a pan.

2/Roast the shallots in a hot oven until they give no resistance to the tip of a paring knife.

3/Let the shallots cool, then peel them.

MACERATED SHALLOTS/MAKES ABOUT 2 TABLESPOONS

One of the most powerful ways to use raw shallot is to macerate it in an acid—here, lemon juice or vinegar—then add it to any sauce or vinaigrette. The acid neutralizes all the harshness in the shallot, without changing its texture; it also infuses the shallot with its flavor. With the addition of 1 tablespoon of these shallots, ½ cup/120 milliliters mayonnaise is transformed into an ethereal dipping sauce for cooked vegetables. Add the shallots to the same amount of crème fraîche or mascarpone, and these creamy dairy concentrations take on a new dimension, perfect for serving with cured salmon (see page 39) on a crouton. A simple combination of sherry vinegar and oil becomes an exquisite vinaigrette to use on a range of vegetables, from lettuce to cooked and cooled green beans or new potatoes. Learn to use the shallot, and your cooking will take a step up. Choose the acid that best complements the food: lemon if adding the shallot to a mayonnaise, lime juice if using in guacamole, vinegar if making a salad dressing.

These are best if macerated just before use.

1 shallot, peeled and minced

Lemon or lime juice or red wine vinegar, white wine vinegar, or sherry vinegar

Put the minced shallot in a small bowl. Add enough lemon juice or vinegar to cover the shallot. Let stand until the harshness of the shallot has completely dissipated, 10 to 15 minutes. Add the shallot to your sauce, either drained of the juice or vinegar, or with it, depending on how sharp you want the finished sauce or vinaigrette to be.

LEMON-SHALLOT MAYONNAISE OR CRÈME FRAÎCHE

MAKES 1 CUP/240 MILLILITERS MAYONNAISE OR CRÈME FRAÎCHE

My favorite dipping sauce for cooked and chilled vegetables is a homemade mayonnaise with lots of shallot macerated in lemon juice—exquisite with asparagus, beans, or an artichoke. The crème fraîche with shallot is a wonderful pairing for cured salmon (see page 39) or would finish a baked potato with elegance.

2 tablespoons minced shallot

1 tablespoon lemon juice

1 cup/240 milliliters Mayonnaise (page 119) or crème fraîche

In a small bowl, combine the shallot and lemon juice and let stand for 10 to 15 minutes. Then mix with the mayonnaise or crème fraîche. Use immediately, or store in the refrigerator, covered, for up to 1 day.

MAC AND CHEESE WITH SOUBISE/SERVES 6

Soubise (sue-BEEZ) is a classic French white sauce that deserves a place in the contemporary kitchen. Simple to make with common ingredients, soubise is defined by the onion, this one including both onion and shallot, blended into a béchamel sauce. Good hot or cold, the versatile sauce goes well with roasted or grilled/barbecued meats and with vegetables. Here I turn it into the backdrop for hearty macaroni and cheese, an excellent side dish or vegetarian main course. Escoffier blanched his onions before adding them to the béchamel, but I think the sauce benefits from the complexity of caramelized onions. Either way, the sauce is great with grilled onions or with seared scallops or sautéed chicken. And it can replace the béchamel base in the Cheddar Cheese Soufflé (page 124).

SOUBISE

4 tablespoons butter

1 medium onion, sliced

Kosher salt

1 shallot, roughly chopped

3 tablespoons all-purpose/plain flour

1½ cups/360 milliliters milk

1 tablespoon white wine vinegar

3 tablespoons sherry

1 tablespoon fish sauce

1 to 2 teaspoons dry mustard

¼ teaspoon freshly ground black pepper

6 or 7 gratings of fresh nutmeg

¼ teaspoon cayenne (optional)

¼ teaspoon smoked paprika (optional, substitute cayenne if you wish)

12 ounces/340 grams macaroni, penne, or cellentani

3 tablespoons butter, melted

1 pound/455 grams Comté, Gruyère, Emmenthaler, Cheddar or a combination of these cheeses, grated

¼ cup/30 grams grated Parmigiano-Reggiano, tossed with 2 tablespoons melted butter (optional)

½ cup/55 grams panko bread crumbs

Continued on the next page.

MAKE THE SOUBISE: Melt half the butter in a medium pan over medium heat and add the onion and a four-fingered pinch of salt. Cook, stirring until the onion is nicely caramelized.

In a small saucepan over medium heat, melt the remaining butter. Add the shallot and a three-finger pinch of salt and cook until some of the water has cooked out of the butter, about 1 minute. Add the flour, stir to mix it with the butter, and cook until the mixture has taken on a toasted aroma, a few minutes. Gradually whisk in the milk and stir with a flat-edged wood spoon or spatula, to make sure the flour doesn't stick to the bottom of the pan, until the sauce comes up to a simmer and thickens, a few minutes more. Stir in a three-finger pinch of salt, the white wine vinegar, sherry, fish sauce, dry mustard, black pepper, nutmeg, cayenne, and smoked paprika (if using). Add the onion to the sauce and stir until heated through. Transfer the sauce to a blender and process until puréed, or purée in the pan with a hand blender. Keep the sauce warm over low heat. You should have about 2 cups/480 ml.

Cook the pasta just until al dente, drain, then return it to the pot. Use 1 tablespoon of the melted butter to spread on a 9-by-13-inch/23-by-33-centimeter baking dish or another appropriately sized, ovenproof vessel. Place the pasta in a large bowl.

Sprinkle half of the Comté cheese into the soubise and stir until melted. Remove from the heat and pour over the pasta. Toss the pasta and pour it into the baking dish. Top with the remaining Comté. The pasta can be baked immediately or later in the day, or it can be covered and refrigerated for up to 3 days before baking.

Preheat the oven to 425°F/220°C/gas 7.

Sprinkle the pasta with the Parmigiano-Reggiano (if using). In a small bowl, toss the panko with the remaining melted butter and spread this over the top. Cover with aluminum foil and bake until heated through, about 30 minutes (longer if it has been chilled in the refrigerator). Remove the foil and bake until the cheese is nicely browned, or turn on the broiler/grill and broil/grill until the top is browned, 15 to 20 more minutes.

Serve immediately.

1/Cooked macaroni is tossed with the soubise and placed into the baking dish.

2/Top with shredded cheese.

5

ACID:
The Power of Contrast

ACIDIC LIQUIDS HEIGHTEN FLAVOR.
If you've cooked any soups or stews, you've already put this critical lever beneath your food to lift it up. The ability to use salt well and the ability to cook foods to the right temperature—these are important skills to have, but are often discussed explicitly in recipes and directives to home cooks. Less often stated is the importance of using acid as a seasoning device. It's second only to salt in its potential for elevating the flavors of your cooking.

The power of acid was the first of many "a-ha" moments I experienced in culinary school. We were making a cream soup (broccoli), but the point was to learn the creamed soup technique and about the last thing I would have thought to put in my lovingly tended soup was a shot of vinegar! Vinegar in cream? I approached Chef Pardus like Oliver approaching Mr. Bumble. He sat behind his desk, paper toque rising high above his brow, grade book and tasting spoons before him. I set the soup down. Pardus drew his spoon through the soup, lifted some with the spoon, and let it fall—evaluating consistency. Good. Then he tasted. He evaluated the seasoning. The soup had the right amount of salt, but something was missing. "I want you to take this back to your station and taste the soup. Then take a spoonful and put a drop of white wine vinegar in it. Taste it, and tell me what you think."

I did as instructed. The spoonful with the drop of vinegar was markedly better, more complex, more interesting—*brighter*. Bright is an element of flavor that takes some imagination. I don't mean literally brighter, but synesthetically brighter: vinegar has a brighter *flavor*—clear, clean, crisp. Some people I've encountered don't "see" this. But put a drop of white wine vinegar in cream of broccoli soup and taste it. The name for the change in flavor is brightness.

The vinegar in cream soup was a great lesson in using acid to season food. All dishes should be evaluated in part for their level of acidity. It's one of the five main taste sensations. Just about everything you make, from a cream soup that begins the meal to a butterscotch sauce that ends it, can be enhanced with acid. In my opinion, the two elements that make a really good butterscotch sauce are not the butter and the sugar, but the salt and the cider vinegar that make the butter and sugar come alive. In these instances, you don't want to taste vinegar; if you can taste vinegar in a butterscotch sauce, it has too much. Just as you don't want to taste the salt in a soup, you don't want to taste the vinegar.

Evaluate your food and think about its acidity. Why do pickles go well on sandwiches? It's not for the flavor of the pickle so much as for the pickle's acidity, which makes the other ingredients taste better. Next time you make a sandwich, think about it, evaluate your sandwich, and ask yourself if a little acidity wouldn't make it taste better. When you taste anything, ask yourself, What would make this better? Often the answer is acid.

Acid is a generic term for anything acidic. You can add vinegar or lemon juice to what you're cooking, and in the same way that you can add anchovies to a pot for their saltiness, you can add, say, sauerkraut to a dish that needs a little acidity. Following are the main categories of acidic ingredients you can use to give your food contrast and brightness.

- Vinegars (Red, white, sherry, and cider are all valuable.)
- Citrus juices (lemon juice, lime juice) or other fruit juices (verjus, which is the juice from unripe wine grapes, or cranberry juice)
- Pickled fruits and vegetables (from cucumbers to capers to kimchi)
- Sour fruits (tamarind, sour cherries, green tomatoes)

- Wines (Use only those you would drink; don't buy "cooking" wine.)
- Mustards
- Sour leafy greens (such as sorrel) or sour vegetables (such as rhubarb)
- Cultured dairy preparations (such as yogurt, sour cream, or goat cheese)

A few forms of acidity deserve special attention.

The first, by a good mile or so, is lemon juice. Lemon juice is one of the most valuable seasoning tools in the kitchen. More foods than not are elevated with the addition of lemon juice. Always have a lemon on hand. Salt, onion, lemon—a kitchen without these items is handicapped.

The second most important acid is vinegar. What's important here is not so much the kind of wine vinegar you use (white, red, or sherry) but the quality. The better your vinegar, the more influential its impact on your food. The larger the proportion of vinegar relative to the rest of the ingredients, the more important that quality is. A vinaigrette is almost wholly dependent on the quality of the vinegar.

You usually get what you pay for. A very cheap vinegar tastes that way. The best vinegars are delicious, not simply harshly acidic. Buy a good sherry vinegar from Spain and taste it—think about the flavor. In my opinion, a sherry vinegar is the most versatile, and good-quality sherry vinegars are widely available. From a seasoning standpoint, wine vinegars are largely interchangeable. You would use a white wine vinegar when a red wine vinegar would alter the color of a dish, but, again, the quality of the wine vinegar is more important than the type of wine it was made from.

Be wary of gimmicky vinegars, those infused with herbs and fruits. I'm not saying they're necessarily bad—just be aware that their claims may be specious. That herbs de Provence vinegar may be delicious, but think about it. If you want herbs in your food, why not put them in yourself? What is the point of a raspberry vinegar? Think about it for a minute. If the taste suits you, terrific, but flavored vinegars like this have limited uses. Better to spend your money on a quality red or sherry vinegar.

Balsamic vinegar is in its own category. This special Italian elixir prized for its flavor and the balance of acidity and sweetness is sometimes so good that it's taken straight as a digestif. Think of balsamic vinegar more as a finishing flavor, in the category of a condiment, rather than an all-purpose seasoning.

Other components that bring acidity to a dish are pickled vegetables and mustards. Swirl a little mustard into a gravy, and that gravy becomes more interesting and complex. Sprinkle pickled chiles on braised meats such as short ribs or pot roast.

Of course, sauerkraut goes great on a corned beef sandwich, but you could also chop sauerraut and stir it into the Winter Vegetable Garbure (page 79) for an interesting acidic counterpoint to the fresh cabbage and smoky bacon flavor.

Acidity can also be the main feature of a dish. In North Carolina, pulled pork is mixed with a vinegar-based sauce and called barbecue. This delicious contrast to the rich, unctuous slow-cooked pork shoulder should not be confused with the tomato-based sweet-sour barbecue sauces that go into pulled pork in the western part of the state, or, farther west and south, the tomato-based sauces mixed with grilled/barbecued or smoke-roasted brisket for barbecue in Texas. All barbecue sauces include a healthy dose of vinegar.

A fish preparation called ceviche uses acid to "cook" fish. The fish is marinated in lemon or lime juice along with other aromatic ingredients and eaten at room temperature.

Acid can help preserve food by debilitating microbes that cause spoilage. Pickles are one common example. Another is an ancient preparation, now referred to as *escabèche* (es-keh-BEHSH), in which cooked fish gets a bath in a warm acidic sauce.

Acid is a fundamental ingredient in some cheese making. Added to warm or hot milk, acid will cause the milk solids to group together and congeal into curds that can then be pressed and aged into cheese.

But here, we are concerned with the impact acidity has on food generally, acidity as it relates to seasoning. Having an authoritative control over the acidity level of everything you prepare is one of the most important skills to develop as a cook.

GROUPER CEVICHE WITH CHILES AND LIME/SERVES 4

This is perhaps my favorite way to eat fish. Ceviche couldn't be easier to make or more impressive to serve. It's also an extraordinary example of the power of acidity. Fresh fish gets fishy only when cooked. When raw, it is mild, clean, and delicious. I like to use grouper, but just about any fish can be prepared this way. Other good choices include sole, fluke, sea bass, and red snapper. Serve the ceviche with something crunchy—crispy flat bread or croutons. It makes a great starter. If you don't like cilantro, you can use mint or simply omit it.

1 pound/455 grams grouper fillets, skin removed, cut into ¼-inch/6-millimeter strips

½ cup/50 grams shaved red onion

½ cup/120 milliliters freshly squeezed lime juice (3 to 4 limes)

1 tablespoon seeded and minced jalapeño chile in teeny tiny dice (brunoise)

1 tablespoon seeded and minced Fresno chile

¼ cup/20 grams cilantro/fresh coriander leaves, chopped or cut into chiffonade

Fine sea salt

2 tablespoons extra-virgin olive oil

In a nonreactive bowl, combine the grouper, onion, and lime juice and toss to combine. Let marinate for at least 10 minutes. Add the chiles and half of the cilantro/fresh coriander and toss again. Season with salt and add the olive oil. Divide among 4 plates and top with the remaining cilantro to serve.

PULLED PORK WITH EASTERN NORTH CAROLINA
BARBECUE SAUCE/SERVES 8 TO 10

When I arrived at Duke University in Durham, North Carolina, from Cleveland, Ohio, I knew the word *barbecue* to be a verb. And you did it on a backyard grill. As a noun, it meant a gathering to eat food cooked on a grill. I think it took me two years to figure out that in this strange new territory, *barbecue* meant pork shoulder cooked over coals until shreddable, then mixed with a vinegar sauce. Barbecue was served, either plain or on a soft white hamburger bun, with hush puppies (deep-fried corn bread), sweet coleslaw, and iced tea. Talk about putting any kind of tomato in the vinegar sauce, and you could find yourself surrounded by an angry mob.

This experience marked the beginning of what would grow into my deep affection for pork generally, and the pork shoulder remains one of my favorite cuts to work with and to cook. Abundant and inexpensive, marbled with a good percentage of fat, and infinitely versatile, the pork shoulder is a go-to cut for big gatherings. (This recipe calls for bone-in shoulder because it's always better to cook meat on the bone, but you can use boneless if you wish.) Here I grill it so that it picks up the flavors of high heat and smoke, then finish it in a low oven with a classic eastern North Carolina barbecue sauce to make it falling-apart tender. Some traditionalists would say that the brown sugar is unnecessary in the sauce, but I think that the acidity needs a little balance. You won't find fish sauce in traditional eastern Carolina barbecue, but it adds depth.

The smoky flavors from grilling give this a great, authentic taste, but it can be simply roasted in the open pot at 425°F/220°C/gas 7 for 20 minutes. Continue cooking, covered in a low oven as instructed.

5 pounds/2.3 kilograms bone-in pork shoulder

BARBECUE SAUCE

1 cup/240 milliliters cider vinegar

¼ cup/50 grams firmly packed brown sugar

1 tablespoon dried red chiles

1 tablespoon fish sauce

Freshly ground black pepper

Kosher salt

Build a hot charcoal or hardwood fire on one side of a grill/barbecue (see technique #18, Grill). Grill/barbecue the pork over direct heat until seared on both sides, about 5 minutes per side, depending on your fire. Move the pork to the cool side of the grill. Cover the grill and continue to cook the pork, turning once, for about 30 minutes. If you want to use wood chips for additional smoke, do so after you move the pork to the cool side of the grill. If using a gas grill, cook only to sear the pork well on all sides.

MAKE THE SAUCE: In a small saucepan, combine the vinegar, brown sugar, chiles, and fish sauce. Season with 1 tablespoon pepper and 1½ teaspoons salt. Bring just to a simmer, stirring to make sure the sugar and salt are dissolved.

Preheat the oven to 225°F/110°C/gas ¼.

Put the pork in a pot that can comfortably contain the shoulder. Add half of the sauce, cover, and cook until the meat shreds easily with a fork, 6 to 8 hours (it will release a lot of juice). Remove and discard the bone. Shred the pork and stir to mix the meat with the juices and sauce. Add the remaining sauce as you wish. Taste, evaluate, and add more vinegar, chiles, salt, or brown sugar as necessary before serving.

Preparation photographs begin on the next page.

1/A bone-in pork shoulder is first grilled over charcoal or hardwood coals.

2/After it has spent many hours covered in a low oven, it will shred easily between two forks.

3/It will have dropped fat and juices into the sauce.

4/The bone should pull out easily and cleanly.

5/The resulting barbecue should have a good smoky flavor from the coals.

6/The shredded pork reheats well, so it can be refrigerated for 3 to 4 days before gently reheating.

LEMON-CUMIN DAL/SERVES 4 TO 6

This thick bean dish is in the style of Indian preparations that often use red or yellow split peas or lentils. Here, I combine mung beans and black-eyed peas because I particularly like the earthiness of the peas. Adapted from a recipe by an Indian chemist turned restaurateur I once wrote about, it's a staple in our house. The dal takes an hour to cook but only about five minutes of prep time. It is finished with a serious dose of acidity, in the form of lemon juice, but if you have access to tamarind pulp, use that in place of the lemon. I like the smokiness of the *kala jeera*, also called black cumin (available at Indian markets), but the dal is delicious without it. In addition to demonstrating the impact of acidity, this recipe cooks the spices and aromatics in butter before they are added to the beans. Once you've seen how powerfully this technique works, it is open to many interpretations and different spice levels. A traditional dal would use ghee, or clarified butter (see page 137), another option. The dal makes a hearty vegetarian meal with some basmati rice and fried bread or pappadams.

1 cup/200 grams mung beans, rinsed and cleaned

⅓ cup/50 grams black-eyed peas, rinsed and cleaned

1 teaspoon ground cumin

½ teaspoon *kala jeera* (optional; see headnote)

1 teaspoon ground turmeric

½ teaspoon cayenne pepper (or more or less depending on your preference)

½-inch/12-millimeter piece fresh ginger, grated

1 garlic clove, minced or smashed with the flat side of a knife

Kosher salt

3 tablespoons butter

2 tablespoons lemon juice, or as needed

¼ cup/20 grams cilantro/fresh coriander leaves, torn or chopped (a delicious garnish, but optional)

In a medium saucepan, combine the beans and peas. Add 3½ cups/840 milliliters water. Bring to a simmer over high heat, cover, reduce the heat to low, and cook until the water has reduced to the level of the beans and the beans are tender, about 45 minutes.

In a small dish, combine the cumin, *kala jeera*, turmeric, cayenne, ginger, garlic, and 1½ teaspoons salt. In a small frying pan over medium-high heat, melt the butter and cook until the frothing subsides and the butter has browned slightly. Add the spice mixture and sauté for 20 seconds or so. Stir into the dal. Bring the dal to a simmer (it should be very moist; add more water and bring to a simmer if it's too dry), remove from the heat, and stir in the lemon juice. Taste for seasoning, and add more lemon or salt as needed. Serve garnished with cilantro/fresh coriander, if desired.

SAUTÉED DUCK BREASTS WITH ORANGE-CRANBERRY GASTRIQUE/SERVES 4

Gastrique (gahs-TREEK) is a French term for a sugar and vinegar reduction that is added to sauces to make what is, in effect, a sweet and sour sauce. Sometimes the sugar is caramelized for different notes of sweetness. The complexity that comes from the intense sourness offset by a parallel sweetness goes especially well with rich poultry and game birds. A small amount of *gastrique* is added to a veal stock, for instance, to serve with sautéed squab/pigeon.

Here the sugar is caramelized and added to an orange-cranberry reduction—sour from the cranberries and sweet from the orange—a classic flavor pairing for rich duck breast. If you can find *magret* (mah-GREH) duck breasts, from ducks raised for foie gras, they are superlative because they are twice as large as other domestic duck breasts and as rich as a strip steak. But the sauce is the point here and will work with all duck parts.

This dish is also a reminder of how wonderful duck is and how little it seems to be used. This recipe is so simple and so delicious that it should be a staple in your repertoire. The key is the crispy skin. The duck is cooked skin-side down over low heat until the fat is rendered and the moisture cooked out, then over high heat to crisp the skin.

The quantities can be scaled up or down as needed; plan on ¼ cup/60 milliliters sauce per serving. Pair the duck with roasted potatoes and cooked and shocked green beans reheated in some of the rendered duck fat.

1 cup/115 grams fresh cranberries

1 cup/240 milliliters fresh orange juice

1 small bay leaf

Kosher salt

Freshly ground black pepper

⅓ cup/65 grams sugar

4 boneless skin-on duck breast halves or 2 *magret* breast halves (see head note)

1 to 2 tablespoons vegetable oil

1 tablespoon sherry or red wine vinegar

1 tablespoon butter

In a small saucepan over medium heat, combine the cranberries, orange juice, and bay leaf and simmer gently until the mixture is reduced by half. Add a generous pinch of salt (about ¼ teaspoon) and some grindings of pepper.

Meanwhile, put the sugar in a small saucepan, add a couple of tablespoons of water, and cook over medium heat until the sugar has dissolved and then begun to brown. Add the caramelized sugar to the sauce and stir to combine (it may seize up, but keep stirring until the sugar dissolves). Remove the bay leaf. Set aside. (The sauce can be made ahead and refrigerated for up to 2 days before serving.)

Score the skin of the duck breasts in a crosshatch and season them liberally with salt and pepper. Heat a sauté pan over low heat, add just enough oil to coat the bottom, and lay the breasts skin-side down in the pan. Cook until the fat has rendered and the skin has browned, 15 to 20 minutes. Raise the heat to high and cook until the skin is crisp, 3 to 4 minutes. Turn the breasts and cook for 1 to 2 minutes longer (they should remain medium-rare). Remove to a plate lined with paper towels/absorbent paper.

Reheat the sauce while the duck rests. Add the vinegar. Swirl in the butter. Taste the sauce—does it have enough salt, pepper, acidity, sweetness?—and adjust as necessary. Serve the breasts whole or sliced, on or beside the sauce.

CIDER VINEGAR TART/SERVES 10 TO 12

I was going to call this a "pie" but couldn't resist the pun. The recipe apparently originated as a pie, and most versions I can find seem to come out of heartland America from an age when lemons would have been an uncommon find in the plains states. The method here is customarily used for a *tarte au citron*, a lemon tart. Critical to the outcome of this simplest of all pies is the use of a good vinegar—the tart is not worth making with bad vinegar. Otherwise, it's better to use lemon juice! This is a very pure and elemental example of the power of acidity to balance sweetness and create an unusual and extraordinary dish.

TART CRUST

Scant 2 cups/280 grams all-purpose/plain flour

¾ cup/170 grams butter, chilled and cut into small pieces

⅓ cup/65 grams granulated sugar

4 tablespoons/60 milliliters cold water

1 teaspoon vanilla extract

1½ teaspoons powdered gelatin

2 tablespoons warm water

2 large eggs plus 3 yolks (save the whites for Whiskey Sours, page 127)

¾ cup/150 grams granulated sugar

2 tablespoons high-quality apple cider vinegar

½ cup/115 grams butter, cut into 6 pieces

¼ teaspoon ground cardamom, or to taste

Confectioners'/icing sugar

MAKE THE TART CRUST: In the bowl of a stand mixer fitted with the paddle attachment, combine the flour, butter, and granulated sugar and mix until the flour is incorporated (this can be done by hand if you don't have a mixer). Sprinkle the water and vanilla over the flour and mix until the dough comes together. Press the dough into a 9-inch/23-centimeter tart pan/flan tin with removable bottom. Neaten the edges and chill in the refrigerator for at least 1 hour and up to 1 day.

Preheat the oven to 350°F/180°C/gas 4.

Place the tart pan on a baking sheet/tray. Put a sheet of aluminum foil over the dough, fill with dried beans or pie weights, and bake for 30 minutes. Remove the beans or weights and the foil and continue to bake until the bottom of the crust is golden brown, 10 to 15 minutes. Let the crust cool.

In a small bowl, sprinkle the gelatin over the warm water. In the top pan of a double boiler (or a makeshift double boiler, see Assorted Vessels and Tools, page 347), combine the whole eggs and yolks, granulated sugar, and vinegar. Beat with a whisk over simmering water until the mixture falls in thick ribbons from the whisk, 5 to 10 minutes. Remove from the heat and whisk in the butter, one or two pieces at a time. When all the butter has been incorporated and the mixture has emulsified, taste it. If you would like to add more vinegar, do so now, in ¼-teaspoon increments. Add the gelatin mixture and cardamom, and stir well until combined. Taste again, and add more cardamom if desired.

Pour into the tart shell and chill in the refrigerator until set, at least 2 hours. Dust with confectioners'/icing sugar before serving.

EGG:

A Culinary Marvel

IF YOU COULD CHOOSE TO MASTER A single ingredient, no choice would teach you more about cooking than the egg. It is an end in itself; it's a multipurpose ingredient; it's an all-purpose garnish; it's an invaluable tool. The egg teaches your hands finesse and delicacy. It helps your arms develop strength and stamina. It instructs in the way proteins behave in heat and in the powerful ways we can change food mechanically. It's a lever for getting other foods to behave in great ways. Learn to take the egg to its many differing ends, and you've enlarged your culinary repertoire by a factor of ten.

You can cook eggs like a brute, and they'll still be eggs, but eggs are best when handled with finesse. Finesse is refinement. Finesse is delicacy. Finesse requires deep thoughtfulness about what you're cooking and what you're attempting to achieve. Working with the egg teaches you these qualities and helps you strengthen them—in your hands, in your eyes, in your mind.

Furthermore, there's no ingredient a cook can bring more honor to than the humble, ubiquitous egg. The egg is the perfect food—an inexpensive package dense with nutrients and exquisite flavor, a food that's both easily and simply prepared and also virtually unmatched in terms of versatility in the kitchen.

Finally, the egg is meaningful simply as a beautiful object, the hard but delicate shell protecting the life within, its elliptical curves symbolic of life and fertility.

The egg is divine.

How do you improve as a cook when you attempt to understand the egg?

First, recognize the main principle of eggs: eggs require gentle heat and gradual temperature change. Certainly you can achieve interesting effects with sudden change using high heat (frying and deep-frying), but the egg is at its most versatile when gentle heat is put to it, whether you're cooking a custard in a water bath, whipping yolks over simmering water, poaching eggs in hot water, and even frying eggs gently in butter (the water in the butter helps keep the temperature down).

Eggs go from fluid to solid when their proteins, all bundled up and separate from one another, uncoil via heat and lock together. The same thing happens when you cook a piece of meat. The proteins lock together and set up. Therefore, a squishy rare steak cooked to well-done becomes stiff and tough. This is why an egg white cooked at 145°F/63°C for an hour will be opaque yet very, very delicate and still partly fluid, but when hard-boiled, it will become rigid. When that transition happens fast in high heat, the proteins lock up too closely because of the heat and the water loss, becoming tough and dry. When the temperature change is gradual, so is their unwinding and leisurely hooking up, with plenty of water in the gaps. This is why custards are smooth and velvety when cooked in a water bath and why some chefs prefer their scrambled eggs cooked in a double boiler, because eggs scrambled this way are almost magically succulent. Gentle heat results in tenderness.

When you recognize this, you can begin to think more clearly and efficiently about cooking your eggs.

Since eggs like gradual temperature change rather than sudden, taking them out of the refrigerator a couple of hours before you intend to cook them would make sense. Doing so makes a little difference but is not critical. How do you cook an egg in its shell? You can drop it into boiling water, but you have more control by starting an egg in cold water and bringing it gradually up to temperature.

To hard-boil eggs, for instance, cover them generously with cold water in an appropriately sized pan (don't cook a single egg in a giant stockpot). Bring them to a complete boil, remove the pan from the heat, cover it, and let the hot water finish cooking them gently. For large eggs, I find that 15 minutes in hot water, followed by a good long chill in an ice bath to prevent the yolk from turning green and smelly, gives me a vivid yellow yolk that is completely cooked through. For all methods of cooking eggs in the shell, you should start timing the cooking at the point when the water reaches a complete boil. To cook soft-boiled eggs, rather than remove the pan from the heat once the water boils, reduce the heat to low and cook 1½ minutes for a true soft-boiled egg, one that's very runny, 2½ minutes for an egg with a set white and a fluid yolk, or 3 minutes for a thickened but not solid yolk, sometimes called *mollet* (moh-LEH). But as with all matters that involve cooking, small variations result, in the end, from small variations at the beginning. The size of the egg and how cold it is can affect cooking times, so it's best to pay attention to your own eggs and how you use them. Keep track of how long it takes to get them the way you like them. Then write it down so you don't forget.

The next most important idea to recognize and embrace is the power of a cooked egg to transform a dish: the supreme power of the egg as garnish. Many dishes are improved by the addition of an egg. A salad becomes a meal when you put an egg on it. Cooked asparagus spears are a welcome side dish; put a poached egg on top, and they become a main dish. Raw or lightly cooked egg yolk is a ready-made sauce. An egg poached in tomato sauce transforms that sauce into a main course (serve it on a piece of toasted bread with a side of sautéed spinach). A steak or burger, a sandwich, a pizza, a soup, a stew—every category of dish is transformed by the addition of an egg. Put another way, if you have an egg and one other ingredient, a last-minute meal can be moments away.

The third thing to understand is the egg's impact on texture: the egg as tool. An egg white is an extraordinary leavener when whipped to peaks. An egg yolk is a powerful emulsifier that keeps microscopic orbs of oil separate so we have mayonnaise rather than cooking oil, Hollandaise sauce rather than melted butter. A custard made with whole eggs is firmer and shinier than a custard made with yolks only. Compare the texture of a crème caramel, a custard made with whole eggs, and a crème brûlée, a custard made with just yolks. The former is sliceable, while the latter is set but creamy. One has egg whites, and the other does not.

And that is all, or the beginning at least, of understanding the egg.

The Remarkable Custard

The custard is a subcategory of egg cooking that, like the egg itself, is so versatile that understanding the way it works and what it can do will expand your range in the kitchen exponentially. We tend to think of custards as being sweet, but savory and salty custards are terrific starters or side dishes. Bread pudding (see page 126) is nothing more than bread that has soaked up a custard. Any cream soup can become a custard—just add eggs and serve at the same point in the meal with a crunchy garnish. A quiche is one of the most delicious savory custards known to humankind. A cheesecake (see page 113) is a custard enriched with cream cheese and sour cream. Vanilla sauce, sometimes called crème anglaise, is a custard you can pour; freeze it, and it becomes ice cream. A famous drink is simply a loose custard: eggnog. Some kinds of cake icings are custards. Expand the boundaries of your thinking, and you see that the cake itself is a custard to which flour has been added.

To keep considerations of the custard grounded, let's break it into three main forms:

whole-egg custards, yolk-only custards, and pourable custards.

Whole-egg custards, such as the crème caramel and the quiche, can stand alone as custards you can slice. The basic rule is that 1 large egg will set ¾ cup/180 milliliters of liquid to a very delicate consistency.

I prefer a little more stability in a stand-alone custard, along with additional richness, and use 1 large egg per ½ cup/120 milliliters of liquid. For a basic vanilla custard in the manner of the crème caramel, the proportions are 4 large eggs and 2 cups/480 milliliters combined milk and cream, plus sugar and flavoring. Omit the sugar, add salt and a little nutmeg, and pour the custard in a high-sided crust filled with bacon and onion, and you have quiche. Pour it over bread, and you have bread pudding. Because all these dishes are sliced when served or are meant to stand alone on a plate, they need the structure provided by the proteins in egg whites.

These custards and others such as crème caramel and Spanish flan are best cooked in a water bath to ensure that their texture remains smooth and delicate. Even cheesecake benefits from being cooked in a water bath; the gentle heating will prevent the rapid expansions and contractions of air responsible for large fissures in the surface. For custards that have lots of interior flavorings, such as a quiche, or are primarily garnish, such as bread pudding, a water bath is not necessary.

Yolk-only custards are my favorite for their unparalleled richness and depth of flavor and their deeply satisfying, voluptuous texture. Crème brûlée is the classic incarnation of the all-yolk custard. Classic lemon curds are yolk-based custards that set when cooled. These custards can be taken in a savory direction with the addition of, say, roasted red pepper or caramelized onion, and served to accompany something very lean such grilled/barbecued fish or a vegetable salad.

Pourable custards are variants of the yolk-only custard. The yolks are cooked over direct heat or over heated water until thick but still pourable. The result is a custard sauce or vanilla sauce. As with other custards, pourable custards can be transformed into rich sauces for savory foods. You might make a lemony, salty sauce for a meaty fish such as salmon or monk fish, or add tarragon, shallot, and black pepper to a sauce for grilled steak. Butter, not milk and cream, is typically used for sauces such as hollandaise or béarnaise. These classic sauces are essentially custard sauces made with butter instead of cream.

The Expansive Egg White

If you like to experiment with food, nothing is more fun than messing around with eggs, and one of the best things to mess with is the egg white. The ability of this combination of proteins and water to trap air is its most dramatic use. Other, more subtle uses, such as the impact of the egg white on a cocktail or its ability to give solidity to a fish or chicken purée, should not be overlooked.

The primary characteristic to know about an egg white is that it has two components: a thin watery part and a thick cohesive part. The thin watery part is what swirls away when you poach an egg (it doesn't matter how much vinegar you put in the water, a common practice I don't recommend). To avoid the unsightly flurry of loose egg white in poaching water, Harold McGee, an authority on the science of cooking, suggests pouring the egg into a large slotted spoon to allow the loose white to fall off, leaving only the viscous part of the white and, as a result, a prettier poached egg. It's a great technique.

By far the most important characteristic of the egg white is its ability to become foam. As a foam, it brings air to food. Normally we wouldn't think that the addition of air would enhance a dish, but such is the importance of texture. A bread that has risen is a pleasure to eat; one that has not is nearly inedible. Cakes are defined in large measure by their soft, airy crumb. A cake without air is not a cake; it's a biscuit. One of the best ways to achieve an airy cake is to separate the yolks, beat the whites to soft peaks, and fold them into the batter. Batters to be fried can be lightened in the same way. The chief attribute of a soufflé is airiness. The dish is named for the French *to breathe*. Cakes and soufflés rise in the oven because the air bubbles trapped by the egg white expand. They fall because the air bubbles contract as they get cooler.

Foamed egg whites are used in many other ways, savory and sweet. Whipped with sugar, they become meringues. Raw meringue often tops a lemon curd for lemon meringue pie. The same meringue can be baked in a very low oven, just to dehydrate it, for crunchy meringues. Or it can be poached or cooked in a water bath to become the French preparation called floating islands. If you add a little flour to a meringue and bake it, you will have an angel food cake.

Egg whites demonstrate that by understanding the properties of an ingredient, of *half* an ingredient, you can improve as a cook in numerous directions.

The recipes in this chapter address the ways that eggs can be cooked and used (the egg as leavener is discussed further in technique #9, Batters). They are grouped into three categories:

GENTLE HEAT = TENDERNESS

- Scrambled Eggs with Goat Cheese and Chives
- Shirred Eggs with Cream and Parmigiano-Reggiano
- Classic New York Cheesecake

THE EGG AS GARNISH

- Pizza Bianco with Bacon and Eggs

TEXTURE: THE EGG AS TOOL

- Mayonnaise
- Aioli
- Cheddar Cheese Soufflé
- Savory Bread Pudding with Caramelized Onions and Gruyère
- The VTR Whiskey Sour

SCRAMBLED EGGS WITH GOAT CHEESE AND CHIVES

SERVES 1 FOR EVERY 2 EGGS USED

These scrambled eggs are ethereal, not because of the goat cheese, but because they are prepared over simmering water rather than an open flame. This ensures that the cooking surface will be around 200°F/95°C. You can use a double boiler or any conductive pan or bowl over simmering water. I sometimes use my well-seasoned wok, which is somewhat nonstick and fits nicely into a big pot. You can use a steel mixing bowl or any saucepan that fits inside a pot. If you have a nonstick pan, you can set it above or in simmering water. Good nonstick pans are helpful for most egg preparations—if you have one, use it here to ease the cleanup.

The second critical point is to know when to remove the eggs from the pan. Stopping the cooking is part of the cooking. The whole point of cooking eggs over hot water is to avoid cooking too much water out of them and binding the proteins too tightly. You want to eat the eggs when they're still wet. The solid curds should look as if they have sauce on them—this sauce is the part of the eggs that's thickening but still fluid. When you see this, take the eggs off the heat and serve them immediately, preferably on plates that are warm and ready.

I like the creamy acidity that little dots of goat cheese bring to gently scrambled eggs, and I like to finish the eggs with the oniony notes and bright green color of sliced chives. You can also try small chunks of fresh mozzarella with a chiffonade of basil, for instance, or you can finish the eggs with a little more butter and torn tarragon, or some grated Parmigiano-Reggiano. Or melt the butter with a little minced shallot, then fold chopped sautéed mushrooms into the eggs as the eggs are cooking. Slices of delicate toast or toasted brioche on the side are always fine. If this is the first time you are cooking eggs this way, you may want to dispense with the garnish and eat them seasoned only with salt and freshly ground pepper.

Try to find farm-fresh eggs; it's worth the effort when eggs are the main ingredient. Two large eggs make one satisfying serving, so cook as many as you need. For each serving, you'll need about 1½ teaspoons butter, 1 teaspoon goat cheese, and ½ teaspoon sliced chives, but these quantities are up to the cook. Fine sea salt is best here.

Large eggs

Butter

Fresh goat cheese, separated into little chunks

Fine sea salt

Freshly ground black pepper

Sliced fresh chives

In the bottom of a double boiler, bring a moderate amount of water to a simmer and put the top pan over the water for long enough to get it hot. If you'll be holding a pan in the water, you can ignore this step.

Crack the eggs into a bowl and whisk until the whites and yolks are completely and uniformly mixed. There should be no clear pools of egg white.

Put the butter into the pan and let it melt completely (or melt it directly over medium-low heat, then hold the pan in or above the simmering water).

Pour the eggs into the pan and stir and fold them continuously with a silicone spatula as they cook. When you sense that they are nearly done, add the goat cheese and season the eggs with salt. Give them another stir before serving. Grind some pepper over each serving and finish with a sprinkling of chives.

Preparation photographs begin on the next page.

1/A sauce pan floating on simmering water allows you to cook eggs (or sauces) gently.

2/Eggs benefit especially from the gentle heat of cooking over water.

3/Pay attention as the curds form.

4/Stir and fold gently as you cook.

5/When there is still plenty of liquid, add the cheese.

6/The curds should look like they are coated with sauce.

7/Wrapping chives in a damp paper towel/absorbent paper makes for easy slicing.

SHIRRED EGGS WITH CREAM AND PARMIGIANO-REGGIANO/SERVES 2 FOR EVERY 2 EGGS USED

When I'm in New York City, and wake frayed and frazzled from the crowds, alone and missing my family, I go to Balthazar in Soho, sit at the bar, and order the shirred eggs and toast. It is infinitely comforting in its simplicity. With that and a few espressos, the day is transformed.

I have *The Balthazar Cookbook*, but much to my sadness, it does not include a recipe for shirred eggs. So here is my version, inspired by Balthazar. Now, I can have the eggs whenever I'm frayed and frazzled and alone at home, or better, I can share them with my wife on a lazy Sunday morning when the *New York Times* is spread out across the dining room table and the day is spread out before us without a plan.

The key to good shirred eggs is to heat the ramekin first, either in the microwave or over direct or indirect heat, so that the bottom of the egg cooks as quickly as the top. It also helps to take the eggs out of the refrigerator an hour or two before you cook them. Finally, it's important to keep an eye on them.

I use ½ teaspoon butter, 1 tablespoon cream, and 1 to 2 teaspoons grated cheese for each large egg. The cream helps ensure gentle cooking. Cooking time depends on the depth of your ramekin. I use shallow oval ramekins that are perfect for two eggs. I like to finish them under the broiler to give the cheese a little color.

These shirred eggs are very simple—very mild and comforting. You can vary them any way you like by adding chives or tarragon, shallot, or tomato, as you wish.

Butter

Large eggs

Heavy/double cream

Finely grated Parmigiano-Reggiano

Kosher salt

Freshly ground black pepper

Preheat the oven to 350°F/180°C/gas 4.

Put the butter in a ramekin. Microwave the dish until it is hot and the butter is melted. Add the eggs, cream, and Parmigiano-Reggiano. Place the ramekin in the oven and bake just until the whites are set, about 10 minutes. If you want to finish the eggs in the broiler/grill, remove them from the oven after 5 to 7 minutes. Heat the broiler/grill and broil/grill the eggs until the cheese has a little color. Season with salt and pepper before serving.

CLASSIC NEW YORK CHEESECAKE/SERVES 16

This easy cheesecake is very dense and rich in the traditional New York style. It's effectively a custard using cream cheese. The custard cooks gently in the heat of the water bath, resulting in a cheesecake with a smooth top and no cracks, worth the extra effort.

CRUST:

1½ cups/150 grams fine graham cracker/ digestive biscuit crumbs (from about 10 whole crackers)

1½ cups/300 grams sugar

6 tablespoons/85 grams butter, melted

FILLING:

2½ pounds/1.2 kilograms cream/soft cheese, at room temperature

½ cup/120 milliliters sour cream

1¾ cups/350 grams sugar

7 large eggs

1 tablespoon grated lemon zest

1 tablespoon lemon juice, or more to taste

2 teaspoons vanilla extract

Preheat the oven to 350°F/180°C/gas 4.

MAKE THE CRUST: In a medium bowl, combine the cracker crumbs and sugar. Pour the butter over the crumbs and sugar and stir until the ingredients are evenly moistened. Press the mixture into the bottom of a 9-inch/23-centimeter springform pan/loose-bottomed tin. Bake until the crust is browned and set, about 10 minutes.

Bring a large pot of water to a boil for a water bath (see page 49). Wrap the bottom of the cheesecake pan in a few sheets of heavy-duty, extra-wide aluminum foil to prevent water from seeping into the crust. It's best if the foil goes all the way up the sides, so that water doesn't get in. Heavy-duty, extra-wide foil works best because you only need one sheet.

MAKE THE FILLING: Using a stand mixer fitted with the paddle attachment, beat the cream/ soft cheese until softened. Add the sour cream and beat on low speed as you add the sugar. Continue to beat until combined. Stop the mixer and scrape down the sides of the bowl with a spatula, and beat again.

In a medium bowl, combine the eggs, lemon zest and juice, and vanilla, and whisk until combined. With the mixer on medium speed, slowly pour the egg mixture into the cheese mixture. Raise the speed to high, and beat to make sure everything is well combined. Taste the filling; if it needs a little more acidity, add some more lemon juice.

Put the cheesecake pan into a roasting pan/ tray and pour the filling into crust. Fill the roasting pan/tray with enough hot water to come halfway up the sides of the cheesecake pan. Put the roasting pan in the oven. Bake until the center is set, 1 to 1½ hours.

Allow the cheesecake to cool, then refrigerate until completely chilled. This can be made up to 2 days before serving, covered in plastic wrap/ cling film. Serve cold or at room temperature.

PIZZA BIANCO WITH BACON AND EGGS

SERVES 3 (IF THERE ARE ONLY 2 OF YOU, YOU'LL HAVE NO PROBLEM POLISHING IT OFF.)

When creating a pizza (or any dish for that matter), think of ingredients that go well together in other circumstances. Is there any pairing more entrenched in American cuisine than bacon and eggs? They are great for breakfast, but I will wager that they are even better when served on a pizza. Eggs and bacon—with melted cheese? To quote Emeril, "Oh, yeah, babe." And the crust makes a handy tool for swiping up the yolk that spills onto the plate. The bacon and egg pizza should be a standard in your house—with the simple pizza dough, there's no reason it shouldn't be.

1 disk Pizza Dough (page 158)

Olive oil

Kosher salt

1 cup/150 grams grated mozzarella

8 ounces/225 grams bacon, cut into strips or ¼-inch/6-millimeter lardons, cooked until tender and lightly browned, drained, and cooled

3 large eggs, each in a ramekin

Parmigiano-Reggiano

Chopped fresh parsley or arugula/rocket (optional)

Preheat the oven to 450°F/230°C/gas 8.

Roll out the dough on floured surface to the desired size. I like to get it as thin as possible. Let the dough rest occasionally if it is difficult to roll. Transfer the dough to a baking sheet/ tray (rimless, if you have one) or a pizza pan. If you cook the pizza on a stone, transfer it to parchment/baking paper.

Rub the dough all over with olive oil and give the periphery a sprinkling of salt. Scatter the mozzarella on the surface, leaving a 1-inch/ 2.5-centimeter rim uncovered. Roll the edges for a hearty crust. Scatter the bacon evenly over the top.

Bake until the pizza is two-thirds done, 15 to 20 minutes in my oven (the cheese should be melted and just beginning to brown). Remove the pizza from the oven, or pull the pan out if you can get complete access to the pizza. Using a ladle, press an indentation into each third of the pizza. Pour 1 egg into each indentation. Give the pizza a generous grating of Parmigiano-Reggiano. Continue to bake the pizza until the egg whites are set but the yolks remain fluid, 7 to 10 minutes more (keep a close eye on them).

Remove the pizza from the oven and garnish with parsley (if using). Cut the pizza into thirds. If serving more than three people, cut through the middle of each yolk.

Preparation photographs begin on the next page.

1/Roll out the dough (let it rest in between rolling if it's very elastic).

2/Coat the dough with olive oil and give it a light sprinkling of salt.

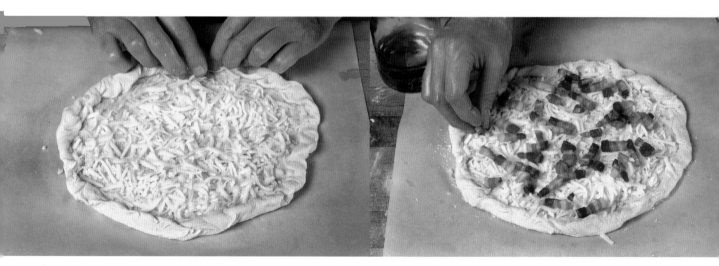

3/Roll the edges for a hearty crust and circular shape. I use parchment paper to transfer the dough to the oven.

4/Put the bacon on the cheese.

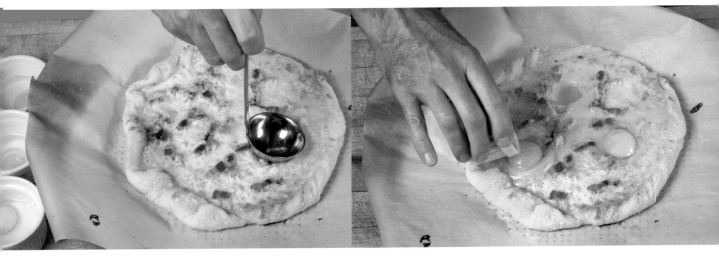

5/Making a divet in the pizza helps to keep the eggs in place.

6/The pizza should be about two-thirds cooked when you add the eggs.

7/Garnish as desired.

8/Slice to serve.

MAYONNAISE/MAKES ¾ TO 1 CUP/180 TO 240 MILLILITERS MAYONNAISE

Surely one of the greatest examples of using the egg as a tool is its potential to change the texture of oil. With some vigorous agitation, you can transform clear, flavorless, fluid cooking oil into a rich, thick, creamy sauce. The key to making this happen is water (or some sort of water-based liquid, such as lemon juice) and a molecule called lecithin, abundant in egg yolk. When, with a whisk or a blade, you break the oil into countless infinitesimal orbs to create a mayonnaise, the reason they don't bunch back up and cohere into one fluid mass is because the teensy orbs are separated by even thinner sheets of water. What keeps the water from giving way is a molecule that has one part attracted to fat (the oil orb) and one part attracted to the water.

The result is one of the most wonderful culinary transformations I know. It's different enough from store-bought mayonnaise that you will want to make the extra effort to prepare it—though very little effort is involved. If you use the hand-blender method, you can make mayonnaise faster than it takes you to walk the length of the condiments aisle at the grocery store. And while you are down that aisle, note that store-bought mayonnaise often contains, in addition to the required ingredients, sugar, vinegar, and "natural flavors," along with preservatives and stabilizers. You can taste the vinegar and sense the sugar, and the consistency has an almost gelled stiffness.

Homemade mayo, on the other hand, is so voluptuous that it's almost sexual. The flavor is so good that you could, and may, eat the mayo straight off the spoon, but add anything you like. A pinch of cayenne pepper gives it a nice piquancy. Macerated shallot will make it an unbeatable dipping sauce (see page 85).

1 teaspoon water

2 teaspoons lemon juice, plus more as needed

½ teaspoon kosher salt

1 large egg yolk

¾ to 1 cup/180 to 240 milliliters canola or other vegetable oil

To make mayonnaise using a whisk: In a large metal or glass bowl, combine the water, lemon juice, salt, and egg yolk. Measure 1 cup/240 milliliters of the oil in a cup with a spout that will allow you to pour it in a thin stream. Whisk the yolk to disperse it and, whisking continuously, add 2 or 3 drops of oil. Continuing to whisk, pour the oil in a steady stream into the bowl. Once you've added about ¼ cup/60 milliliters, you can pour the oil a little faster until all of the oil is incorporated.

If the mayonnaise breaks, as it will occasionally, pour it into the measuring cup, clean the bowl, put 1 teaspoon water in the bowl, and begin again, first whisking in a few drops of the broken sauce, then increasing the rate you add the remainder.

To make mayonnaise using a hand blender: Combine the water, lemon juice, salt, and egg yolk in a 2-cup/480-milliliter glass measure (the blender's blade must get close enough to the bottom of the measure to blend the yolk; if yours doesn't, use the whisk attachment). Mix briefly with the blender. Measure ¾ cup/180 milliliters of the oil in a cup with a spout that will allow you to pour it in a thin stream. With the blender running, pour the oil into the yolk mixture, moving the blender up and down to incorporate all the oil.

To make mayonnaise using a food processor: Combine the water, lemon juice, salt, and egg yolk in the bowl of a food processor. Measure 1 cup/240 milliliters of the oil in a cup with a spout that will allow you to pour it in a thin stream. Turn on the processor and pour in the oil.

Taste the mayonnaise and add more lemon juice if you wish.

Preparation photographs begin on the next page.

1/No matter how you mix your mayonnaise, the *mise en place* is the same: egg yolk, lemon, oil, and salt.

2/Wrap a towel around the base of the bowl to keep the bowl from moving if you whisk by hand.

3/Pour the oil into the bowl in a thin, steady stream, whisking continuously.

4/The result should be thick enough to hold its shape.

5/Making mayonnaise with a hand blender is the fastest way to make mayonnaise.

6/Add the oil in a thin stream while lifting the blade up and down.

7/Use only ¾ cup/180 milliliters of oil if using the blade attachment.

8/Using the whisk attachment saves on muscle power when making more than ¾ cup/180 milliliters of mayonnaise.

Continued on the next page.

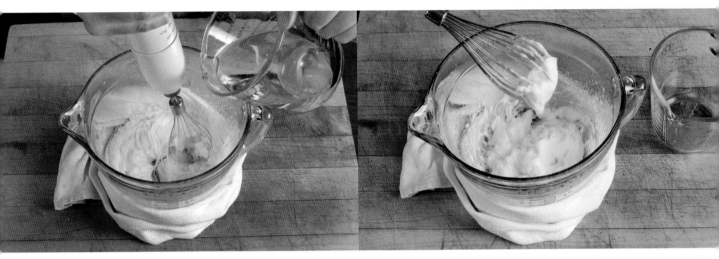

9/Add the oil slowly as you whisk continuously.

10/Using the hand blender with the whisk attachment, you can add as much oil as you wish—just make sure you have lemon juice or water in proportion to maintain the emulsion.

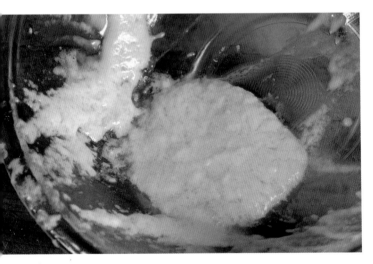

11/This is a broken mayonnaise—pourable and unappetizing.

AIOLI/MAKES 1 CUP/240 MILLILITERS AIOLI

Aioli, mayonnaise made with garlic and olive oil, is a fabulous sauce for, well, just about anything, from hot or cold vegetables to a steak sandwich, and fried foods such as fish tempura. Traditionally, it was prepared in a mortar using a pestle. I did this once, and it was well worth the effort, as the aioli was exquisitely textured. But I did it only once. I don't want to have arms like Popeye. Be sure your olive oil tastes good—it's often rancid or bitter (I find it's best to buy good olive oil in cans, as light damages olive oil). If it doesn't taste good plain, it's going to taste especially poor when it's emulsified. I find that most aiolis made with 100-percent olive oil are too strongly flavored, so I combine the olive oil with canola or other neutral-tasting oil.

2 teaspoons lemon juice

1 garlic clove, germ removed, mashed to a paste or crushed

1 large egg yolk

½ teaspoon kosher salt

1 teaspoon water

1 cup/240 milliliters olive oil (or a combination of ½ cup/120 milliliters olive oil and ½ cup/ 120 milliliters other vegetable oil)

Following any of the methods for making mayonnaise (see page 119), combine the lemon juice, garlic, egg yolk, salt, and water. Measure the oil in a cup with a spout, and mix as directed.

CHEDDAR CHEESE SOUFFLÉ

SERVES **8 AS AN APPETIZER** OR **4 AS A MAIN DISH**

The soufflé is a preparation famed for being temperamental, though I don't know why. Cooking soufflés is simple. Making them is what takes a little doing. The soufflé is a great example of putting the air-trapping capacity of the egg white to use, while also taking advantage of the richness of the egg yolk.

There are three parts to a great soufflé: the vehicle for the soufflé's flavoring (often referred to as the base), the flavoring, and the egg whites, whipped to glossy peaks. The base is made first, typically a flour-thickened sauce such as béchamel for savory soufflés or pastry cream for sweet ones. Yolks are added to a béchamel and often are part of the pastry cream. The flavor, often something rich such as cheese or chocolate, is then folded into the sauce, followed by the whipped whites. The mixture is put into ramekins and baked.

The timing is important—soufflés should be served immediately, before the trapped air begins to cool and contract. Fortunately, soufflés can be made ahead and frozen and then baked straight from the freezer in not much more time than it takes to bake them when they're at room temperature.

This traditional cheese soufflé makes a perfect appetizer or light main dish, served with a salad and a glass of white wine. Because the recipe calls for Cheddar cheese (quality matters here, so buy a good one), I think of it as an American version of the French cheese soufflé, which uses Gruyère. Feel free to use that instead. Or you can experiment—make the béchamel sweet, fold in the same weight of chocolate and let it melt to incorporate it, and then fold in the egg whites for a chocolate soufflé.

Butter for greasing ramekins, plus 2 tablespoons

Finely grated Parmigiano-Reggiano for dusting ramekins

1 shallot, minced (about 2 tablespoons)

Kosher salt

2 tablespoons all-purpose/plain flour

1 cup/240 milliliters milk

Cayenne pepper

6 large eggs, separated

1 teaspoon lemon juice

4 ounces/115 grams farmhouse Cheddar cheese, grated (about 1½ cups/170 grams)

Preheat the oven to 350°F/180°C/gas 4.

Butter eight ½-cup/120-milliliter ramekins (or spray them with vegetable oil). Dust the insides with the Parmigiano-Reggiano. Put the ramekins on a baking sheet/tray.

In a small saucepan over medium-high heat, melt the 2 tablespoons butter. Add the shallot and sweat it, stirring, for 1 minute. Add a pinch of salt. Add the flour and stir until the butter and flour are combined and the flour cooks a little. Whisk in the milk and bring to a simmer, continuing to whisk until it becomes thick. Add another pinch of salt and a pinch of cayenne. Remove the béchamel from the heat and let stand for a few minutes.

Meanwhile, in a large bowl, beat the egg whites until frothy. Add the lemon juice and a three-finger pinch of salt. Continue beating until the whites form stiff, glossy peaks.

Beat the egg yolks into the cooled béchamel. Stir in one-fourth of the cheese, followed by about one-fourth of the beaten whites. Fold the béchamel into the remaining beaten whites, sprinkling the remaining cheese over the mixture as you do. When all the ingredients are uniformly combined, spoon the mixture into the ramekins, filling the ramekins about two-thirds full.

Place the baking sheet/tray in the oven and bake until the soufflés are light and airy but set, and the tops are nicely browned, about 25 minutes. Serve immediately.

To freeze soufflés: Fill the ramekins three-fourths full (the freezing has a small impact on the end volume), cover with plastic wrap/cling film and freeze for up to 2 weeks. When ready to cook them, move them straight from the freezer to the hot oven on a baking sheet/tray and bake for 35 to 45 minutes.

SAVORY BREAD PUDDING WITH CARAMELIZED ONIONS AND GRUYÈRE/SERVES 8

This is comfort food at its best. What I also like about the bread pudding is that it's a further example of the power of the egg to transform ordinary ingredients into a special dish. Bread puddings, sweet or savory, are simply custard that has soaked into bread and been cooked, giving richness, flavor, and body to the bread. This recipe works perfectly fine with day-old bread; if using a fresh loaf, toast the bread until dry.

I've flavored this bread pudding with the same ingredients that flavor the water for onion soup, the only difference being that the custard replaces the water. The flavor profile of the pudding is similar to that of the soup—which combines the richness and sharpness of the cheese with the sweetness of the onions and the tang of the sherry. This is one way you can teach yourself to improvise. You can look at the bread pudding as blank canvas, as you would a quiche—think bacon and onions (Lorraine), spinach (Florentine), or, in a more dramatic direction, chorizo and roasted red and green peppers.

I like serving the bread pudding with roast chicken (see page 249). Leftovers can be refrigerated for several days, then sliced and sautéed in butter to reheat.

1½ cups/360 milliliters heavy/double cream

1½ cups/360 milliliters milk

6 large eggs

¼ cup/60 milliliters sherry

½ teaspoon freshly ground nutmeg

Kosher salt

Freshly ground black pepper

2 large onions, cut into slices and caramelized as for onion soup (see page 69)

1 loaf Pullman or good-quality sandwich bread, cut into ¾- to 1-inch/2- to 2.5-centimeter cubes and lightly toasted (about 10 cups/570 grams)

3 cups/340 grams grated Gruyère cheese

½ cup grated Parmigiano-Reggiano

Preheat the oven to 325°F/165°C/gas 3.

In a blender, combine the cream, milk, eggs, sherry, nutmeg, two three-finger pinches of salt, a few grindings of pepper, and one-third to one-half of the onions. Process until combined.

In a large bowl, toss the remaining onions with the bread until the onions are evenly dispersed. Spread a layer of bread and onions in the bottom of a 9-by-13-inch/23-by-33-centimeter baking dish. Sprinkle about one-third of the Gruyère over the bread. Spread another layer of bread over the cheese, followed by another layer of cheese. Spread the remaining bread over the cheese and then the rest of the Gruyère over the bread. Top with the Parmigiano-Reggiano.

Pour the cream mixture over the bread. Press the bread down to help it begin absorbing some of the liquid. Let sit for 15 minutes or so, then bake until the custard is set, about 1 hour. Serve immediately.

THE VTR WHISKEY SOUR/SERVES 2

The Velvet Tango Room, a bar on the near West Side of Cleveland, Ohio, takes its cocktails seriously. Here is where I had my first Ramos gin fizz, which contains an egg white. As I went on to explore more of the bar's offerings, I paid close attention to the impact of the egg white on the cocktails. Proprietor Paulius Nasvytis has on his menu a variety of cocktails that include egg white. An egg white gives a cocktail excellent body and a cohesive texture on the palate. It also can be argued that egg white turns the cocktail into food, obviating the argument that it's 5 P.M. somewhere. The egg certainly makes this cocktail more nourishing than a martini.

Here, all the ingredients except the whiskey are added to a shaker and given a preliminary sturdy shake to ensure that the egg white gets mixed enough. Then bourbon is added and shaken hard to further loosen the egg white, followed by the ice. If you don't have a cocktail shaker, you can whip the ingredients with a whisk until frothy, pour the mixture over ice and stir, and then strain into glasses when the cocktail is cold.

This version, served straight up, is adapted from Paulius's recipe to make two cocktails and to provide an easy simple syrup. The exact recipe for the VTR whiskey sour, measured out on a scale at the bar, is 1 egg white, 20 grams simple syrup (2 parts sugar dissolved in 1 part water), 15 grams lemon juice, 5 grams lime juice, and 30 grams Maker's Mark. The quantities here can be halved or doubled as needed.

1 large egg white

1 tablespoon sugar dissolved in 1 tablespoon water

2 tablespoons lemon juice

2 teaspoons lime juice

3 ounces/90 milliliters Maker's Mark or bourbon of your choice

Ice cubes

Orange slices and cherries for garnish (traditional but very optional as far as I'm concerned)

Chill two martini glasses.

Put the egg white in a cocktail shaker and shake thoroughly 20 to 30 times. Add the sugar water, lemon and lime juices, and bourbon and shake again until well combined. Fill the shaker with ice and shake gently to chill the cocktail completely. Strain into the chilled glasses. Garnish if desired.

BUTTER:

"Butter. Give me butter!
Always butter!"

THE SUBTITLE TO THIS CHAPTER, immortal I pray, was written by Fernand Point, chef proprietor of La Pyramide, one of the great restaurants of the twentieth century. A man of extraordinary generosity, he trained a generation of the chefs who would transform French cuisine. He was not only a gifted cook and chef, but an observant and thoughtful man, as his cookbook-cum-memoir, *Ma Gastronomie*, clearly shows.

> *"The duty of a good cuisinier is to transmit to the generations who will replace him, everything he has learned and experienced."*
>
> *"Success is the sum of a lot of little things done correctly."*
>
> *"Before judging a thin man, one must get some information. Perhaps he was once fat."*

Point was a large man in every way, and there's no better reflection of his spirit and his culinary wisdom than his exclamation on butter. Every chef knows why he would say such a thing. This magical, mystical gift from the cow makes almost *everything* taste better.

As chefs also know, and preach, *fat is flavor,* and few fats are as flavorful or as useful as this dairy fat. Slowly and surely, America is learning that fat is not bad, that it might even be good, that fat doesn't make us fat. (What does? Eating too much! Surprise!)

Butter is the most useful and most common fat for cooking and eating, and understanding how to use it makes you a better cook. Butter sits in a covered dish on the kitchen counter, is offered wrapped in foil in a dish of ice at a hotel buffet, and is stacked in boxes in the refrigerator case at the grocery store. This easy availability is yet another facet of its usefulness. Unlike other flavorful fats, such as duck fat or mascarpone, butter is always on hand. But because it is ubiquitous, we scarcely stop to think about how truly valuable it is.

Thinking about butter allows us to see it, and use it, as a tool. It shortens the dough that will hold your pie filling or form the cookie you serve with tea. It enriches a sponge cake and also becomes part of the frosting on that cake. It cooks and flavors the meat in your roasting pan/tray. Basting the meat with butter simultaneously helps the meat cook and flavors it, then enriches the pan sauce you later make for the meat. The solids in butter take on extraordinary flavors when gently browned. Butter is a ready-made sauce—serve it soft with a roast chicken, along with a little Dijon mustard. Add aromatics, such as a little shallot and lemon, and it becomes a more complex sauce. Knead some flour into butter, and the mixture becomes the perfect thickener for sauce.

Butter is critical in the sweet kitchen; indeed, it's hard to imagine a pastry kitchen without it. When asked about butter's single most important attribute in the pastry kitchen, chef and writer David Lebovitz said, "For me, the most important quality of butter is its flavor. Since baked goods usually have few ingredients, the flavor of the butter is paramount. A second important effect butter brings to doughs and batters is aeration—fluffing up the butter with the sugar creates air pockets that cause cakes, and other batters, to rise so nicely."

Butter is every bit as critical in the savory kitchen. As Tony Bourdain, chef, writer, and television personality, puts it, "In a professional kitchen, it's almost always the first and last thing in a pan." Butter is a great cooking medium, flavoring and giving color to sautés. Added at the end, it completes a dish, making it more luscious, and it smoothes out the texture and flavor of the finished sauce (see technique #11, Sauce).

Here is a truism that makes the uncertainties and stresses of life a little more manageable: few things cannot be made better with the addition of a little (more) butter. All cooks should rejoice in this happy circumstance.

First Things First: What Exactly Is Butter?

To harness the magic of butter, you need to know its parts and how those parts work. Butter is primarily milk fat, 80 percent usually. The fat is what contributes great flavor and texture to so many foods. This fat is hard and opaque at room temperature but melts into translucency. When the fat is separated from the other components of butter, it can be heated to 400°F/200°C before it starts to smoke, which makes it a superlative medium for cooking. Butter fat will do things that other fats do—shorten or make more tender a dough or pastry crust, add richness and flavor to a sauce, or be the main component of a sauce. Water makes up about 15 percent of butter. This is why butter is soft and spreadable at room temperature; pure butter fat is not. Water is what makes it froth when you heat butter in a pan, and it is what keeps the pan cool. The remaining weight of butter is composed of solids (proteins, salts, lactose). Once the water has been cooked out of butter, these solids become brown and flavorful, but they can turn black and bitter if you cook them too long.

Think about the three components that make the butter, and you will have more control over your cooking and a better understanding of why your food is behaving as it does.

Butter as a Cooking Medium

As a cooking medium, butter has a few different tiers of use. The first is simply gentle heating. Melt a little butter over medium-low heat and cook food in it until the food is heated through—this can be an egg, a thin piece of fish, or green beans that you've boiled and shocked (see technique #20, Chill).

Salted vs. Unsalted Butter: Does It Matter?

Generally speaking, no. It's a matter of choice. Originally salted to help preserve it, butter is now salted because salt improves flavor. If you don't want extra salt in whatever you're cooking, use unsalted butter. I almost always use salted butter because that's what I've always used and I like it. For a preparation in which I want to have great control over the salt level (in a sweet pastry) or where salt might not be desirable (in a buttercream icing, say), I may choose unsalted butter.

Chefs, especially pastry chefs, tend to prefer unsalted butter because it gives them more control over the salt levels in their food.

More important to me than salt or no salt is the quality of the butter. At home, use the type of butter you like best.

Raising the heat a little alters the situation. The higher heat cooks off the water in the butter more rapidly. Once that happens, the butter solids brown, and some adhere to the food, coloring it and flavoring it. The only thing to do once this happens is to make sure the solids don't burn. One of the advantages of cooking food this way is that the butter can be used as a baste. Basting, spooning butter over what you're cooking, does two things: it flavors the food with the butter fat and the browning butter solids, and it cooks the food from the top down while the hot pan cooks it from the bottom up.

You can use butter to cook at very high temperatures—it is a very effective cooking fat—but you must first remove the solids that would otherwise turn black and ruin the butter. The process is called *clarifying* butter. As butter is melted over low heat, the solids rise to the top and are spooned away as the water cooks off until all you are left with is pure butter fat. Clarified butter is wonderful for sautéing fish and beef, and it may be the best fat for cooking potatoes.

The fourth level of butter as a cooking method is using it as a poaching liquid. Butter is whisked into a bit of water and melted to retain the solids, water, and butter fat in a homogenous but liquid state. This dense, flavorful medium cooks food very gently and is thus well suited to cooking ingredients that need gentle heat such as lobster or shrimp (see page 141). (See also Using Whole Liquid Butter, following.)

Butter as a Shortener

When we combine butter and flour, the butter shortens the strands of gluten that make some flour-based preparations chewy, such as bread, resulting in a tender crumb, which you want in a pastry crust or in shortbread. The reason to choose butter as opposed to another fat, such as lard or vegetable shortening or even olive oil (a fat that's fluid at room temperature), is flavor. The flavor of butter is a natural partner for flour. Try the shortbread for a vivid expression of this.

Remember that butter is composed of 15 percent water, which encourages the formation of gluten, especially with a lot of kneading. Gluten is desirable in a bread or a noodle, but not in a pie crust. Butter will thus have less shortening power than the same weight of a pure fat, such as lard.

Brown Butter

One of the wonderful components of butter is the milk solids, which turn brown as they cook and develop rich nutty, salty, sweet flavors. These flavors enhance the taste of many foods, especially starchy foods. Pasta, bread, potatoes, polenta, and risotto all make a great canvas for the complexity of brown butter. Brown butter is a traditional sauce for lean white fish, seasoned with lemon juice and parsley, a preparation called à la meunière (mew-nee-AIR). The roasted cauliflower on page 246 owes most of its deliciousness to the butter that melts down through the florets, browns in the pan, and then flavors the cauliflower as a baste. Brown butter pairs perfectly with sweet pastries, creams, and cakes. You can even try browned butter on popcorn. It's fabulous.

The only thing you need to be careful about is overcooking the butter, in which case it goes from brown to black, and black rarely tastes good. When you know that the butter in your refrigerator can be transformed into a versatile, delectable sauce, you have a last-minute way to finish almost any dish.

Using Whole Liquid Butter

If you take care not to let the water and solids separate from the fat when you melt butter, you will have a product completely different from butter in any other form. In restaurant kitchens, it's often referred to as *beurre monté* (burr mohn-TAY), "mounted butter," from the French phrase *monter au beurre*, to mount, or whisk, butter into a sauce. The butter is ready to enrich sauces at the last minute when the kitchen is busy and time is tight. It also makes a great baste and an incomparable cooking medium.

Beurre monté is made by whisking chunks of butter into a tablespoon or two of hot water over medium heat. Butter is already an emulsification of fat and water. By melting the butter this way, you maintain the emulsion so that the butter is liquid but opaque, creamy, and homogenous. If you were simply to melt the butter without the continual whisking, the clear fat would separate from the water and solids.

As a cooking medium, *beurre monté* is especially suited to foods that require gentle heat, especially lobster and shrimp. Lean, firm white fish such as halibut are likewise excellent poached in butter. It can be spooned over pan-roasted meats as a baste, and it can be added to sauces in the same way that whole solid butter is swirled into sauces.

Butter as a Finisher, Enricher, and Thickener

Most hot, stock-based sauces are improved when you finish them by swirling in a little butter just before serving. In professional kitchen parlance, this is called mounting a sauce with butter, or *monté au beurre*. The butter smoothes out the texture of the sauce, making it more voluptuous and satisfying.

If you work an equal volume of flour into solid butter, you will have something called kneaded butter, *beurre manié* (burr man-YAY), which is whisked into a sauce. A loose, broth-like sauce will become opaque and thicken as the flour grains, separated from one another by a coating of butter, expand in the hot liquid. It's a terrific way to enrich a sauce while improving its texture.

Butter as a Garnish

One of the best ways to put the qualities of butter to work is as a garnish. Butter and mustard make a great finish for a roasted chicken. Radishes with butter are a traditional French hors d'oeuvre. Butter on bread is even a kind of garnish.

A preparation called compound butter is a terrific do-ahead garnish for most grilled/barbecued or roasted meats and fish. Simple to make, it can be varied according to your whim. Let the butter soften, then mix in aromatics, fresh herbs, minced shallot, or lemon. One traditional variation is "hotel butter"—*beurre maître d'hôtel*—which includes parsley, shallot, and lemon (see page 136). Compound butter is usually rolled into a log using plastic wrap/cling

film, then is sliced and placed atop hot meat or fish, over which it slowly melts. For a grilled steak, I like to make a compound butter with chipotle chiles, cilantro/fresh coriander, shallot, and lime juice (see page 136).

Butter as Preserver

In the same way that duck fat and lard are used to make confits—poaching duck or pork in fat, then allowing it to cool submerged in the fat, preserving the meat—butter can act as a preserver. My friend and teacher Michael Pardus suggests a couple of approaches to using butter for this purpose.

You can make salmon confit by poaching a salmon fillet in *beurre monté* (see page 137) that's about 145° to 150°F/63° to 65°C. A thin piece will take about 5 minutes, a thick piece about 7 minutes. Let the salmon cool in the pan. Or transfer it to a dish and pour the butter in the pan over the salmon so that it is completely submerged. Refrigerate the salmon until you're ready to use it. It can be warmed and eaten as is, or you can make salmon rillettes: bring it to room temperature and stir it so that it shreds, season with salt and lemon, add some of the poaching butter, and then put the salmon in a ramekin and pour a layer of butter on top.

The preservative effects of butter also work with summer berries. Beat room-temperature butter with a rubber spatula until soft and creamy. Stir in berries as if making a berry compound butter. Roll the butter into a log with plastic wrap/cling film and freeze to use later in the year for baking, making a sauce, garnishing, or finishing a dessert. "Berry compound butter on waffles is awesome!" Pardus exclaims.

Fats, Generally

When you learn to cook, you learn to group foods and techniques in ways that may not be obvious. One of the most useful groupings is fat. When professional cooks taste a dish, in addition to evaluating it for seasoning (salt) and acidity/sweetness, they ask themselves, Does this dish have the right amount of fat? Fat gives food depth of flavor, succulence, and fine texture. Think of sorbet on your tongue, and then think of ice cream on your tongue. Fat is the primary difference in the experience. When you taste something you're working on, ask yourself, Does this sauce have the depth of texture and satisfying nature that I'm after? If not, fat may be the solution.

The next question is, What kind of fat? Butter is the most common and useful finishing fat. But for a tomato sauce, emulsifying some olive oil may be what you're after (though I like butter in fresh tomato sauces as well). Cream, in effect butter with a lot more water, is another fat that can enhance a dish. Animal fats—bacon fat or duck fat, for instance—can add great flavor to a sauce such as a vinaigrette.

Fat as a cooking medium allows you to get food very, very hot, so hot that it can become crispy. Your choice of fat makes a difference in the finished dish. Potatoes fried in duck fat have a different flavor than potatoes fried in canola oil, a neutral oil; they also seem to get especially crispy. Clarified butter gets hotter than most other flavorful fats and so makes a great fat for sautéing. Duck poached in duck fat will give you a delicious preparation called duck confit, preserved duck that's unparalleled in its rich flavor and succulence. A simple batter of eggs, flour, and milk cooked in hot beef fat makes luxurious, savory Yorkshire pudding.

The type of fat you use in a pastry dough affects the dough. You can make a pie crust using butter (rich and flavorful, with some water), vegetable shortening (neutral flavor), or lard (a rich savory flavor with greater shortening capacity because of its lack of water).

Some fats should only be used as finishing fats. Extra-virgin olive oil would be ruined in a hot sauté pan. Use it cold or warm for its elegant flavor.

Choose fat according to the results you want. A factor in your decision may be the desire to make your wallet happy—the most flavorful fats are often more expensive than the neutral ones. It's fine to use less expensive oils for big jobs such as deep-frying and daily sautéing. Canola oil and other neutral oils tend to have less saturated fat and are considered better for your body.

CULTURED CREAM AND BUTTER/MAKES ABOUT 1¼ POUNDS/
570 GRAMS BUTTER AND 1¼ CUPS/300 MILLILITERS CREAM

Want to prepare your own butter? It's simple. A food processor or stand mixer is a powerful churn. Cream behaves as it did when our forebears churned their own butter. Given enough agitation, the fat separates from the liquid (the buttermilk). The butter fat must then be kneaded to squeeze out the remaining water.

To make excellent butter, however, you can culture it, just as you can culture milk to make yogurt. The acidity from the lactic bacteria gives depth and flavor to the butter. The leftover buttermilk is tangy and delicious. If you have access to fresh cream from a local dairy, making your own exceptional butter is a snap.

Yogurt cultures are now widely available at health-food stores. Filling your stomach with these beneficial bacteria is also considered to be salubrious.

The following instructions are for making cultured cream, or crème fraîche, and then making butter from the cream. To make yogurt, rather than crème fraîche, substitute whole milk for the cream.

This is a fun exercise that lets you get a better sense of what butter is. You might want to add some salt for flavor.

4 cups/960 ml organic heavy/double cream (avoid ultrapasteurized cream)

2½ tablespoons yogurt culture

Fine sea salt (optional)

In a medium saucepan over medium heat, heat the cream to 170° to 180°F/77° to 82°C. This helps the proteins set up. Transfer to a non-reactive container, such as a glass measuring cup. Let the cream cool to below 110°F/43°C. Add the yogurt culture and stir to mix. Cover and keep in a warm place for 24 to 36 hours; the ideal temperature is about 105°F/40°C. In the summer, I put the mixture in the sun. In winter, I put it in a warmed oven (don't forget it's in there and turn the oven on—I've killed millions of friendly bacteria this way!). The bacteria will be less effective when the temperature begins to rise above 110°F/43°C and will eventually die.

The cream should be thick, and you should smell and taste a pleasant green-apple tanginess. Allow the cream to cool to room temperature if it's warm. The ideal temperature for churning it is between 60° and 70°F/15.5° and 21°C. Put the cream in a food processor or the bowl of a stand mixer fitted with a whisk. Process until the butter fat separates from the buttermilk. This can take several minutes.

Line a strainer with cheesecloth/muslin and place over a bowl. Pour the butter and buttermilk into the strainer. Refrigerate the buttermilk and save it for another use, such as pancakes or biscuits. Squeeze the butter in your hands until you have removed most of the buttermilk. If you want to salt the butter, add about ¾ teaspoon/ 3 grams fine sea salt and continue to knead the butter until the salt has dissolved and is uniformly distributed throughout the butter.

Both the cream and butter can be stored in the refrigerator, covered, for up to 1 week.

COMPOUND BUTTER /MAKES ABOUT ½ CUP/115 GRAMS BUTTER

Compound butter combines butter's rich texture and various dynamic aromatics into a perfect sauce that's especially good on lean meat and fish. The first recipe is for the most traditional compound butter. The second adds the vibrant flavors of lime and chipotle. The butter can be made several days ahead or can be wrapped in aluminum foil and frozen until needed.

TRADITIONAL HOTEL BUTTER

2 teaspoons minced shallot

2 teaspoons lemon juice

½ cup/115 grams salted butter, at room temperature

2 teaspoons grated lemon zest (optional)

2 tablespoons minced fresh parsley

LIME-CHIPOTLE-CILANTRO BUTTER

2 teaspoons minced shallot

2 teaspoons lime juice

½ cup/115 grams salted butter, at room temperature

2 chipotle chiles in adobo sauce, seeded and minced

3 tablespoons chopped cilantro/ fresh coriander

To make either butter, combine the shallot and citrus juice and allow the shallot to macerate for 10 minutes.

Combine all the ingredients in a bowl with room to work the butter. Using a stiff, rubber spatula, stir, smash, and fold the ingredients into the butter. The butter should eventually get very creamy and pliable. When the ingredients are uniformly dispersed in the butter, transfer the butter to a serving dish.

If you want to create a roll of butter, spoon the butter into the center of a piece of plastic wrap/cling film. Fold the plastic over the butter to form a cylinder. Press a flat edge (a small cutting board or a baking sheet/tray) into the bottom of the roll to tighten the cylinder. Hold the plastic at either end of the butter and roll the butter to make it tight and remove air pockets. Tie the ends of the plastic together or tie a knot at either end. To maintain the cylinder shape, submerge the rolled butter in ice water; this will prevent the cylinder from acquiring a flat side when placed in the refrigerator. When the roll is firm, remove it from the ice water and refrigerate until ready to use. Cut the butter into slices to serve.

CLARIFIED BUTTER AND INDIAN GHEE

MAKES ¾ CUP/170 GRAMS CLARIFIED BUTTER OR GHEE

Clarified butter is a superlative cooking medium: it is delicious, and it can get very hot before it starts to smoke and break down. It's terrific for cooking fish, meat, and potatoes.

Ghee is an Indian preparation originally used to preserve the dairy fat in a hot climate. Cream is cultured, like yogurt, then churned into butter. The butter is then cooked until golden brown, and the solids are strained out of it. It is then used primarily as a flavoring fat for dals and curries. The dal on page 99 uses the basic method with whole butter, but ghee would make it more authentic.

The only difference between the two preparations is that clarified butter is cooked gently so that it doesn't develop color.

1 cup/225 grams butter

To make clarified butter, melt the butter in a medium pan over medium heat. Reduce the heat to low and continue to cook the butter. The water will slowly cook off; skim off the white solids that float to the top of the butter and any skin that forms on the surface. When the water is cooked off and you've skimmed the solids, strain the butter through a fine-mesh strainer or cheesecloth/muslin to extract any remaining impurities. You should be left with pure yellow butter fat. Refrigerate until ready to use.

To make ghee, cook the butter as for clarified butter but don't skim off the solids. Line a strainer with cheesecloth/muslin and set it over a heatproof measuring cup or other container. As soon as the water has cooked off, the butter fat will get hot quickly and brown the solids fast. When the butter solids are a rich, golden brown, strain the butter. Refrigerate until ready to use.

Preparation photographs begin on the next page.

BEURRE MONTÉ/MAKES 1 CUP/240 MILLILITERS *BEURRE MONTÉ*

The technique for making *beurre monté* (see page 132), whisking butter into a small amount of water, is the basis of beurre blancs, white wine–based pan sauces. It can also be used for a large quantity of butter, as here. The butter makes an extraordinary baste—it's the foundation for the lemon tarragon baste for grilled/barbecued chicken (see page 295), or it can be spooned over pan-roasting meat, such as pork tenderloin (see page 255).

I give exact measurements, but *beurre monté* can be made with as much or as little butter as you need. No matter how much butter you're working with, you only need a little water to get the butter melting.

1 cup/225 grams butter, cut into 2-tablespoon chunks

Put 2 tablespoons water in a small saucepan over medium-high heat. When the water is hot and just beginning to bubble, add a chunk of butter and continuously swirl or whisk it in the pan over the heat. When the first chunk is nearly melted, add one or two more chunks, continuing to stir or whisk. When the butter is almost melted, add more chunks, stirring, whisking, or swirling until all the butter is melted. Cover and keep warm until ready to use.

1/The clear fat separates from the water and the solids.

2/Water makes up about 15 percent of the total whole butter, and causes the melted butter to foam.

3/The white butter solids and foam are skimmed off to leave only the butter fat.

4/The copious foam indicates that the water is nearly gone.

5/Once the water has been cooked out of the butter, the fat will become hot enough to brown the solids.

6/Solids left to cook a little longer develop more complex, nutty flavors.

7/One stick of butter, browned and clarified, will reduce by about 20 percent.

BUTTER-POACHED SHRIMP WITH GRITS/SERVES 4

Shrimp/prawns, so often overcooked in boiling water, are beautiful poached in butter—they remain tender, do not become rubbery, and develop an almost unfamiliar sweetness. What better pairing for buttery shellfish than butter-loving grits? One of the great regional American dishes, it is a specialty of low country, South Carolina.

In this recipe, the grits are cooked with bacon and onion, and the seafood is gently poached in butter, which then enriches the grits.

If you haven't had grits in a while, make these, and you'll ask yourself why they aren't part of your pantry and cooking routine. They require at least the 30 minutes of cooking called for in this recipe, but can be cooked longer; in fact, they're best cooked over very, very low heat for hours and hours so that they fully hydrate. The grits can also be cooked all day in a slow cooker, if you have one.

4 ounces/115 grams bacon, cut into small dice

1 medium onion, cut into small dice

Kosher salt

1¼ cups/250 grams high-quality stoneground grits (see sources, page 352)

2 cups/480 milliliters milk or homemade vegetable or chicken stock (page 65; optional)

Freshly ground black pepper

1 cup/225 grams butter, cut into about 12 chunks

1 pound/455 grams shrimp/prawns, peeled and deveined

4 lemon wedges

In a medium saucepan over medium heat, combine the bacon and water to cover. Cook until the water has cooked off, then reduce the heat to medium-low and cook until the bacon is lightly colored and enough of the fat has rendered to cook the onion. Add the onion, season with a three-finger pinch of salt, and cook until softened.

Add the grits and stir. If using milk or stock, add it along with 2 cups/480 milliliters water. If not using milk, add 4 cups/960 milliliters water. Raise the heat and bring to a simmer. Reduce the heat to low and cook the grits, stirring, for about 30 minutes. Give the grits several grinds of black pepper. Add more milk or water as needed (about 2 cups/480 milliliters) to keep the mixture fluid. You should use enough water so that the grits don't stick to the pan and they can absorb the moisture they need. You can cook off additional moisture, so err on the side of using too much liquid. Keep the pan covered on low heat over a heat diffuser for up to 12 hours; monitor the moisture level, adding milk or water as needed. (You can also put the grits in a slow cooker on low or in a covered pan in a low oven, 150° to 200°F/65° to 95°C, for up to 12 hours.)

When the grits are ready, put 2 tablespoons water in a saucepan that is just large enough to hold the butter and shrimp/prawns. Bring the water just to a simmer over medium-high heat. Add a chunk of butter and whisk continuously as the butter melts. When the butter has begun to melt and emulsify into the water, add three more chunks and continue to whisk. (Or you can swirl the butter in the pan; it needs to keep moving—how you do it is up to you.) When all

Recipe continues on page 145.
Preparation photographs begin on the next page.

BUTTER/p.**141**

1/Heat a small amount of water, add a chunk of butter, and whisk continuously.

2/Add more chunks of butter once the emulsion has been established.

3/Swirl the butter to keep it moving.

4/Don't let it boil or you will cook all the water out.

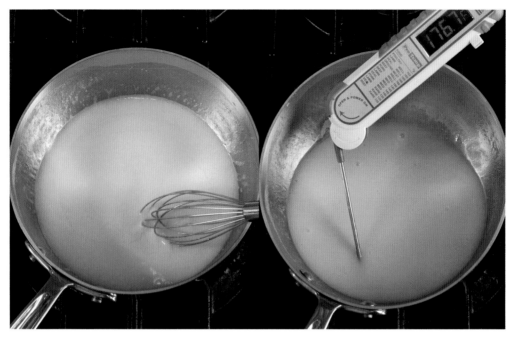

5/The *beurre monte* is done when all the butter is melted.

6/To butter-poach shellfish, get the butter hot, 170° to 180°F/75° to 80°C.

7/Add the shrimp/prawns.

8/The shellfish will cook slowly, flavoring the butter. The low heat will keep them tender.

Continued on the next page.

9/Gently toss and stir to ensure that they cook evenly.

10/If you're unsure about doneness by squeezing them, cut into one.

11/Finish the grits by stirring in some of the poaching butter.

the butter is incorporated, add the shellfish and stir. Keep the pan on medium-high heat until the butter gets hot again. Use an instant-read thermometer to maintain a temperature just below a simmer, 170° to 180°F/77° to 82°C. Don't let the butter boil. Cook for 3 to 5 minutes. Remove a shrimp, cut it open, and check that it's just cooked through. It should be white at the center, not translucent gray, and tender and juicy.

Put the grits over medium-high heat to get them up to temperature. They should be loose but thick. Taste and add more salt if needed. Stir about a third of the poaching butter into the grits.

Spoon the grits onto plates, and arrange the shellfish on or beside the grits as desired. Garnish with more butter, freshly ground pepper, and a squeeze of lemon.

BROWN BUTTER MASHED POTATOES/SERVES 4

This recipe is a great example of the power butter has when you cook its solids until they turn a caramel, nutty golden brown. Brown butter added to any plain starch is transformative. Serve the potatoes with roasted chicken (see page 249), fried chicken (see page 307), or prime rib (see page 296).

1 pound/455 grams russet/baking or Yukon gold potatoes, peeled and cut into large pieces

1 cup/240 milliliters milk, plus more if needed

Kosher salt

½ cup/115 grams butter

Put the potatoes in a medium saucepan and add water to cover. Bring to a simmer over high heat, then reduce the heat to medium-low and cook until the potatoes are tender throughout, about 20 minutes. Don't boil the potatoes; this can disintegrate the exterior. Drain the potatoes and set aside to let the moisture steam off.

In the same saucepan, combine the milk and 2 teaspoons salt and set over medium heat. When the milk is hot, return the potatoes to the pan. You can mash them in the pan with a masher (I like them chunky so I prefer this method), or mash them directly into the pan with a ricer or food mill. Stir the potatoes just to combine with the milk; don't overmix. Taste and season with salt if needed.

In a small saucepan over medium-high heat, melt the butter. When the foaming subsides, stir the butter and note the color of the solids. When the solids are golden brown, add half of the butter to the mashed potatoes. Taste for seasoning. If you prefer the potatoes thinner, add a little more milk.

Serve the potatoes topped with a spoonful of the remaining brown butter.

SCOTTISH SHORTBREAD/MAKES 15 TO 20 PIECES

This recipe is adapted from the one passed down to my friend Stephanie by her Scottish grandmother. What I love about this shortbread is its simplicity: flour, butter and sugar. The flavor of the shortbread is almost entirely dependent on the butter. Try to use a cultured butter, made from cream that has been cultured like yogurt, or, better yet, make your own cultured butter (see page 135) and use that. It will have a more complex flavor and is worth the added expense. I prefer a lightly salted butter here; if you use unsalted butter, you may want to add ¼ teaspoon salt to the dough.

A key feature of shortbread is its tender, almost crumbly crumb. This is achieved by reducing the gluten, the protein in flour that can make flour-based preparations chewy (such as bread). Stephanie's grandmother used a combination of rice flour and regular flour. This version is made with a low-gluten flour. The recipe works if you just combine everything in a bowl and stir, but I think creaming the butter—that is, paddling or beating the butter and sugar together until the sugar has begun to dissolve and the butter becomes light and fluffy—makes for a better distribution of the sugar and a better finished texture. I like the way Shuna Fish Lydon, a.k.a. Eggbeater, a pastry chef, fine writer, and creaming advocate, describes shortbread: "The best shortbread in the world calls absolutely no attention to itself. It's as humble as the rough terrain it hails from."

2 scant cups/225 grams cake/soft-wheat flour

¾ cup/170 grams cultured butter or other high-quality butter, at room temperature

½ cup/100 grams sugar

Preheat the oven to 350°F/180°C/gas 4.

Combine the flour, butter, and sugar in the bowl of a stand mixer fitted with the paddle. Beat on the lowest speed until the dough comes together. This can take a few minutes.

Press the dough into an 8-inch/20-centimeter cake pan/tin or other baking pan. The dough should be about ½-inch/12-millimeter thick.

Bake until cooked through and lightly browned, about 30 minutes. Cut into servings while still hot.

DOUGH:

Flour, Part One

DOUGH IS FLOUR THAT'S BEEN GIVEN shape by water. Without some form of liquid, it remains powder, a collection of individual, distinct granules of starch and protein. Add water, and the proteins in the flour—tightly curled strands collectively called *gluten*—can stretch out and connect with one another, forming long strands of proteins and a single mass of dough.

Sometimes the water in a dough is contained in a fat (butter) that is combined with the flour. Fat shortens the long strands of gluten created by the water, resulting in a tender, flaky pie dough, rather than a loaf of bread or a noodle with some bite. Fat coats the particles of flour, so if only fat is added to the flour, the granules can be shaped using a mold such as a tart pan/tin or ring mold and then baked. The flour will cook and set up, but the pastry will be very crumbly. Eggs are more than half water; flour and eggs will thus create an elastic dough much like bread, but we tend to boil this dough rather than bake it.

Understanding the behavior of these proteins is what gives you control over dough. The proteins allow us to shape dough, and they are what account for its elasticity. Protein is what allows dough to stretch without breaking, giving us delicious pastas and trapping gas to give us leavened bread.

When you work dough, mixing it or kneading it, you encourage these strands of protein to elongate and connect, both end to end and side to side, with each other. The more they connect and line up, the more smooth, elastic, and strong the dough becomes.

Another facet to understand is that this protein network relaxes, meaning that at first, if you stretch the protein strands, they want to snap back, but if you leave them alone for a while, you can stretch them and they won't stretch back quite so strongly. This is why bread and pasta doughs should rest before you shape or roll them out.

Fat interacts with the proteins by keeping them separate, thereby preventing them from linking up and forming long, elastic chains. This is why pie doughs are tender, not chewy, and why cookies crumble rather than tear.

The final piece of the flour puzzle, and it's an important one, is the fact that depending on a number of unpredictable conditions, the weight of specific volumes of flour differs. That is, on one day, 1 cup of flour may weigh 4 ounces/ 115 grams, and on another day, it may weigh 6 ounces/170 grams. If there is a single reason why people fear baking, why bread seems daunting, and why a simple sponge cake can seem an arch enemy, it is because measurements of flour are almost always given as a volume, which is guesswork.

Given that a cup of flour can differ by 50 percent, it's no wonder that some recipes "don't work." If your recipe asks you to put 4 cups flour into a bowl, you might have 1 pound of flour in there, or you might have 1½ pounds. Who knows?

This is why recipes that give the weight of flour are more likely to work than those that give the volume of flour. Also, recipes using the weight of flour are more successfully doubled or tripled. I urge you to buy a scale and use it (see Sources, page 352). Scales also provide a much cleaner and easier way to measure, in addition to being accurate. Most digital scales offer ounce and gram measurements. If you have a scale, I recommend following the metric recipes in this chapter.

The recipes here focus on three fundamental dough preparations: bread, pie, and cookie.

Bread Dough

Once you can make a great loaf of bread, whole worlds seem to open up. For the most part, bread is bread, meaning there's not a lot of variation in basic breads—baguettes, sandwich bread, pizza dough, ciabatta, flatbread. They are variations on the same thing—roughly a five-to-three ratio of flour to water by weight, plus yeast and salt. Fabulous bread is no more difficult than that. I've found that most recipes have too many instructions, overcomplicating what is a simple business: flour, water, salt, and yeast, mixed until the dough is good and elastic.

Any wheat flour will work: cake/soft-wheat flour, bread/strong flour, all-purpose/plain flour. There are some differences using a low-gluten flour (cake) rather than a high-gluten flour, or using a whole-wheat/wholemeal flour, which will give you a denser bread, but not so much that you should worry about making bread if you don't have bread/strong flour in the pantry.

The only time you should not attempt bread is when you need to eat in an hour. Bread can't be rushed. Bread takes time. The longer you give it, the better it is.

FLOUR AND WATER: You need about five parts flour and three parts water by weight; that will give you a good consistency and result in a versatile dough, not so wet that it sticks to everything and not so dry that it's difficult to mix. That would amount to 5 ounces of flour and 3 ounces of water, for a very tiny loaf. I use 20 ounces of flour for a standard loaf, with 12 ounces of water, for 2 pounds of raw dough (in metric, it's even easier: 500 grams flour, 300 grams water).

For those who don't have a scale, I have translated 5 ounces of flour to equal 1 cup of flour.

SALT: Salt is what gives the dough flavor. That's why it's there. Bread with no salt is insipid. The general rule of thumb is to multiply the weight of the flour by 0.02 and that is the amount of salt to use; in other words, salt should equal 2 percent of the weight of the flour. For 20 ounces of flour I use 0.4 ounces (again metrics shine: for 500 grams

flour, 10 grams of salt). You can also use a scant ½ teaspoon of coarse kosher salt per 1 cup of flour if you aren't weighing your ingredients.

For those who don't have a scale, I recommend using Morton's coarse kosher salt, which has a near equal volume to weight ratio, that is, 1 tablespoon equals ½ ounce.

YEAST: Yeast is what makes it bread rather than hard tack. The amount of yeast can vary considerably; the more yeast you put in, the faster the dough will rise. I use active dry yeast, but instant dry yeast is fine, too (it's a little more active than active!). I use 0.5 percent of the weight of the flour. You can also use ¼ teaspoon of yeast per 1 cup of flour.

Many bread recipes are fussy about adhering to various temperatures, such as blooming yeast in 110°F/43°C water or adding 75°F/24°C water to flour. Bakers will concur that variables in bread baking are many and that a yeast dough is alive and responds to the environment. But for basic bread at home, you don't need to drive yourself crazy with temperatures. Just know that if you use warm water, or the day is very hot and humid, the yeast is going to act faster than if the dough is chilly.

Three phases require your attention for good basic bread: the mixing, the first rise, and the second rise.

Mixing is what develops the gluten network that will give the dough its structure and the elasticity that will allow it to rise. Aligning all those proteins is the work of mixing. A properly mixed dough should be smooth and so elastic that you can stretch it to translucency.

The first rise , also called fermenting, allows the yeast to propagate, eating the sugars that compose the starch granules and releasing gas as a result. This not only begins the leavening process but also develops flavor. You should let the dough rise until it doubles in size; the longer it takes to do this, the more flavorful the bread will be. The first rise is finished when you press a finger into the dough and the dough does not spring back. If you let the dough rise too long, it can become slack, and you won't get a proper final rise.

The second rise is what gives the dough its final structure. It's especially important not to let the dough overrise, or your bread may be flat and dense.

The following doughs—for Dutch Oven Bread and the pizza dough—use exactly the same ingredients in exactly the same proportion. They differ only in how they're shaped and how they're baked. The same dough can be used to make herbed bread, sandwich bread, flat bread, focaccia, and ciabatta.

Pie Dough

Perhaps due to the ubiquity of the frozen pie crust, many have stopped making dough for pies. This is a shame because it's easy and so much tastier, especially if you make it with butter rather than with flavorless vegetable shortening/lard (though that's an option if you prefer it).

Pie dough can be used in many ways—for savory pies such as quiches or chicken potpie, as well as sweet pies and tarts. Meat or fillings can be enclosed in pie dough and sautéed or baked or fried, as for empanadas. Leftover dough can be sprinkled with cinnamon and coarse sugar, baked, and eaten like cookies (which is really all it is).

The secret to tender, flaky crusts is three-fold. First, keep the butter or other fat in pieces of varying sizes, from tiny to peanut sized. When the dough is rolled out, the chunks of fat create layers within the dough, which results in flakiness. Second, add just enough liquid to bring

the dough together. Using more than you need encourages more gluten to form, which makes dough tough. Finally, working and kneading the dough strengthens the gluten network, so work and knead the dough only enough to bring it together.

Some preparations require you to blind-bake dough, for custard pies, for instance. This means that the dough is baked before the filling is added. You can buy pie weights, which keep the dough from buckling and cracking in the oven. It's just as easy to line the dough-filled pan with aluminum foil and weight it with dried beans. Bake at 325°F/165°C/gas 3 for 20 to 30 minutes, then remove the foil and beans to finish baking.

Cookie Dough

The most basic cookie is simply pie dough with sugar replacing the water. Butter is used for a shortbread style of cookie. The water in the butter helps hold the dough together. This results in dry, crumbly cookies, what a friend calls "adult" cookies, excellent after dinner or as a midmorning snack with a hot beverage. The cookies can be flavored with citrus juice or zest and poppy seeds, or dusted with confectioners'/icing sugar or decorative granular sugar. But most important is that cookie dough shows how doughs in general work. Add more fat, and the cookies spread out and become thin. Add more sugar, and they retain more moisture and are chewy (depending on proportions of other ingredients, this can also spread them out more and increase crispiness). A cookie with a high fat content will be crisper if you increase the sugar. On the other hand, you don't want a cookie that is cloyingly sweet. Increasing the flour makes them crisper, drier, and more crumbly. Eggs make cookies cakier. Cookies are all about balance.

CINNAMON BUNS/MAKES 12 TO 15 BUNS

This is an example of a soft yeasted dough, a dough that has pillowy crumb from the butter, egg, and sugar. The recipe can be made to the point of cutting the dough and arranging the pieces on the pan. The dough can be covered with plastic wrap/cling film and the pan placed in the refrigerator overnight. In the morning, let the dough rise and bake the buns as directed. The rise will take at least 90 minutes because the dough is cold.

DOUGH

5 cups/700 grams bread or all-purpose/plain flour

2 teaspoons active dry yeast

2 teaspoons kosher salt

¼ cup/50 grams granulated sugar

2 large eggs

1¼ cups/300 milliliters buttermilk, warmed for 40 seconds in a microwave

4 tablespoons/55 grams butter, melted

FILLING

¼ cup/50 grams granulated sugar

4 teaspoons cinnamon

4 tablespoons/55 grams butter, softened

GLAZE

2 cups/200 grams confectioners'/icing sugar

1 teaspoon vanilla extract

¼ to ⅜ cup/60 to 90 milliliters milk, warmed

MAKE THE DOUGH: In the bowl of a stand mixer fitted with the paddle attachment, stir together the flour, yeast, salt, sugar, and eggs. Add the buttermilk and melted butter. Mix until the dough comes together. Switch to the dough hook and knead until the dough is tacky but not sticky, and can be stretched to translucency, 6 to 7 minutes.

Turn the dough out onto a work surface. Shape the dough into a ball and place in an oiled bowl, rolling the dough around the bowl to coat it lightly with oil. Cover with plastic wrap/cling film or a kitchen/tea towel and let rise until doubled, 60 to 90 minutes.

Place the dough on the work surface. Roll out into a rectangle about 14 by 12 inches/35 by 30 centimeters. It should be about ½ to ⅔ inch/12 to 17 millimeters thick. Don't roll out the dough too thinly. If it resists rolling, cover it with a towel and let it rest for 5 minutes or so.

MAKE THE FILLING: In a small bowl, mix together the granulated sugar and cinnamon.

Spread the softened butter all over the surface of the dough and sprinkle with the cinnamon sugar. Roll the dough up from a long edge into a log. Pinch the seam closed, then rock the roll slightly to finish the seal. Using a serrated knife, cut the dough at about 1¼-inch/3-centimeter intervals.

Coat a baking sheet/tray with vegetable oil or cover with parchment/baking paper. Arrange the rolls on the pan. (They should not touch, but may be touching after the next rise.) Cover with a kitchen/tea towel and let rise until roughly doubled in size, 60 to 90 minutes.

Preheat the oven to 350°F/180°C/gas 4.

Place the pan in the oven and bake until the buns are golden brown, 20 to 30 minutes. Let cool until barely warm.

MAKE THE GLAZE: In a small bowl, mix together the confectioners'/icing sugar, vanilla, and enough milk to form a thick glaze.

Brush the buns with the glaze and let cool completely before serving.

DUTCH OVEN BREAD/MAKES 1 LOAF

This is the most basic kind of loaf, simple to make and to shape, beautiful to look at, and delicious to eat. I believe that baker Jim Lahey initiated the idea of baking bread in a pot, and it's a brilliant one. The moisture trapped in the closed pot results in a fantastic crust. The pot is uncovered for the second half of baking. The dough can be made a day before it is baked. Proceed up to the second rise, and instead of letting the dough rise at room temperature, refrigerate it overnight. Remove it an hour before baking it. This recipe can be halved, doubled or tripled provided you weigh all the ingredients.

TO MEASURE BY VOLUME
4 cups all-purpose/plain flour

1½ cups water

1 teaspoon active dry yeast

2 teaspoons kosher salt, plus more for sprinkling

Vegetable oil or vegetable oil spray

Olive oil

TO MEASURE BY WEIGHT
500 grams all-purpose/plain flour

300 grams water

10 grams kosher salt, plus more for sprinkling

2 grams yeast

Vegetable oil or vegetable oil spray

Olive oil

Combine the flour, water, yeast, and salt in the bowl of a stand mixer fitted with a dough hook. Mix on medium speed until the dough is smooth and elastic, 5 to 10 minutes. Depending on the size of the bowl, you may need to stop the mixer and remove the dough from the dough hook if the dough is not developing thoroughly. When the dough looks smooth, cut off a piece and stretch it. If it stretches to the point of transparency, it's mixed enough. If not, continue mixing until it will.

Remove the bowl from the mixer and cover it with a pot lid or plastic wrap/cling film. Allow the dough to rise until it has doubled in size and does not spring back when you push your finger into it, 2 to 4 hours.

Turn the dough out onto a work surface and knead it to release the gas and redistribute the yeast. Shape it roughly into a ball, cover it with a towel, and let stand for 10 minutes or so to allow the gluten to relax.

Shape the dough into a tight ball—the tighter the better—by rolling it on the work surface between your palms.

Coat the bottom and sides of a large Dutch oven or other heavy ovenproof pot (5½ quarts/ 5.2 liters or larger) with vegetable oil. Put the dough in the center of the pot and put the lid on. Allow the dough to rise again, 30 to 60 minutes (less if it's very hot and humid, more if it's cold).

Preheat the oven to 450°F/230°C/gas 8.

Rub 1 tablespoon olive oil, or more if you like, gently over the surface of the dough. Score the bread with a sharp knife or razor, making an X or a hash mark; this will allow the dough to expand freely. Sprinkle the dough with salt. Cover the pot and put it in the oven.

After 30 minutes, remove the lid, reduce the oven temperature to 375°F/190°C/gas 5, and continue baking until the bread is nicely browned and cooked through. It should have an internal temperature of 200°F/95°C or so when done.

Allow the bread to rest on a rack for at least 30 minutes before serving so that the interior finishes cooking.

Preparation photographs begin on the next page.

1/Use a scale to measure flour and water.

2/Mix the flour, water, yeast, salt combination using a dough hook.

3/If the dough tears rather than stretches, as this dough does, it needs more kneading.

4/I like to finish kneading by hand.

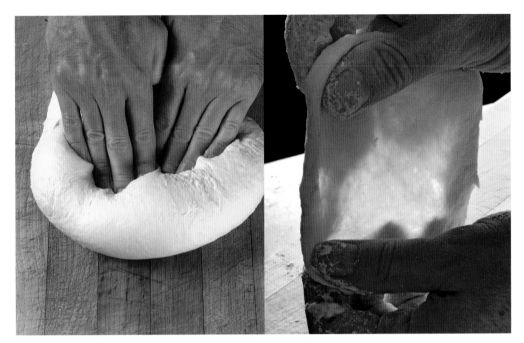

5/Take the time to appreciate the feel of the dough.

6/The dough is kneaded enough when a piece of it can be stretched to translucency.

7/A finger inserted into the dough after the first rise should leave an indentation.

8/Before baking, rub with olive oil, sprinkle with kosher salt, and score with a knife.

PIZZA DOUGH/MAKES 2 PIZZAS

Make the dough at least 3 hours before you need to bake it. The dough can also be prepared up to a day ahead and refrigerated, or it can be frozen for a month or so. This recipe will yield enough dough for two medium pizzas. This recipe can be halved, doubled or tripled provided you weigh all the ingredients.

TO MEASURE BY VOLUME

4 cups flour

1½ cups water

1 teaspoon active dry yeast

2 teaspoons kosher salt or coarse sea salt

TO MEASURE BY WEIGHT

500 grams flour

300 grams water

2 grams active dry yeast

10 grams kosher salt or coarse sea salt

Combine the flour, water, yeast, and salt in the bowl of a stand mixer fitted with a dough hook. Mix on medium speed until the dough is smooth and elastic, 5 to 10 minutes. Depending on the size of the bowl, you may need to stop the mixer and remove the dough from the dough hook if the dough is not developing thoroughly. When the dough looks smooth, cut off a piece and stretch it. If it stretches to the point of transparency, it's mixed enough. If not, continue mixing until it will.

Remove the bowl from the mixer and cover it with a pot lid or plastic wrap/cling film. Allow the dough to rise until it has doubled in size and does not spring back when you push your finger into it, 2 to 4 hours.

Turn the dough out onto a work surface and knead it to release the gas and redistribute the yeast. Cut the dough in half and press each half into a disk. Cover the disks with a towel and allow to stand for about 15 minutes.

Preheat the oven to 450°F/230°C/gas 8.

Stretch each disk, or roll it with a rolling pin, until it is as thin as desired (the thinner the better). Top as desired and bake on a rimless baking sheet/tray or baking stone until the edges are golden brown and the bottom is crisp, about 20 minutes. Serve immediately.

COOKING TIP:

If you don't have a bread peel and are baking a pizza on a stone, put the dough on a sheet of parchment/baking paper before topping it. The paper will make it easier to transfer the pizza from work surface to oven.

PIE DOUGH / MAKES ENOUGH DOUGH FOR ONE DOUBLE-CRUST PIE OR TWO 9-INCH (23-CENTIMETER) TARTS

Pie dough can be made in a stand mixer, but if you need enough for only one or two pies, it's faster to mix it by hand. I believe that pastry dough prepared in a food processor results in a tough rather than delicate crust.

The dough can be wrapped in plastic wrap/cling film and stored in the refrigerator for up to 24 hours, or in the freezer for up to *1 month*. If frozen, thaw in the refrigerator before using.

2 cups/300 grams all-purpose/plain flour

14 tablespoons/200 grams cold butter, vegetable shortening, or lard, chopped into ½-inch/12-millimeter chunks

Kosher salt (optional)

¼ to ½ cup/60 to 120 milliliters ice water

Combine the flour and butter in a large bowl. If using unsalted butter, add a three-finger pinch of salt. Mix the butter into the flour with your fingers, pinching it, until the butter is in chunks not bigger than peanuts. Add ¼ cup/60 milliliters of the ice water and mix until the dough comes together. Add as much of the remaining water as you need to bring the dough together if the first addition isn't enough. Shape the dough into a disk about 1 inch/2.5 centimeters thick. Wrap the dough tightly in plastic wrap/cling film, and refrigerate for at least 1 hour or up to a day. If you need a top and bottom crust, divide the dough and wrap the disks separately.

Roll out the dough as needed on a work surface dusted with flour.

CHARLOTTE'S APPLE JACK/SERVES 8

This is a favorite dish from childhood when my grandmother visited. Charlotte Addison Spamer was an excellent baker and mostly worked by intuition, so when I asked for the recipe, she told me she made a pie dough and used apples. When I asked for the amount of sugar, she said, annoyed, "Oh, I don't *know*." She did most things by sight, which, sadly, she lost at age ninety-four. But she remembers that a bakery not far from her longtime home on Sumner Road in Detroit, Michigan, sold squares of what it called Apple Jack. The family liked it so much that Charlotte started making her own. "Mine was better," she says. She also made sure to note her apple choice: Macintosh. She doesn't like cooked apples that retain some bite; she wants a completely soft apple. Macintosh delivers this quality, but I think such sweet preparations need the acidity of a tart apple, such as Granny Smith. Use Macintosh for soft and sweet, Granny Smith for a more balanced flavor and sturdier bite.

I make Charlotte's Apple Jack in a quarter sheet pan/tray or small jelly-roll/Swiss roll pan, both of which have rims and measure 13 by 9 inches/ 33 by 23 centimeters. If you don't have a pan this size, you can also make the apple jack in a 9-by-13-inch/23-by-33-centimeter baking dish.

Pie Dough (page 159)

10 Granny Smith apples, peeled and sliced as desired

⅓ cup/65 grams granulated sugar

1½ teaspoons ground cinnamon

Juice of 1 lemon

Freshly grated nutmeg

3 tablespoons packed brown sugar

GLAZE

2 cups/200 grams confectioners'/icing sugar

1 teaspoon vanilla extract

¼ to ⅜ cup/60 to 90 milliliters heavy/double cream, warmed

Preheat the oven to 350°C/180°C/gas 4.

Roll out half of the dough to the dimensions of the pan (see head note). Lay the dough in the pan.

In a large bowl, toss the apple slices with the granulated sugar, cinnamon, and lemon juice. Spread them in the pan. Generously sprinkle with nutmeg (I use plenty), then with the brown sugar. Roll out the remaining dough. Lay it over the apples, trim the excess, and seal it as desired. This is a rustic preparation, so if the dough cracks or breaks, patch it as needed. Prick all over with a fork.

Cover the edges of the dough with foil, place on a larger sheet tray to catch any drips, and bake for 30 minutes. Remove the foil and continue baking until the crust is golden brown, 30 to 45 more minutes. Allow the apple jack to cool completely.

MAKE THE GLAZE: In a small bowl, mix together the confectioners'/icing sugar, vanilla, and enough cream to form a thick glaze.

When the apple jack has cooled, brush the glaze on the crust. Serve immediately.

SNICKERDOODLES/MAKES ABOUT 12 COOKIES

This is adapted from a recipe by my friend Shuna Fish Lydon, a pastry chef and a fine writer. The cookies were originally slated for the sugar chapter because their structure is so dependent on that ingredient, but I found they did such a good job of showing how a cookie behaved that I decided to showcase them here. Shuna uses less sugar, which results in a very traditional cookie. More sugar makes these chewier and thicker. If you want them thin, simply double the butter. These are simple, delicious cinnamon-sugar cookies.

¼ cup/55 grams butter, at room temperature

½ cup/100 grams firmly packed brown sugar

1½ cups/300 grams granulated sugar

1 large egg

1 cup/140 grams all-purpose/plain flour

1 teaspoon baking powder

Kosher salt

CINNAMON SUGAR
¼ cup/50 grams granulated sugar

4 teaspoons ground cinnamon

Preheat the oven to 350°F/180°C/gas 4.

In a large bowl, combine the butter and sugars. Using a stiff spatula, stir and paddle the ingredients until uniformly combined. Add the egg and whisk rapidly until it is combined into the butter mixture.

In a small bowl, combine the flour, the baking powder, and a three-finger pinch of salt. Stir to distribute the baking powder. Fold the flour mixture, in a few batches, into the butter mixture until completely incorporated.

Scoop out tablespoons of the dough and arrange them about 3 inches/7.5 centimeters apart on a baking sheet/tray. Cover the top of a glass with a damp towel. Press the covered opening of the glass down onto each cookie.

MAKE THE CINNAMON SUGAR: In a small bowl, stir together the granulated sugar and cinnamon until the cinnamon is uniformly distributed.

Sprinkle the cookies with the cinnamon sugar (save any leftover for cinnamon toast!). Bake until the cookies are cooked through, and the edges are golden, about 15 minutes.

BATTER:
Flour, Part Two

BATTER IS FLOUR MADE FLUID. YES, WE
can call any thick mixture a batter, such as that
for a flourless chocolate cake. But technically
speaking, a flourless chocolate cake and its ilk—
preparations whose structure relies exclusively
on egg and fat—are custards, not batters. Batters
involve a starch. Although fine batters can be
made with gluten-free flours (rice flour, in
tempuras for instance), I focus exclusively on
batters that involve wheat flour. Wheat flour
brings texture and bite to a cooked batter that
no other substance does—tender cakes and
muffins, tempura with just a little bite along
with the crunch, and crêpes that have a pleas-
ingly delicate chew.

Batters lie on the opposite side of the
flour-liquid fulcrum from doughs: a batter is
a flour mixture that you can't shape; it is flour
you can pour.

There are all kinds of batters—ones of
varying thickness, ones that include fat, those
that use egg or a leavener—but a basic starting
definition of batter is equal parts flour and liquid
by weight. Batters can use liquids other than
water (milk, sauce, juice), depending on what
you're after. Most batters contain some egg, with
the white providing structure and the yolk adding richness. Butter adds flavor and richness.
Sugar adds sweetness and flavor, creates structure, and affects texture. Batters can be leavened
naturally, with whipped egg white, for instance,
or chemically, with baking powder. But the basic
composition of a batter is flour in liquid—flour
that, once heated, provides a structure for the
other ingredients.

Gluten remains a dynamic player in batters but not to the extent that it does in doughs.
Indeed, a critical way that doughs and batters differ is that in a dough you aim to develop gluten,
but in a batter you avoid it as much as possible.

Preventing the formation of gluten—the
network of proteins created by vigorous mixing—
is the key to successful batters, whose excellence
is defined in part by tenderness. You do this simply
by not overmixing. Try mixing pancake batter in
a blender, and you'll see the impact of gluten in a
cake—you will have one tough pancake.

Thus, we mix flour into a batter gently. In
a cake, it's folded in last; in a batter bread or pancake, it's mixed just until incorporated. In a tempura batter, it's mixed at the last minute, so that
the starch molecules don't have time to soak up
the liquid, resulting in a crisp coating. In a popover, absorption is desired, so the batter rests
before you cook it, resulting in a popover with
an almost creamy interior.

Most batters have egg. Egg adds nutrition,
richness, flavor, and structure. Eggs are exciting
players in batters because the way you mix them
in many respects determines the end result.

In a simple batter, say, for batter breads
and griddle cakes, eggs are simply mixed together
with the liquid. In a cake, though, they can be
mixed with the sugar first, then the flour is folded
in. In a basic sponge cake, the eggs are beaten
vigorously until they are fluffy from trapped
air bubbles, which will leaven the cake. An even
lighter cake can be made if the yolks and whites
are beaten separately. For a rich pound cake, which
includes butter, the butter and sugar are mixed
(*creamed* is the term), and the eggs are beaten
into the butter mixture. If eggs are part of a
batter, the way they are handled shapes the finished product.

Sugar, equally complex in its effects, has
an impact on flavor, texture, moistness, and
color. When sugar is dissolved into the liquid
ingredients to become a syrup, it makes a cake
sweet. It also adds some structure, and it helps
the cake to retain moisture. You can best see this

in an angel food cake, which combines equal amounts of egg whites and sugar, then about a third as much flour, folded in at the end.

Butter adds richness and depth of flavor to a batter, it helps prevent gluten networks from forming, and it can also make a cake dense. I use plenty of butter in a pound cake, but I prefer cakes without butter, in favor of those made simply with eggs, sugar, and flour.

Batter is one of the most common preparations in baking. The following recipes explore the basic batter types: a cake batter with whole eggs (for a batter using whites only, see Angel Food Cake, page 183), a batter bread, and a thin, airy batter for popovers.

CLASSIC LAYER CAKE WITH CHOCOLATE BUTTERCREAM ICING AND CHOCOLATE GLAZE

MAKES **ONE 8-INCH/20-CENTIMETER** TWO-LAYER CAKE (SERVES **12 TO 16**)

The processed food industry has trained many of us to believe that making a cake is too hard to do on our own, so we'd better buy an easy cake mix. To be honest, not all cake mixes are bad, but they usually have a generic flavor, often contain trans-fats and an unnecessarily high amount of sugar, and typically use chlorinated flour. For a moist, uncommonly flavorful cake, try making one on your own. It's a piece of cake.

This cake has no butter, which can make cakes heavy. (Don't worry, there's plenty in the icing!) The yolks and whites are mixed separately, with the beaten whites giving the cake the majority of its aeration.

Perhaps the most important part of baking a cake is thinking—having good *mise en place*, that is, having everything ready to go, especially a preheated oven and prepared pans. Also, if you have a digital scale, use that to weigh your flour in grams.

9 large eggs, separated

2 cups/400 grams sugar

2 teaspoons vanilla extract

2 tablespoons lemon juice

2 cups/280 grams cake/soft-wheat flour, sifted

Chocolate Buttercream Icing (page 171)

Chocolate Glaze (page 171)

Preheat the oven to 325°F/165°C/gas 3.

Prepare two 8-inch/20-centimeter cake pans/tins (or one 9-inch/23-centimeter springform pan) by coating with butter or vegetable oil and then flouring the bottom and sides, shaking out any excess flour. Line the bottoms with parchment/baking paper (see page 170).

In a large bowl, combine the egg yolks with half of the sugar and the vanilla. Whisk until the yolks are light and bubbly and the sugar is combined, about 1 minute.

Combine the egg whites and the lemon juice in the bowl of a stand mixer fitted with the whisk attachment. Beat on high speed for 1 to 2 minutes. With the motor running, slowly add the remaining sugar. Continue to beat until the whites have tripled in volume and formed soft peaks.

Fold half the egg white mixture into the egg yolks, then fold in half the flour. Fold until well combined, then fold in the remaining egg whites followed by the remaining flour.

Pour the batter into the prepared pans. Bake until set and a toothpick inserted into the centers comes out clean, 30 to 40 minutes. Allow the cakes to cool in the pans for 10 minutes, then invert on racks, remove the paper, and gently turn the cakes right-side up to cool completely.

Slice the top off what will be the bottom layer. (If you used a springform pan, slice the cake in half horizontally to make two layers.) Ice the top of the first layer with the buttercream, then add the second layer and ice the top and sides of the cake. I recommend giving the cake a crumb coat, a very thin first coating of icing, refrigerating it until the icing sets, finishing the icing, and then coating with the glaze.

Preparation photographs begin on the next page.

1/Whip the egg yolks.

2/Add the sugar to the egg yolks.

3/Whip until tripled in volume.

4/Whisk the whites in a spotlessly clean bowl.

5/When the whites are foamy, sprinkle in the sugar.

6/The whites will quadruple in volume.

7/The whites are done when they hold a soft peak.

8/Gently fold half of the whites into the yolks.

9/Fold in half of the flour.

10/Alternately fold in the remaining whites and flour.

11/Immediately pour the batter into the cake pans.

12/Fill the pans three-quarters full.

Continued on the next page.

13/Cool the cakes on a rack for 10 minutes, then peel off the paper.

14/Frost with a thin layer of buttercream, called the crumb coat.

How to Cut a PARCHMENT ROUND

Fold a square of parchment/baking paper in half. Fold it in half again to make a square. Working from either crease, fold the paper over as if making a paper airplane, with the tip being where the two creases meet (if you were to open the paper, the tip would be the paper's center). Continue to make the triangular fold until you reach the other edge. Place the tip of the triangle in the center of the cake pan/tin and hold a finger on the other end of the triangle where it meets the side of the pan. Cut the triangle off at the side of the pan with a knife or scissors. Unfold the paper, and behold your parchment round. To cut the parchment for a tube pan, before unfolding it, hold the point in the center and make a second cut at the edge of the tube to create a hole in the center of the round.

Chocolate Buttercream Icing/MAKES 5 CUPS/1.2 LITERS BUTTERCREAM

When you try this awesome concoction, it will forever shame you for having been tempted to buy the artificially flavored icing from the store. French buttercream is distinguished from Italian buttercream by the use of yolks rather than whites. Italian buttercream is the supremely white icing you see on fancy cakes. German buttercream uses pastry cream, which is thickened vanilla sauce. They're all good, but I like the richness of the yolks in this icing.

¾ cup/150 grams sugar

6 large egg yolks

1 large egg

2 cups/455 grams butter, at room temperature, cut into about 30 pieces

2 teaspoons vanilla extract

6 ounces/170 grams semisweet/plain or bittersweet chocolate, melted, and slightly cooled

In a small saucepan, combine the sugar and ½ cup/120 milliliters water. Bring to a boil over high heat and cook for 3 to 5 minutes. (The sugar syrup should register between 230° and 240°F/112° and 115°C on a candy thermometer if you have one.)

While the sugar syrup cooks, combine the egg yolks and whole egg in the bowl of a stand mixer fitted with the whisk attachment. Whip the eggs on high speed until tripled in volume. This will take about as long as needed to cook the sugar syrup.

Continuing to whip the eggs, pour the sugar syrup slowly into beaten eggs. Continue to whip until the outside of the bowl has cooled, 8 to 10 minutes. Reduce the speed to medium and add one piece of the butter. After it begins to become incorporated, add the remaining butter, one piece at a time. The butter may look as if it's breaking, but keep whipping it, and the mixture will come together.

When all the butter is incorporated, add the vanilla and chocolate, return the speed to high, and beat until the icing comes together (it will change from visibly grainy and unappetizing to smooth and luscious).

Ice the cake while the buttercream is at room temperature.

Icing preparation photographs begin on the next page.

Chocolate Glaze/MAKES ABOUT ¾ CUP 180/MILLILITERS GLAZE

3 ounces/85 grams butter, cut into 3 pieces

3 ounces/85 grams semisweet/plain chocolate, melted

Stir the butter into the chocolate until it is completely incorporated. Cool to room temperature. Spoon over the top of the cake, allowing the excess to run down the sides.

1/Boil your sugar syrup for 3 to 5 minutes.

2/Whip the egg yolks until they triple in volume.

3/Whip the sugar syrup into the egg yolks.

4/Ready the final ingredients while the syrup-egg mixture cools.

5/When the bowl is not warm to the touch, add the butter a few pieces at a time.

6/Add the melted and slightly cooled chocolate.

BANANA-BLUEBERRY BREAD

MAKES **ONE 8-INCH/20-CENTIMETER** LOAF

In deciding what kind of batter bread I wanted to include, I simply combined my favorite batter bread with my favorite muffin. I started with the basic batter ratio of equal parts liquid and flour by weight, half as much egg, then scaled back on the liquid to account for the very moist banana.

2 cups/280 grams all-purpose/plain flour

2 teaspoons baking powder

½ teaspoon baking soda/bicarbonate of soda

Kosher salt

3 large eggs

¼ cup/60 milliliters buttermilk

⅓ cup/65 grams sugar

¼ cup/60 grams butter, melted

2 bananas, mashed

1 teaspoon vanilla extract

1 teaspoon grated lemon zest

1 cup/140 grams blueberries, tossed with 1 tablespoon flour

Preheat the oven to 350°F/180°C/gas 4. Butter an 8-inch/20-centimeter loaf pan/tin or coat it with vegetable oil.

In a medium bowl, combine the flour, baking powder, baking soda/bicarbonate of soda, and 1 teaspoon salt. In a large bowl, combine the eggs, buttermilk, sugar, melted butter, bananas, vanilla, and lemon zest and mix well. Add the flour mixture and whisk just to combine. Stir in the blueberries.

Pour the batter into the prepared pan. Bake until a paring knife or toothpick inserted into the bread comes out clean, about 1 hour. Cool in the pan on a wire rack for 15 minutes. Turn the bread out of the pan onto the rack and let cool.

Store at room temperature, well wrapped, for up to 3 days.

BASIC POPOVERS/MAKES ABOUT **4** POPOVERS

POPOVERS and YORKSHIRE PUDDING

Popovers are showoffs. True to their name, they pop out of their pan like a girl out of a cake, as the water in the batter vaporizes. For popover batter, you want the flour to fully hydrate, so it's best to mix the batter at least an hour before you cook it. The recipe will work if you can't wait, but I've found that the popovers are better with the rest—crisper on the outside and creamier inside.

For an excellent savory preparation, try traditional Yorkshire pudding, which is popover batter poured into a pan with beef drippings (or into cups containing melted rendered beef fat).

Popovers are wonderful for Sunday morning breakfast with jam or apple butter or honey. They're most dramatic when baked in a popover pan, but you can make them in ½-cup/120-millimeter ramekins if you wish.

1 cup/240 milliliters milk

2 large eggs

Scant 1 cup/120 grams all-purpose/plain flour

Kosher salt

4 tablespoons/55 grams butter, melted

In a bowl, combine the milk, eggs, flour, and ½ teaspoon salt. Mix with a whisk or hand blender until uniformly combined. Let the batter rest for 1 hour at room temperature (or refrigerate overnight, removing it at least 30 minutes before baking).

Place a popover pan in the oven and preheat the oven to 450°F/230°C/gas 8.

After about 10 minutes, remove the pan from the oven. Pour about 1 tablespoon of the melted butter in each cup. Fill each cup three-fourths full with the batter. Bake for 10 minutes. Reduce the oven temperature to 400°F/200°C/gas 6 and continue to bake until the popovers are golden brown and hot in the middle, about 20 minutes. Remove from the pan and serve immediately.

MARLENE'S YORKSHIRE PUDDING/MAKES 6 TO 8 PUDDINGS

Marlene Newell, who tested all the recipes in this book (and oversaw secondary testers), feels these are best done in a very hot oven. Be sure your oven is clean, to avoid smoking yourself out of the kitchen, or reduce the heat somewhat. If you don't have a popover pan, you can use a standard muffin pan. Or it can even be done in a large baking dish with hot beef fat—it rises and bubbles and curls dramatically.

1 cup/140 grams all-purpose/plain flour

1 teaspoon mustard powder

4 or 5 large eggs

1 cup/240 milliliters whole milk

6 teaspoons vegetable oil or beef fat drippings

Sift the flour and mustard powder together into a large bowl. Add the eggs and milk and blend on high speed with a hand mixer until fully incorporated. Let the batter rest for about 2 hours, reblending it now and then.

Preheat the oven to 475°F/240°C/gas 9.

Place 1 teaspoon of vegetable oil in each cup of a popover pan. Place the pan on a baking sheet and slide it into the oven for a few minutes, until the oil is hot.

Remove the pan and pour the batter into the cups, dividing it equally and filling the cups three-fourths full. Place the pan in the oven, and turn on the light so you can watch the pudding rise. After 10 minutes, reduce the oven temperature to 450°F/230°C/gas 8. Continue to bake, without opening the oven door, until the pudding is puffed, golden brown, and hot in the center, 15 to 20 more minutes. Serve immediately.

10

SUGAR:

From Simple to Complex

SUGAR IS ONE OF THE MOST IMPORTANT and complex ingredients in the kitchen. It is critical not just because of its capacity to sweeten—which is huge and pervasive in itself—but also because of its impact on the structure of cooked batters and doughs.

Furthermore, the permutations sugar undergoes at varying temperatures are more numerous than for any other single ingredient. Heat it to 240°F/115°C, and it will be clear and pliable when cooled. Heat it a little more, and it will harden completely and stay clear. Take it above 300°F/150°C, and it begins to brown, or caramelize, taking on increasingly intricate flavors. Pour a little of this clear, amber sugar in a ramekin, and it will harden to glass but then melt when a custard is cooked on top of it so that the sugar cascades down the custard's sides when the dessert, crème caramel, is upended on a plate. Add dairy fat to liquid caramelized sugar, and you have a thick, pourable caramel sauce. Add butter, cook the sauce some more, and it will become sweet brittle toffee.

Sugar is a study in contradictions. Getting sugar very hot results in hardness in a finished preparation, whether a cookie or a candy; yet freezing it results in softness. Sugar, not fat, is the reason ice cream is pliable (consider how hard water and butter get when you freeze them). It is also why lemon bars do not become rock hard and instead take on a pleasing chewiness. Sugar has an affinity for opposites: marrying vinegar in a barbecue sauce that makes pork sing (see page 97), welcoming salt when used as caramel on a sundae (see page 43).

Once sugar is incorporated into food, its impact goes far beyond making something sweet. Sugar attracts and binds with water, water that might otherwise get soaked up by the flour. Its affinity for water helps make cookies crisp and keep many baked goods moist. Sugar contributes to the shortening of gluten and so can help make baked foods tender. It prevents crystallization in many frozen desserts. Try to reduce calories in a recipe by cutting the sugar, and you may have a mess on your hands. Sugar helps hold food together. It pulls moisture out of fruits to make a kind of syrup and concentrate the fruit flavors. Sprinkle strawberries liberally with sugar, and in an hour you will have a delicious topping for strawberry shortcake.

By carefully controlling the warming and heating of sugar, you can create sculptures as complex and compelling as blown glass.

That unassuming white stuff in the bowl next to the coffee and cream is a wonder.

In many ways, mastering sugar is all about balance, whether in terms of the flavor of a dish or in relation to other structural ingredients, such as flour, egg, and butter—or in terms of other flavoring ingredients, especially acidic ones.

Among the most important skills to learn as a cook is the balancing of flavor. Often, sugar added to a sauce or a braise helps round it out and balance acidity. When you evaluate any dish, sweetness should be considered. Would a little sweetness enhance this sauce, for instance? Not sure? Put some on a spoon add a little sugar and taste. As with salt, you shouldn't taste sugar or allow it to overpower; you wouldn't want to turn a savory sauce into a dessert sauce. Vinaigrettes are an excellent example of sugar's capacity to balance. Make a standard 3:1 vinaigrette with sherry vinegar and oil, diced shallot, and a little Dijon mustard. Then add a little brown sugar or honey, and taste the vinaigrette. Barbecue sauces and the French techniques for *gastrique* and *aigre-doux* are all sweet-and-sour savory dishes that rely on an aggressive balance of vinegar and sugar.

When seasoning dishes, white table sugar is only one of many alternatives. Brown sugar and honey are good examples of seasoning options, as is a relative newcomer, agave nectar, a liquid derived from the agave plant and now widely available in grocery stores.

White table sugar, seemingly so plain, so ordinary, becomes an enormously powerful player once it's put into action with water or heat. Cooked, it takes on extraordinary complexity with a range of aromas and flavors. Learning the fundamentals of sugar, especially in baking and pastry, can make you a more confident cook.

CARAMEL SAUCE/MAKES ABOUT 1¾ CUPS/420 MILLILITERS SAUCE

Made with just sugar and cream, caramel sauce is one of the great renditions of sugar. I grew up with a jar of store-bought caramel sauce in the door of the refrigerator, never realizing that my own, more delicious and more-fun-to-make caramel sauce could be finished in the time it took me to find the opener to get the stuck lid off the jar. It is as easy as melting a little sugar until it's amber, then adding the same amount of cream. Cool the sauce a little by setting the pan in water for a warm caramel sundae, or let it cool completely so it doesn't melt the ice cream.

Technically, you don't even need cream. You can make a good caramel sauce with sugar, butter, and water, all of which we commonly have on hand, so it can be a last-minute creation.

And it can be varied. Make caramel sauce with brown sugar. Cook brown sugar with half as much butter until it's brown and frothy, add the cream, season with a few drops of lemon juice and salt, and you've got an amazing butterscotch sauce.

Caramel is not just for topping ice cream, or for making Caramel-Pecan Ice Cream (page 332). It can be featured in a rich caramel and chocolate tart, or drizzled over cakes or brownies.

Caramel works great in savory preparations, too. There's no reason you couldn't improve on any barbecue sauce by replacing the sugar with caramel, or use caramel in a sauce for miso-glazed pork (see facing page).

Caramel is a cooking basic. There are two ways to begin the process: melting the sugar dry by itself in the pan or melting the sugar by adding just enough water to make it look like wet sand. Both work fine. I prefer the wet approach because I feel it gives me a little more control as the water first dissolves the sugar, then cooks off. Resist the urge to stir too much. Wet or dry, stirred sugar will clump up into grainy pebbles.

If this happens, be patient—the clumps will eventually melt along with the rest of the sugar. Use a silicone spatula or a flat-edged wooden spoon to stir the hot sugar.

Simple though caramel is, it comes with a major warning. Sugar can get hot, as hot as oil, and worse than oil, if you spill it on yourself, it will stick like tar. Some of the worst burns in the kitchen are sugar burns, so be careful. Use a high-sided, heavy saucepan (enameled cast iron is a good choice). When adding other ingredients such as cream, be watchful—some of the water will vaporize on contact, and the sugar will foam up in steamy violence during the first several seconds. Have a source of cold water within arm's reach, whether a faucet or a bowl of water just in case. (Cooling the pan with water is also a good way to stop a caramel from overcooking if you sense it's going to burn.) Lastly, never leave melting sugar unattended on the stove.

The following proportions can be doubled or halved as needed.

1 cup/200 grams sugar

1 cup/200 milliliters heavy/double cream, warmed in a microwave

Put the sugar in a small, heavy-bottomed saucepan. Add 3 tablespoons water, if desired. Set the pan over medium heat and cook the sugar without stirring until it liquefies and begins to brown. Stir gently with a heatproof spoon until the sugar turns amber, 5 to 10 minutes. Carefully add the cream (the sugar is so hot that the cream will boil on contact, which is why you need a high-sided pan) and stir to incorporate. Allow the sauce to cool before using, or refrigerate, covered, for up to 2 weeks. If the sauce is very stiff, rewarm it gently in a microwave.

EASY CARAMEL-BUTTER SAUCE

MAKES ABOUT ½ CUP/120 MILLILITERS SAUCE

If you don't have cream, but still feel like making caramel sauce, try this recipe, which requires only sugar and butter. I use the dry caramel method here, but feel free to add a little water at the start when melting the sugar.

½ cup/100 grams sugar

4 tablespoons/55 grams butter

Put the sugar in a small, heavy-bottomed saucepan over medium heat and cook without stirring. When the edges are melting and turning brown, gently swirl the pot to distribute sugar or give the sugar a delicate stir. When the sugar is a dark amber, add the butter and then ¼ cup/60 milliliters water, and stir until the bubbles subside. Continue to simmer for another minute or so. Remove from the heat, pour the sauce into a heatproof container, and let cool. The sauce can be refrigerated, covered, for up to 2 weeks.

CARAMEL-MISO GLAZE/MAKES 1 CUP/240 MILLILITERS GLAZE

There are many ingredients here, but the key players are the caramel sauce and miso. Miso, a fermented paste made from rice, barley, and/or soybeans, adds great flavor and depth to many savory dishes and is a staple in Japanese cuisine. The stock distributes the ingredients, and the vinegar balances the sweetness of the caramel and miso. Shiro miso is sweeter and less salty than regular miso. Use the glaze for braised pork belly (see page 269) or with any pork preparation.

1 tablespoon butter

1 tablespoon minced shallot

1 teaspoon minced garlic

Kosher salt

Freshly ground black pepper

½ cup/120 milliliters pork cooking liquid (see page 269), or pork or chicken stock

¼ cup/60 milliliters Caramel Sauce (facing page) or Easy Caramel-Butter Sauce (above)

2 tablespoons shiro miso

3 tablespoons red wine vinegar

1 tablespoon soy sauce

1 tablespoon fish sauce

In a small sauté pan, melt the butter over medium heat. Add the shallot and garlic and sauté until translucent. Season with a two-finger pinch of salt and some pepper. Add the cooking liquid, caramel sauce, miso, vinegar, soy sauce, and fish sauce. Bring to a simmer and cook for 30 seconds or so, then remove from the heat. The glaze can be used immediately or refrigerated for up to 2 days.

ANGEL FOOD CAKE WITH WHIPPED CREAM AND TOFFEE/SERVES 12

When I was a boy, this was the cake my mom always made for my birthday because I loved it so much. It continues to be a favorite. If there is such a thing as dessert comfort food, this soft angel food cake covered with toffee-studded whipped cream is it.

I don't have a tube pan, and even if I did, I wouldn't use it for this recipe. Instead, a springform pan makes the work of extricating the cake from the pan a snap—no small issue with very sticky angel food cake batter. Pour the batter into the pan and press a tapered drinking glass, bottom down, into the center so that the batter is forced up around it. If you prefer a tube pan, line the bottom with parchment/baking paper.

TOFFEE
½ cup/100 grams granulated sugar

½ cup/115 grams butter

CAKE
1½ cups/300 grams granulated sugar

Scant 1 cup/120 grams cake/soft-wheat flour

10 large egg whites

½ teaspoon cream of tartar

1 tablespoon lemon juice

2 teaspoons vanilla extract

Kosher salt

WHIPPED CREAM
2 cups/480 milliliters heavy/double cream

1 to 2 tablespoons brown sugar

1 teaspoon vanilla extract

1 teaspoon Frangelico liqueur (optional)

2 ounces/55 grams semisweet chocolate, finely chopped

MAKE THE TOFFEE: Place a 15-inch/38-centimeter square of parchment/baking paper on a wood cutting board or other heatproof surface. Put the granulated sugar and butter in a small saucepan over medium heat. When the butter begins to melt, stir to make sure the sugar cooks evenly. The mixture will be very frothy, and the sugar on the bottom of the pan will brown. Stir only occasionally as the mixture turns the color of caramel, 5 to 10 minutes. Pour it onto the paper and allow it to cool completely. Don't worry if some of the butterfat breaks out.

MAKE THE CAKE: Preheat the oven to 350°F/180°C/gas 4. Combine ¾ cup/150 grams of the granulated sugar and the flour in a food processor and pulse a few times. Put the egg whites in the bowl of a stand mixer fitted with the whisk attachment and beat on high speed until frothy. Add the cream of tartar, lemon juice, vanilla, and a three-finger pinch of salt, and mix on high. Slowly pour in the remaining sugar. When the egg whites form soft peaks, remove the bowl from the mixer. Fold in the flour-sugar mixture until completely incorporated. Pour the batter into the prepared pan. Bake until a skewer or paring knife inserted into the center comes out clean, 40 to 50 minutes. Remove the pan from the oven and invert it over a bottle or other suitable stand or on the inserted glass so that the cake cools upside down for 1 hour or more before removing it from the pan.

MAKE THE WHIPPED CREAM: Combine the cream, brown sugar, vanilla, and liqueur (if using) in the bowl of the stand mixer fitted with the whisk attachment and beat on high speed until the whipped cream holds its shape.

Coarsely chop the toffee. Fold all but about 2 tablespoons into the whipped cream.

Remove the cake from the pan and cut it in half horizontally to make two layers. Ice the cut side of the bottom layer with the whipped cream and add the top layer. Ice the top and sides of the cake. Sprinkle the top with the remaining toffee and the chopped chocolate.

Preparation photographs begin on the next page.

1/First whip the egg whites.

2/Then add sugar, lemon juice, and cream of tartar.

3/Whip on high speed.

4/Stop whipping when soft peaks form.

5/Fold in the flour.

6/Gently pour into the cake pan.

7/You can use a tube pan or a springform and a pint glass.

8/The cake is golden when finished baking.

9/Cool the cake upside down.

10/For the toffee, cook the butter and sugar together.

11/Pour onto parchment/baking paper when caramel in color.

12/Some butterfat may render out.

Continued on the next page.

13/Coarsely break, then chop the toffee into bits.

14/Frost all around with the whipped cream and toffee mixture.

15/Garnish with chopped toffee and chocolate.

COOKING TIP:

To make the cake in advance, hold the baked cake at room temperature. Make the whipped cream and hold in the fridge. When ready to serve, combine the toffee with the whipped cream and ice the cake as directed.

LEMON-LIME SORBET/

Sugar is the key in a sorbet, not only to balance the intense acidity, but also to keep the sorbet pliable. Use too much water relative to the sugar, and the sorbet will be nearly as hard as a block of ice. I also add a little alcohol for textural reasons. My dad was a gin drinker so that's why it's here, but you can use vodka if you must.

1 cup/200 grams sugar

½ cup/120 milliliters lime juice (about 4 limes)

½ cup/120 milliliters lemon juice (2 or 3 lemons)

⅓ cup/75 milliliters gin (optional)

Combine the sugar and 2 cups/450 milliliters water in a medium saucepan over high heat, bring to a simmer, and cook just long enough for all the sugar to dissolve. Add the lime and lemon juices and the gin (if using). Refrigerate the mixture until completely chilled, then freeze in an ice-cream maker. Transfer to a container and freeze for at least 4 hours before serving.

CANDIED ORANGE PEEL

MAKES **FIFTY TO SIXTY** ¼-INCH-/5-MILLIMETER-WIDE STRIPS

I like candied orange peel because it makes use of something we normally throw away, and also because it tastes so good. You can coat the strips of peel in decorative sugar or dip them in melted chocolate. I like some bite and chewiness to the strips, so after I blanch them, I cut off a layer of pith. For very fine peels, remove all the pith.

2 oranges

1 cup/200 grams granulated sugar

Decorative sugar or melted chocolate

Working from one end of each orange to the other, make four or five cuts through the peel just to the flesh. Remove the peel and reserve the flesh for another use. Cut the peel into strips about ¼ inch/6 millimeters wide, or as you wish.

Bring a large pot of water to a boil. Blanch the peels for 60 seconds. Remove them with a strainer and run under cold water. To reduce the bitterness of the pith, you can blanch the peels again and rinse them one or two more times.

Put the peels, the granulated sugar, and 1 cup/240 milliliters water in a saucepan. Bring to a simmer over medium heat, then reduce the heat to low and cook the peels, stirring once or twice, until the peels are cooked and saturated with the syrup, about 1 hour. Spread the peels on a rack and allow them to dry overnight.

Roll the peels in decorative sugar or dip them in melted chocolate. Store in an airtight container for up to 2 weeks.

1/The peels are simmered in a 1:1 water-to-sugar syrup.

2/Dry for 8 hours or overnight.

3/Toss the peels in decorative sugar.

4/The finished peels.

SAUCE:
Not on the Side!

A KEY REASON THAT THE FOOD YOU MAKE at home tastes different from the food you're served in a decent restaurant is that the restaurant makes its own stock. That's why stock is called *fond de cuisine*, the "foundation of cooking." One might also say that the main way a chef's plate differs from a plate you serve is sauce.

About midway through my culinary school adventures, I began to notice the ubiquity of sauce. Everything, but *everything*, got a sauce. You didn't even *think* about a dish without a sauce to go with it, whether you were making a canapé, an appetizer, a main course, or a dessert. Even soups got sauced! That's what the dollop of crème fraîche in a curried butternut soup is: it is the finishing flavor, enriching, smoothing, piquing with its acidity, as well as adding a final visual flourish.

For this reason, "sauce on the side" is a request that drives most chefs bananas. Sauce is a fundamental part of a dish, not an accessory. And that's how you should think of it. Sauce completes a dish, adding succulence, seasoning, and color to something that, one hopes, is already delicious. That's how you turn something good into something fantastic.

Sauces at fine-dining restaurants are often based on stocks, and although stock-based sauces are considered by some to be one of the pinnacles of the chef's craft, they are but one branch of the sauce tree. If you have a little bit of stock, you're moments away from a delectable sauce. But if you don't have stock on hand, you don't need to go sauceless.

Butter is a ready-made sauce that is delicious with roasted chicken and a little Dijon mustard. You can add several different flavors to make it even better (see Compound Butter, page 136). Cream, the mother of butter, is likewise one step away from being a sauce, whether it is added to a mixture of shallots, peppercorns, and cognac, or to caramelized sugar for a dessert.

Chopped tomato with onion and lime, *salsa crudo*, is a great simple sauce for all kinds of food (see fish tacos, page 312).

There are whole categories of roux-thickened sauces. Stock thickened with roux and milk thickened with roux (covered in technique #13, Soup) are categories comprising countless derivative sauces.

Vinaigrettes are such an important kind of sauce that they have their own chapter.

Emulsified sauces such as Mayonnaise (page 119) and Hollandaise (page 199) are oil- and butter-based sauces that are far more easy to make than their reputation suggests.

Puréed vegetables make splendid sauces (see Sautéed Scallops with Asparagus, page 233). Cooked puréed tomatoes are a terrific all-purpose sauce that goes well beyond the world of pasta; tomato sauce is also an excellent medium for braising, for instance, especially if you don't have stock. Braises and stews make their own sauce as a by-product of the cooking method. The sauce for the braised veal breast (see page 327) is in effect the kind of reduction sauce you get in restaurants—it is meat stock reduced to sauce consistency.

I address the main sauce categories here: cream sauce, emulsified butter sauce, vegetable-based sauce, and tomato sauce.

I focus first on pan sauces, last-minute preparations made in the same pan that the meat cooked in, and on other sauce techniques that don't require stock or long cooking times. These sauces enhance all kinds of dishes and work like steroids on your cooking muscles. Learning how to produce a last-minute sauce is an invaluable skill, taking advantage of what you are already cooking. With little effort from the cook, they become an elixir that can bring the whole meal together. Making a pan sauce while a roasted chicken rests teaches many lessons in how a pan sauce works. Water, as discussed in technique #3, is your main tool for drawing flavor out of cooked vegetables and browned protein stuck to the pan. Wine, an ally here too, provides instant flavor and acidity, exactly what you want in a sauce. Issues of finesse and tools will tighten your control over cooking sauces, but for the most part, there are only a few basic ideas to understand.

The first is that when you remove meat from the pan, the pan holds some of the flavor that you want to use in the sauce. In the case of this chicken, skin should be stuck to the pan. The skin is largely connective tissue, or protein, and will contribute gelatin that gives your sauce body. The golden brown color of the skin will provide flavor. Juices that the chicken released during cooking will have collected in the pan and turned brown. And there will be fat rendered from the chicken. The pan may also have salt and any other seasonings you put on the bird.

All these elements are ready to go to work for you. If you simply add water, bring it to a boil, and let the mixture cook down a little, you'd have a tasty liquid.

But you can make the sauce much better. First, before you add anything, make sure all the juices have cooked down to a glaze on the pan, that the chicken skin is fully browned, and that the fat is clear, indicating that most of the water has cooked off.

Depending on the size and kind of chicken you roasted, you may not need all the rendered fat. Pour off all but a few tablespoons. This is *schmaltz*, which you can save. It's tasty, and you can cook with it or use it as the fat in *pâte à choux* (paht ah SHOO) dough for chicken and dumplings.

Return the pan to the heat, add sliced onion, and cook just to sweat the onion if you're in a hurry or cook it deeper if you have a little more time. This will give the sweetness of the onion a little more complexity.

Now that you've captured the flavors in the pan, add 1 cup/240 milliliters water to make those flavors liquid and catch even more of them. This is often called *deglazing*, lifting the glaze of fat and flavor off the bottom of the pan. Bring the water to a boil. The hot water will immediately begin extracting sugars from the onion and amino acids from the chicken skin. When you cook the water off to make a reduction, the tasty molecules will remain in the pan, browning, getting increasingly flavorful. When the liquid is nearly gone, the fat has begun to crackle, and the onions are browning further, stir the contents of the pan and add another 1 cup/240 milliliters water. Bring the water to a simmer, and you will have a sweet savory sauce for the chicken. You can pour it from the pan onto the chicken, using a spoon to hold back the solids.

Now that we have isolated the key dynamics of the basic pan sauce, we can begin to bring even more flavor to it.

- Instead of using water for the first deglazing, use white wine.

- Do a third deglazing and reduction.

- Finish the sauce with some acidity: a shot of red wine or sherry vinegar or a squeeze of lemon juice.

- Stir in a couple of teaspoons of fish sauce for umami.

- Add aromatic ingredients: fresh herbs such as parsley, tarragon, or chives, or a tablespoon of minced Lemon Confit (page 33).

- Add a variety of aromatics to the hot fat along with the sliced onion. Using a vegetable peeler, cut a carrot into thin strips, for faster flavor extraction, and add to the onion. Add a smashed garlic clove or two; cracked peppercorns; a bay leaf or some thyme; and a teaspoon of tomato paste/purée. (If you do this, you're making a mini batch of your own chicken stock!)

• Include chicken parts, such as the wing tips, neck, gizzard, and heart (not the liver), either before roasting the chicken or before the first deglazing.

Soon all of the preceding will be too easy for you, and you'll want to make the sauce even better. After the final deglazing, pass the sauce through a fine-mesh strainer into a small saucepan. Now you have a very fine sauce, and you can refine it further. Swirl in some butter to enrich it and give it a voluptuous texture. Sweat a little minced shallot in the saucepan before you strain the sauce into it. Adjust the consistency with a couple of teaspoons of *beurre manié* or a cornstarch/cornflour slurry. Stir in some finely minced herbs—fines herbes are a common and delicious pairing: parsley, tarragon, chervil, and chives. Taste your sauce again for seasoning and acidity.

Once you do this, you'll see that the technique works for any meat that leaves some of its browned protein and fat in the pan. Home cooks are often led to believe that in order to make great meat-based sauces, they must spend weekends laboring over enormous pots of stock and vats of steaming bones and, afterward, a piled-high sink. Not true: Some water and a pan in which you cooked meat are all you need.

A traditional hollandaise sauce is a preparation to revel in, not to fear. Like mayonnaise, hollandaise is an emulsified sauce—lots of butter emulsified into a small amount of liquid with the help of some enriching egg yolk. Many recipes use only lemon juice for flavor, but a vinegar reduction is included in the version described by Escoffier, and adds some complexity to the end flavor.

A reduction is basically a mini stock that you quickly prepare before making the sauce by combining vinegar and aromatics, cooking off the vinegar, and then reconstituting it with water.

Vegetable-based sauces are great as well. You can quickly sauté chopped mushrooms and shallots, season them with salt and pepper,

deglaze the pan with white wine, and add just enough water to bring all the ingredients together. Finish with a pat of butter, and you've got a delicious sauce for white fish such as halibut, sautéed chicken, or grilled/barbecued meats. Add a squeeze of lemon or a pinch of curry for a tantalizing accent.

Tomato sauce is not only an excellent all-purpose sauce—it's also a great cooking medium. I suspect it's not prepared nearly enough at home because of the heavy marketing of tomato-sauce makers. You can't make tomato sauce at the last minute—the fastest you can bring it together is about an hour—but tomato sauce is simple and practically cooks itself once the ingredients are in the pan. It's little more than puréed tomatoes cooked down. You can flavor it, you can enrich it, and you can make it more complex in any number of ways.

My favorite tomato sauce is simply plum tomatoes (also known as Roma tomatoes), onion, and butter. This results in a very fresh-tasting sauce that is equally fine on pasta or as a braising liquid for pot roast. If I want more complexity, I char the tomatoes under a broiler/grill. For the recipe in this section, you can roast them in a hot oven for 20 minutes. They could be grilled/barbecued first for a smoky tomato sauce. In winter, when good fresh tomatoes are scarce, I use canned whole tomatoes (I prefer Muir Glen organic tomatoes and San Marzano tomatoes).

When flavoring the sauce with hard herbs (herbs with tough stems), such as oregano or marjoram, add them at the beginning (tie them in a bunch with kitchen string to make them easy to remove later). When using soft herbs, such as basil, add them just before serving to keep their flavor vivid and fresh (the flavor will be lost if you cook them).

The following recipes are examples of how quickly sauces can come together. With one exception, the following sauces don't rely on stock.

PAN SAUCE FOR ROASTED CHICKEN

MAKES ABOUT ¾ CUP/180 MILLILITERS **SAUCE**

This sauce relies on little more than the flavors already in the pan in which you cooked the Perfect Roasted Chicken (page 249) and can be made while the chicken rests. You can serve it rustic and plain, or you can lift it up with a little extra effort. If you have fresh chicken stock on hand, using it instead of water will result in an especially rich sauce, but the sauce is delicious with water alone.

RUSTIC SAUCE

½ Spanish onion, thinly sliced

1 carrot, thinly sliced

½ cup/120 millimeters white wine

REFINED SAUCE

2 tablespoons butter

1 shallot, minced

2 teaspoons minced fresh tarragon

1 teaspoon minced fresh parsley

1 teaspoon minced fresh chives

Squeeze of lemon (optional)

2 teaspoons Dijon mustard (optional)

MAKE THE RUSTIC SAUCE: Put the pan in which you have just roasted a chicken over high heat and cook any remaining skin for 1 minute or so. The juices will cook down and stick to the bottom of the pan. Pour off all but 1 or 2 tablespoons of the rendered fat if you wish. Add the onion and carrot and stir with a flat-edged spoon to coat the vegetables with the fat. Cook until the onion is translucent, 3 to 4 minutes. Add the wine and deglaze the pan, scraping up the caramelized bits. Cook all the wine off (the fat will begin to crackle). Continue to cook until the onion and carrot are caramelized, 1 to 2 minutes. Add 1 cup/240 milliliters hot water, deglaze the pan again, and let the water cook down completely. When the crackling begins, stir the onion and carrot until they become nicely caramelized. Add another 1 cup/240 milliliters hot water and cook until reduced by about two-thirds.

MAKE THE REFINED SAUCE: While the wine and water are cooking down, melt the butter in a small saucepan over medium heat, adding the shallot as the butter melts. Cook the shallot gently until translucent. Remove the pan from the heat. Strain the sauce into the saucepan with the shallot and bring to a gentle simmer. Add the remaining butter and swirl it in the pan until completely incorporated into the sauce. Stir in the herbs. (While the sauce is reducing, separate the legs from the chicken. You can add any juices accumulated on the carving board to the pan sauce.)

Add the lemon juice or mustard, if you wish. Arrange the chicken on plates. Holding back the solids in the pan, pour the sauce over the chicken, or spoon the sauce over the chicken.

Preparation photographs begin on the next page.

1/Start with the tasty fat, skin, browned bits, and juices leftover from cooking the chicken.

2/Add the onion and carrot.

3/Deglaze with wine.

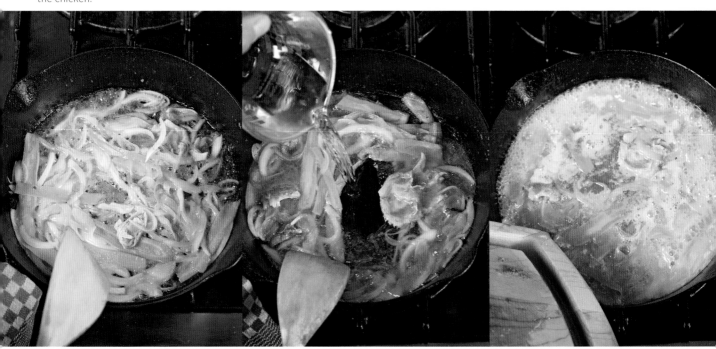

4/The longer the ingredients caramelize, the more flavorful the sauce.

5/Deglaze again with water.

6/Add any chicken juices from the cutting board.

7/Cook off the water and juices.

8/Deglaze a final time.

9/When the water comes to a simmer, the sauce is ready.

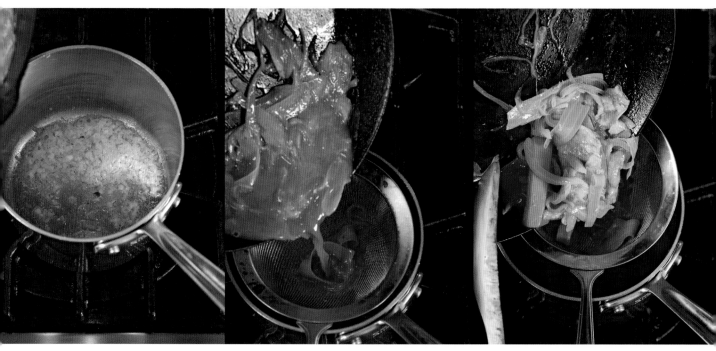

10/For a tastier sauce, sweat shallots in butter.

11/Strain the pan sauce into the shallots.

12/Discard the onion, carrot, and skin.

Continued on the next page.

13/Bring the sauce to a simmer and add the butter.

14/Add the herbs.

15/A perfect pan sauce.

HOLLANDAISE SAUCE/MAKES ABOUT 1 CUP/240 MILLILITERS SAUCE

Hollandaise is one the great transformations of butter. It can be varied any number of ways. Use dried tarragon in the reduction and add chopped fresh tarragon to the finished sauce for one of the greatest sauces ever made, béarnaise, which is excellent with beef. Or simply season the sauce with lemon juice to make an all-purpose hollandaise for vegetables and fish.

Two phases follow: cooking the egg yolks and emulsifying the butter. It's easiest to cook the eggs over simmering water. If you use direct heat, be careful not to overcook the eggs. After the eggs are airy and hot, you remove the pan from the heat and whisk in melted butter. Some cooks use whole butter and keep the sauce over heat, but I think you have more control using melted butter.

1 tablespoon minced shallot

10 or more peppercorns, cracked

1 bay leaf, crumbled

¼ cup/60 milliliters white wine vinegar or sherry vinegar

Kosher salt

¼ cup/60 milliliters water

3 large egg yolks

2 to 3 teaspoons lemon juice, or more to taste

1 cup/225 grams butter, melted in a vessel from which you can pour it in a thin stream

Cayenne pepper (optional)

Combine the shallot, peppercorns, bay leaf, vinegar, and a three-finger pinch of salt in a small saucepan over medium-high heat. Cook until the vinegar is gone, leaving a damp glaze in the pan. Add the water and bring to a simmer, then strain into a medium saucepan, which you'll be using to make the sauce.

Bring a large pot of water to a simmer. Add the egg yolks to the vinegar reduction. Hold the saucepan in the simmering water and whisk the eggs continuously until they are fluffy and warm, 1 to 2 minutes. Whisk in 2 teaspoons of the lemon juice.

Take the pan out of the simmering water. Whisk in the butter, beginning with a few drops, then adding it in a steady stream, just until all the fat is incorporated (it's fine if some of the watery whey goes into the sauce). If the sauce begins to look rough, add a few drops of cool water to smooth it out. If the sauce breaks (turns from thick to watery), put 1 teaspoon water in a clean bowl or pan and whisk the broken sauce into the water, first in a few drops, then in a steady stream. Taste the sauce. Add more lemon if you wish. Season with cayenne (if using). Cover the sauce with plastic wrap/cling film to keep it warm, but do not leave it over heat. The sauce can be made 1 hour ahead, covered, and reheated gently before serving.

SIMPLE BUTTER SAUCE

MAKES ¾ TO 1 CUP/180 TO 240 MILLILITERS SAUCE

One of the easiest sauces to make is simply butter, flavored with wine and herbs, that you've kept emulsified by whisking it into a liquid. In French cuisine, it's called *beurre blanc* and usually follows some variation of whisking butter into reduced white wine (or, for a *beurre rouge*, into reduced red wine). Classically, the sauce is a reduction of wine and vinegar, in effect, hollandaise without the egg, and was served with lean white fish, but there's no reason to overcomplicate matters. You can omit the tarragon for a plain butter sauce, but I love the tarragon (parsley, chives, or chervil can also be used). The version here is made in the pan in which you have sautéed chicken or fish.

2 tablespoons minced shallots

Kosher salt

½ cup/120 milliliters white wine

2 tablespoons lemon juice

½ cup/110 grams butter, cut into 8 pieces

2 tablespoons chopped fresh tarragon (optional)

Remove the meat or fish from the pan and keep warm. Add the shallots to the pan and sweat over medium heat for about 30 seconds, adding a three-finger pinch of salt. Add the wine and lemon juice, bring to a simmer, and reduce by about half. Reduce the heat to medium-low and whisk in the butter, one piece at a time. Stir in the tarragon (if using), just before serving.

PEPPERCORN AND COGNAC CREAM SAUCE

MAKES 1 CUP/240 MILLILITERS SAUCE

Cream is practically a ready-made sauce. All it needs is a little reduction and a flavor. Here, peppercorns and shallot are sautéed in the pan in which beef has been cooked. The pan is deglazed with cognac, and then cream is cooked down to the desired consistency. The sauce is usually served at restaurants with pricey cuts, but I recommend buying a lesser cut, such as a top sirloin, and elevating it with this sauce. Sear the meat and serve it rare, cut into slices.

1 tablespoon minced shallot

2 garlic cloves, minced

2 teaspoons peppercorns, cracked beneath a pan, then coarsely chopped

¼ cup/60 milliliters cognac

1 cup/240 milliliters heavy/double cream

Kosher salt

1 to 2 teaspoons Dijon mustard

2 or 3 teaspoons fresh thyme leaves (optional; use if you have handy)

While the steak rests, pour off the excess oil from the sauté pan. Place over medium-high heat, add the shallot, garlic, and peppercorns, and sweat the shallot and garlic, stirring, for 30 seconds or so. Add the cognac, deglaze the pan, and simmer until reduced to about 1 tablespoon. Add the cream and simmer until reduced by half. Taste the sauce, and season with salt. Stir in the mustard and the thyme (if using). Spoon over the steak to serve.

MUSHROOM SAUCE/MAKES ABOUT 2 CUPS/450 MILLILITERS SAUCE

Mushrooms are a great all-purpose ingredient when seared to give them flavor. I like to make what the French call a *duxelles*, finely diced mushrooms (they cook better when diced, but you can finely chop them if you wish), sautéed and flavored with wine and shallot. This versatile preparation can be used as a stuffing for ravioli or to sauce meat; blended with cream for a mushroom soup or a mushroom cream sauce; or simply served as a bed for sautéed or roasted fish, which is what I recommend here. If you have beef or chicken stock, you can add that, too, but it's not necessary. Don't be shy with the pepper—it pairs well with the seared mushrooms.

3 tablespoons canola oil

1 pound/455 grams button mushrooms, finely diced

2 shallots, minced

Kosher salt

Freshly ground black pepper

½ cup/120 milliliters dry white wine

¼ lemon

¼ teaspoon curry powder

2 tablespoons butter

Heat a large sauté pan over high heat until very hot. Add the oil and swirl it in the pan to coat the bottom. When the oil begins to smoke, add the mushrooms in a single layer and press them down with a spatula to sear them well, about 30 seconds. Add the shallots and stir the mushrooms, cooking them for another 30 to 60 seconds. Add a three-finger pinch of salt and several grindings of pepper. Add the wine and cook, stirring, until the wine is nearly gone. Season with a squeeze of lemon and the curry powder. Taste and adjust the seasoning if you wish. If the sauce has become too dry (it should be liquidy but not soup), add ¼ cup/60 milliliters water (or cream!) and return to a simmer. Swirl in the butter and serve.

TOMATO SAUCE / MAKES ABOUT 3 CUPS/720 MILLILITERS SAUCE

Homemade tomato sauce is leagues better than anything you can find in a jar at the grocery store, however fancy the jar might be. Fresh tomato sauce can be made well in advance or even frozen. It should be a regular part of your repertoire.

1 tablespoon olive oil

1 Spanish onion, cut into medium or small dice

Minced garlic (optional)

Kosher salt

3 pounds/1.4 kilograms plum tomatoes, stem ends removed and tomatoes halved, or one 28-ounce/800-gram can whole plum tomatoes

4 tablespoons/55 grams butter

2 bay leaves or 1 bunch fresh oregano (optional)

Basil or other soft herb

In a large saucepan over medium-high heat, warm the olive oil. Add the onion and garlic (if using) and sweat, adding a three-finger pinch of salt and stirring, until the onion is soft and translucent.

Put the tomatoes in a blender or food processor and blend until completely puréed. Pour into the saucepan. (You can also put them into the saucepan with the onion and purée with a hand blender.) Add the butter and bay leaves (if using) and bring the sauce to a simmer, then reduce the heat to medium-low and cook until thick, about 1 hour. Taste and season with salt, adding the basil just before serving.

CHICKEN OR TURKEY GRAVY

MAKES 3½ TO 4 CUPS/840 TO 960 MILLILITERS GRAVY

French sauces based on stock reductions aren't practical for everyday cooking, so the sauces I make at home rely on ingredients I have on hand (wine, butter) or are a by-product of cooking (the skin and juices of a chicken). A notable exception is gravy, an emblem of home cooking that nevertheless strikes many with fear, especially on feast days when gravy is a requirement. But gravy is a breeze if you have good stock, because that's all gravy is—thickened stock. For the gravy to be good, the stock has to be good. Therefore you must make your own stock. Follow the instructions for Easy Chicken Stock (page 65). If you're not using a chicken carcass, substitute 2 pounds/910 grams chicken or turkey bones (preferably roasted, for flavor) and 8 cups/2 liters water.

Once you have stock, you whisk in enough cold roux until you get the consistency you want. Roux is simply equal parts by volume of butter and flour. The butter coats the granules of flour, keeping them from joining and clumping, and the granules then expand in the hot liquid environment of the stock. If I'm roasting a turkey, I use fat that renders from the turkey instead of the butter. You can use a slurry, cornstarch/cornflour and water, to thicken the stock, but roux gives it better body and flavor.

You can season the gravy any way you want. Add rosemary or tarragon, chopped onion, or sautéed giblets. Start with a good stock, and it's difficult to go wrong.

4 tablespoons/55 grams butter

4 tablespoons/30 grams all-purpose/plain flour

4 cups/960 milliliters chicken or turkey stock

Kosher salt

Freshly ground black pepper

Melt the butter in a small sauté pan over medium heat. When it's bubbling, add the flour and cook, stirring until the flour and butter are evenly combined and the flour takes on the aroma of a baking pie crust, about 4 minutes. Allow it to cool completely.

In a large saucepan over high heat, bring the stock to a simmer, then reduce the heat to medium. Whisk in the cooled roux. Continue to whisk until the roux thickens the stock. Lower the heat so that the gravy simmers gently for another 10 minutes, stirring occasionally with a flat-edged spoon to scrape up any flour that may adhere to the bottom of the pan. Taste the gravy and season with salt and pepper before serving.

12

VINAIGRETTE:
The Fifth Mother

FOR DECADES IN THE UNITED STATES, we've known this tart combination of oil, vinegar, and flavorings as salad dressing. Yet what I grew up seeing in store-bought bottles in the refrigerator door in the 1970s can be a fantastic sauce on *anything*—on steak, on pork, on chicken, on green vegetables, on starchy vegetables, with cheese, and, in principle at least, on desserts. It even works, yes, on salad.

The principle is simple. One of the key flavor components in any dish is acidity, along with salty, sweet, bitter, and savory flavors. We also evaluate the pleasure of a dish according to textural categories: crunchy or soft, smooth or coarse, fat or lean. A vinaigrette combines two of the most important of those qualities, acidity and fat. After that, it's simply a matter of flavoring a vinaigrette. The vinaigrette is so variable and so versatile that one way to think about it is as a mother sauce.

In culinary school, chefs in training learn the French system of sauce classification created in the nineteenth century by Antonin Carême, who divided sauces into four broad categories of mother sauces, each of which had myriad offspring. Brown sauce, or *sauce Espagnole*, could become any number of sauces depending on what you add to it—a wine reduction for a Bordelaise sauce, mustard for a *sauce Robert*—and a milk-based béchamel (see page 124) could become Mornay if you add cheese and Nantua if you add reduced shellfish stock. Such classifications were born of restaurant cooking and the ability to produce many different dishes quickly. Mother sauces could be made in the morning and finished *à la minute* when they were needed. Carême listed four mother sauces. Escoffier got rid of one (sauces enriched with yolk and cream) and added tomato sauce, calling them "foundation" sauces. Some authorities also include the emulsified butter sauce, such as hollandaise, among the mothers.

The vinaigrette deserves to be in this group of utilitarian sauces. It's the most important sauce for the home cook. Its effects are powerful; it can be made from what we commonly have on hand (oil and vinegar); it's a sauce that doesn't require stock; and it's most in line with the contemporary palate, which eschews high-fat butter sauces and protein-dense stock reductions. Think of vinaigrette as a base for countless variations.

A vinaigrette is traditionally made of three parts oil and one part acid. This baseline, always a good place to start, makes a perfect classic red wine vinaigrette (see page 211). After you mix it, taste it and evaluate its acidity. If you like a sharper vinaigrette, add a little more vinegar. The basic vinaigrette can be enhanced with other flavors—minced shallot, garlic, fresh herbs (added at the last minute). You might want to balance it with something sweet, a few pinches of brown sugar, a roasted shallot, a hit of balsamic vinegar.

The vinaigrette is infinitely variable. Replace the neutral oil with a flavorful nut oil. Alter the vinegar, from red wine to white wine or any of the countless flavored vinegars now available. Use a citrus juice instead of vinegar. Consider adding spices—cumin, cayenne, coriander, or allspice, clove, or cinnamon. Consider other flavoring elements as well, mustard, say, or peanut butter, or anchovies, or roasted peppers, or ginger.

My Cleveland colleague Michael Symon, restaurateur and Iron Chef, includes a *salsa verde*, "green sauce," in his book, *Live to Cook*, which he spoons generously over roasted chicken. The sauce is thick with ingredients—parsley and mint, anchovies, garlic, shallot, capers, jalapeño, and red pepper flakes. But with the juice of a lemon and ½ cup/120 milliliters olive oil, it is, at its core, a vinaigrette, and it's fabulous on a roasted chicken.

We don't have pan juices to initiate a sauce for grilled/barbecued meats, but a flavorful vinaigrette is often a perfect complement. Think of a mint-garlic vinaigrette for grilled lamb or a spicy oregano vinaigrette for grilled steak.

The final consideration in a vinaigrette—after you've determined your acid and oil, your seasonings, and your flavoring ingredients—is texture. A classic vinaigrette is emulsified: the oil is whipped or blended into the vinegar and seasonings so that it's thick and stable, and does not separate back out. If you stir all the ingredients together at once, the vinaigrette will be loose, which may be what you want.

Finally, there are creamy vinaigrettes. They can use cream but more commonly are based on emulsions. A creamy vinaigrette is, in effect, a loose acidic mayonnaise.

Learning how to put the vinaigrette to use in your kitchen will ratchet up your entire cooking repertoire.

On Making a Vinaigrette

Of the several ways to mix a vinaigrette, none is better than another. The method you choose depends on your situation and what effect you're after.

Simply combining the ingredients and stirring them just before you use them is the easiest and most common way to mix vinaigrettes. Some people combine everything in a jar and shake. That works fine, but the oil will quickly separate from the vinegar, so you need to pour the vinaigrette immediately.

Many home cooks have immersion blenders or hand blenders. I do—it's probably my most-used small appliance. I highly recommend it. Immersion blenders usually come with a cup-and-blade attachment, ideal for making small quantities of vinaigrettes. Just combine all the ingredients and process briefly. Immersion blenders also come with a whisk attachment, which saves a lot of effort.

Traditionally, vinaigrettes are emulsified, that is, the oil is evenly dispersed and won't separate from the vinegar. In the same way that you make a mayonnaise, you can mix a vinaigrette. Depending on how vigorously you whip the oil, and whether you include an emulsifier such as an egg yolk or a high proportion of mustard, the thicker it will be.

Creamy vinaigrettes, typically mayonnaise based, are made in the same way mayonnaise is mixed (see page 119), but depending on how you're using them, they're considerably thinner than mayonnaise.

Vinaigrettes can be made in a standard blender, which can result in a vinaigrette you can stand a spoon in. For large quantities of vinaigrettes, a stand mixer with the whisk attachment is excellent.

However you mix, the vinaigrette is all about the type of acidity, the amount of acidity, often a sweet component (onion, sugar) to balance that acidity, and additional aromatics and spices added to what can be the home cook's most versatile and valuable sauce.

LEMON-PEPPER VINAIGRETTE, TWO WAYS/SERVES 4

This all-purpose last-minute dressing is ideal for crunchy lettuces. With two small additions, you can turn it into a luxurious Caesar vinaigrette.

VINAIGRETTE WITH CRISP LETTUCE:

3 tablespoons lemon juice

1 large garlic clove, finely minced or smashed with the flat side of a knife

Kosher salt

Freshly ground black pepper

½ cup/120 milliliters olive oil or canola oil

Zest from ½ lemon

¾ pound/340 grams crisp lettuce such as wedges of iceberg lettuce or romaine/Cos

½ cup/60 grams grated Parmigiano-Reggiano (optional)

CAESAR VARIATION:

3 tablespoons lemon juice

1 large egg yolk

1 large garlic clove, finely minced or smashed with the flat side of a knife

1 or 2 anchovies, chopped to a paste if whisking in a bowl, left whole if using a blender

½ cup/120 milliliters olive oil or canola oil

Kosher salt

Freshly ground black pepper

¾ pound/340 grams romaine/Cos lettuce

½ cup/60 grams grated Parmigiano-Reggiano

Croutons

MAKE THE VINAIGRETTE WITH CRISP LETTUCE: In a small bowl, combine the lemon juice and garlic and season with salt and pepper. Add the lemon zest. Whisk in the oil. Toss the vinaigrette with the lettuce, season with more pepper, and garnish, if desired, with the Parmigiano-Reggiano.

MAKE THE CAESAR VARIATION: Combine the lemon juice, egg yolk, garlic, and anchovies in a bowl or blender. Whisking continuously or with the blender running, pour in 2 or 3 drops of the oil, then continue pouring the oil in a continuous stream until all the oil is emulsified into the vinaigrette. Season with salt and pepper. In a bowl, toss the lettuce with three-fourths of the vinaigrette. Taste and add more dressing if you wish. Garnish with the Parmigiano-Reggiano and croutons.

LEEKS VINAIGRETTE/SERVES 4

This recipe uses a classic red wine vinaigrette. Pairing it with a member of the onion family results in a great bistro dish, Leeks Vinaigrette. The dish showcases the power of red wine vinaigrette to illuminate cooked cold vegetables. The quality of the vinegar is critical, so it's worth buying a good one. The vinaigrette will also work well with a good Spanish sherry vinegar.

4 large leeks or 8 small leeks

¼ cup/60 milliliters red wine vinegar

1 tablespoon Dijon mustard

1 tablespoon honey

Kosher salt

Freshly ground black pepper

¾ cup/180 milliliters canola oil

¼ cup/170 grams minced shallots

4 hard-boiled eggs (see page 330), yolks and whites finely chopped separately

1 tablespoon sliced fresh chives

Trim the roots from each leek but leave the root end intact. Cut off the dark tops so that you have only white and pale green parts (save the tops to add to Easy Chicken Stock, page 65, or beef stock). Cut the leeks in half lengthwise, being careful not to cut through the root ends. Wash the leeks thoroughly under cold water, checking for dirt between the layers of leaves.

Bring a pot of water with a steamer insert to a boil. Cook the leeks until tender, 10 to 15 minutes. (They can also be boiled if you don't have a steamer.) Remove the insert from the pot and run the leeks under cold water to cool them, then put them on a plate lined with paper towels/absorbent paper to drain. Refrigerate until you're ready to serve them.

Put the vinegar, mustard, and honey in a blender. Add a two-finger pinch of salt and several grinds of pepper. With the blender running, pour in the oil in a steady stream. Transfer the vinaigrette to a glass measuring cup. About 10 minutes before serving, stir in the shallots.

Cut the root end off each leek. Arrange the leeks on plates and spoon the vinaigrette over the leeks. Garnish each plate with the chopped egg white, followed by the chopped yolk and chives.

GRILLED STRIP STEAKS WITH CHILE-OREGANO VINAIGRETTE/SERVES 4

Vinaigrettes are excellent on every manner of grilled food, and I especially like them with red meats such as steak and lamb, which are naturally rich and benefit from the contrasting acidity and, here, from the heat of chiles. I add some balsamic vinegar because I like the way its sweetness balances the charred flavors of the meat. The vinaigrette is dominated by the oregano, but replace it with mint, and you have a fabulous vinaigrette for grilled lamb.

Please buy steaks thick enough to grill well, at least 1 inch/2.5 centimeters. If they're too thin, they can overcook before the exterior is properly seared. The same is true of lamb chops, though the bones give you a little leeway (see technique #18, Grill). Another excellent method is to use two strip steaks, each 1¾ inches/4.5 centimeters thick. Cook as instructed, cut on the bias into six or seven thick slices, divide among plates, and top with the vinaigrette.

VINAIGRETTE:

3 tablespoons red wine vinegar

2 teaspoons balsamic vinegar

1 teaspoon fish sauce

1 tablespoon minced shallot

1 garlic clove, minced

2 tablespoons chopped fresh oregano

1 red chile such as Fresno, serrano, or Thai, seeded and finely chopped

1 jalapeño chile, seeded and finely chopped

Kosher salt

Freshly ground black pepper

¼ cup/60 milliliters canola oil

2 tablespoons chopped fresh parsley

4 strip steaks, at least 1 inch/
2.5 centimeters thick

Kosher salt

MAKE THE VINAIGRETTE: In a bowl, combine the vinegars, fish sauce, shallot, garlic, oregano, and chiles. Season with a two-finger pinch of salt and several grinds of pepper. Add the oil and stir to mix well. Let the vinaigrette stand for at least 30 minutes or up to half a day before using. Just before serving, stir in the parsley.

Remove the steaks from the refrigerator 2 hours before grilling/barbecuing them. Give both sides an aggressive salting if you haven't already done so. If they're the proper thickness, they can take a nice crust of salt.

Build a very hot fire in a grill/barbecue. Spread the coals over an area large enough to grill/barbecue the steaks over direct heat. Put the grill rack over the coals and let it get very hot, 5 to 10 minutes. Grill/barbecue the steaks until their internal temperature reaches 120°F/48°C on an instant-read thermometer for rare, about 3 minutes per side over a blazing-hot fire. Allow the steaks to rest for 5 minutes or so. Serve as desired, either individually or sliced, topped with the vinaigrette.

CHORIZO VINAIGRETTE/MAKES ABOUT 1 CUP/240 MILLILITERS VINAIGRETTE

Spanish chorizo is perhaps my favorite dry-cured sausage. It's smoky and spicy and redolent of Spanish *pimentón*, one of the best paprikas on Earth. Try to find chorizo produced in Spain and available in specialty markets. Here it adds a deep red color to the vinaigrette and a rich smoky flavor that pairs perfectly with pan-roasted cod (see page 254) or grilled fish; it's even excellent on steamed new potatoes.

¼ cup/60 milliliters canola oil

¼ cup/40 grams finely chopped red onion

¼ cup/30 grams finely chopped red bell pepper/capsicum

¼ cup/30 grams finely chopped cubano or jalapeño chile

¼ cup/60 grams chopped Spanish chorizo

Kosher salt

3 tablespoons sherry vinegar

Heat the oil in a small saucepan or sauté pan over medium-high heat. Add the onion, bell pepper/capsicum, chile, chorizo, and a three-finger pinch of salt. Sauté until the vegetables are tender. Remove from heat and allow to cool slightly. Stir in the vinegar. The vinaigrette should taste fairly acidic. Adjust the seasonings as desired.

The vinaigrette can be stored in the refrigerator, covered, for up to 5 days.

13

SOUP:
The Easiest Meal

NOT LONG AGO, I WAS ON A PANEL WITH erstwhile *Gourmet* editor and author Ruth Reichl when chicken stock came up. "You know what they say," she said. "If you've got chicken stock, you've got a meal."

And it's *true*. Soup nights are the easiest meal night. In the winter, a day or two after a roast chicken dinner, having kept a pot of Easy Chicken Stock (page 65) on the stove top, I strain the stock over some sautéed chopped onion; add left-over vegetables and chicken, and sometimes dried pasta or potatoes; and season with salt and a squeeze of lemon or some drops of vinegar. In short order, the soup is ready to go. Soup like this is infinitely variable. Want some delicate Asian flavors? Sauté garlic, scallions, and a chunk of ginger, strain in the stock, season with salt or soy sauce, fish sauce or miso, rice vinegar, and a drop of sesame oil, add chicken or tofu or wontons, and you have a great meal. Want a spicy soup? Add red pepper flakes to sautéing onion, then your stock, and finish with chopped escarole/Batavian endive and sausage.

These are reason enough to have chicken stock on hand. But soups are a breeze, a deeply satisfying breeze, even without stock. Milk can make a great soup base, and vegetables can be puréed and thinned for soups.

Soups warm us when it's cold and cool us when it's hot. They nourish us by capturing all the nutrients in the ingredients and transferring them to us spoonful by spoonful down to the last swipe of a crust of bread.

What makes this happen is the magic of water, its ability to extract flavor and nourishment and disperse them throughout the soup, to carry any garnish, and to receive any seasoning. Soups are often so basic that seasoning is the key factor in how good they turn out to be.

The most important skill in making delicious soups of any kind is learning how to evaluate a soup. *Think* about it. *Taste* it, and think some more. As always, ask yourself if you've got the right amount of salt. The soup should taste seasoned rather than flat or dilute, but you should not taste salt. Flatness can also be fixed with fish sauce, which makes the flavor seem to fill the mouth more. You do not want to use so much that you taste fish sauce.

Ask yourself if the soup would benefit from a little acidity. Not sure? Take a spoonful and put a drop of vinegar or lemon juice in it and taste. Does the soup taste a little brighter, a little more interesting? Then add a little vinegar or lemon juice to the pot.

If you are making a clear soup with garnish, like chicken noodle, ask yourself if you have the right proportion of liquid to solids and adjust it as necessary.

For a creamy or thick soup, ask yourself if the texture is right. You are evaluating the soup as you would any other dish or preparation. Does it have a balance of textures? Soups are soft, but we love crunchy (that's why we have soup crackers). Perhaps your soup would be delicious garnished with some croutons or fried tortilla.

Some soups are meant to be lean and are a pleasure in their leanness. But even lean soups are enhanced with a little fat—perhaps finish the soup with a few drops of extra-virgin olive oil, sesame oil, or truffle oil, or with some crème fraîche or mascarpone cheese. This would be considered a finishing garnish.

Think about what other garnishes would be appealing. If you make a puréed vegetable soup such as asparagus, a final garnish of cooked asparagus tips would be good. Does the soup need a little color? How about some lemon zest?

Finally, think what you're serving with the soup. You want an appropriate food to serve beside it—garlic toast with white bean soup, for instance, or pappadams with curried soup.

In culinary school, soups are among the first techniques taught because they put so many basic cooking skills to good use. In this context, soups are broken down into categories, and although they can vary and overlap, thinking about the categories gives you flexibility and agility. Don't think of a classic chicken noodle soup as being different from a Mexican corn-tortilla soup, or an Asian wonton soup, or a Thai pho. They're all the same, broth with different garnishes and seasonings—or, in chef speak, flavor profiles, a term that is useful but has yet to find its way into the home kitchen. I like the term because it acknowledges that cooking does not depend on knowing thousands of recipes but in understanding a set of manageable categories within which there are thousands of variations.

In the most basic terms, there are two types of soup, the clear soup and the puréed soup. The puréed soup is often broken down into the cream soup (cream of broccoli was the example we learned in culinary school) and the vegetable purée (black bean soup, for instance, or split pea). The puréed soups overlap in many ways—most cream soups are puréed in some way, and many vegetable purées are finished with cream.

CLEAR SOUP: The clear soup, the most basic kind of soup, involves little more than sautéing some onion (and other aromatic vegetables depending on the soup), then adding stock and any other ingredients, such as meat, vegetables, starches, or dairy. The clear soup is simple and boundless. Clear soups are all about featuring the garnishes, using the stock as a platform.

PURÉED SOUP: The puréed soup is simply food you'd normally eat solid transformed into a liquid. Why would we do this? Because the food is often better this way. A black bean soup, to my palate, is better than a scoop of black beans. Diced cooked celery root, or mashed celery root, is a nice accompaniment to braised beef, but if you want to feature celery root, you do so in a soup by cooking the celery root in an appropriate liquid, puréeing it, and seasoning it.

Sweet soups, fruit soups, are another form of puréed soup. When you have good fruit, you can simply purée and strain it. If you like cooked fruit, such as poached peaches, pears, or apples, the fruit can be puréed with some of the poaching liquid (simple syrup, white wine, and a vanilla bean/pod, for instance) for a terrific fruit soup, appropriate for dessert or, when made less sweet, a starting course.

With a puréed soup, the garnishes are secondary.

The All-Important Garnish

The garnish, the nonsoup ingredient, is what makes a soup fun, distinguished, and memorable. I'm tempted to compare garnish in a soup to sartorial accessories: a plain dress, or slacks and shirt, can stand out with the right necklace, jewelry, earrings, belt, hat, scarf, or brooch. But garnish is more essential, more like shoes and a jacket. It is a fundamental and integral part of the soup. That I probably have more to say about garnish in soup than I do about soup itself attests to the critical nature of the garnish. As for soups, it is useful to break garnishes into categories.

VEGETABLE GARNISH: Vegetables are a primary garnish, contributing flavor, color, and body. Any vegetable can be added to a soup. The only consideration is whether you want to pre-cook the vegetable. Most vegetables are best cooked in the soup; this makes flavor and nutrition sense. If you are entertaining or want the garnish to stand out—diced carrots in a fresh pea soup, for instance—you can blanch and shock the garnish vegetable first. In the Cream of Celery Root Soup (page 221), the diced celery root garnish is cooked until tender and the soup is added to it, so that the garnish stands out.

Leafy vegetables—spinach, escarole, sorrel—make a great garnish, adding flavor, nourishment, and color. Onion is considered an aromatic rather than a garnish, unless it's featured in some version of onion soup.

MEAT GARNISH: Meat, in all its forms, makes a powerful and substantial garnish. If soup were a chess board and garnishes the pieces, meat would be a rook. Chicken in a chicken soup, shredded beef in a beef soup, and sausage in just about any kind of soup can't be beat. Don't limit yourself to the standard use of leftovers (though that's a fabulous way to make use of food). Meat attached to bone is a fine addition—not only are spareribs in a soup great to eat, but they add flavor and body. Skinless chicken wings, sautéed with the onions, would make a flavor-enhancing garnish. Finer cuts work well—if you cut your own beef tenderloin, you're left with a lot of trim, which can be diced and added raw to a hot beef soup. Pot-au-feu is a soup-as-meal with meat at its center.

STARCH GARNISH: Noodles and rice are the most common starch garnishes. Potatoes and other starchy vegetables are an excellent garnish. Corn is a kind of starch-vegetable garnish that makes for superlative and hearty soups. Bread—soft for body and substance, or hard (whether three-day-old or baked into croutons) for substance and texture—is one of the best things to add to soup. Bread is also easy and economical.

EGG GARNISH: Almost every soup is improved by the addition of an egg. No garnish is at once so easy and so impressive. To use a raw egg, make sure your soup bowls are hot and your soup is boiling hot. Crack an egg into each bowl and add the soup. You can also poach the eggs ahead of time to add as a garnish. Or cover whole eggs with cold water, heat the water, and remove the eggs as soon as the water comes to a boil; they're ready to be cracked into bowls of hot soup.

CRISP GARNISH: I almost never serve a soup without putting something crunchy in it, on it, or with it. If you're serving a very refined consommé and want to focus on the clarity and flavor of the broth, you might forgo the crunch. But most soups benefit from something crunchy. This can be as simple as serving a toasted baguette or crackers alongside the soup, or more elaborate, such as a fried celery root chip along with a celery root soup. Or the added texture can be something that's naturally crunchy, such as a raw vegetable.

ENRICHING GARNISH: One of the pleasures of soups is that they are both lean and satisfying. But on occasion a soup might need an additional something, a soupçon of richness to balance the lean and clean. A common garnish is a tart dairy product such as sour cream or crème fraîche. These add acidity and richness along with some visual contrast. Flavorful oils make visually enticing garnishes—olive is the most common, but a range of delicious nut oils is now available to cooks. A less common enricher for soups, and one that has a powerful impact on flavor, is grated Parmigiano-Reggiano—it adds richness and a serious flavor kick.

Seasoning: Making Good Soup Great

Seasoning a soup is mostly about training yourself—tasting and thinking and remembering what you experience.

One of the best ways to teach yourself about how to season is to taste the soup and then taste a spoonful with a little of the seasoning you're considering. If the seasoning is salt, take a spoonful of soup, add a few grains, and taste and compare. Follow the same method to understand the impact of a drop of vinegar, especially in cream soups. Add a drop of vinegar or lemon juice and compare. Now you can sense the impact of acidity.

Seasoning a spoonful of soup also helps you know whether you've chosen the right seasoning. Maybe the soup doesn't need salt or acid. Taste it in a spoon before you change the flavor of the whole pot.

Another powerful seasoning device is fish sauce (see page 22). It's salty, but gives soups depth. Again, use the spoonful method to sense it for yourself.

You might consider adding a little heat, such as cayenne pepper or Espelette powder.

Soup Strategy: Soups for Entertaining, Soups for Busy Weekday Meals

Because soup is so easy to make, it's a practical choice for weeknight dinners. Soups come together in a snap, are delicious and nutritious, and put leftovers to good use.

Because soups hold so well, they can be made a day ahead. They also make a great first course for entertaining. They can be simple creamy soups, cold or heated at the last minute and served. For something fancier, you can set out bowls containing a cooked garnish and pour the soup at the table.

Soups make a terrific canapé. Thomas Keller at The French Laundry was among the first chefs to serve soups in demitasse cups. This is easy to do at home, as a canape. The soup should be rich and satisfying, focusing on the main ingredient, or should be lean with a compelling featured garnish.

Soup is food manipulation at its best and most powerful.

> ## COOKING TIP:
> **Before adding a powerful ingredient to a whole batch of soup or sauce, try a drop of what you want to add with a spoonful of soup or sauce and taste it. This way, if you're wrong, you haven't changed the entire batch.**

SAUSAGE AND ESCAROLE SOUP/SERVES 4

I could have made any number of clear soups because the method used here is infinitely variable. Use any kind of sausage you like: bratwurst; spicy sausage; lamb, chicken, or pork sausage; or a smoked sausage such as kielbasa. You could replace the sausage with chicken, and cooked white beans could be used as a garnish to add more heft to the soup. For a corn tortilla soup, cook corn and garlic, season heavily with lime, and finish with chunks of avocado, cilantro/fresh coriander, and fried corn tortillas. Replace the sausage with mushrooms and the chicken stock with vegetable stock for a vegetarian soup. If you want a very lean wonton soup, substitute scallions for the onions, sauté along with garlic and ginger, and add stock and cook to infuse the stock with the aromatics. Then strain the resulting broth into a clean pan, add wontons, and finish with finely sliced scallion.

I accompany this soup with a baguette. If you like, you can garnish it with croutons made by sautéing cut-up day-old bread in olive oil until crisp.

1 large onion, cut into small or medium dice

1 tablespoon minced garlic

Canola oil as needed

Kosher salt

4 cups/960 milliliters Easy Chicken Stock (page 65)

1 pound/455 grams sausage, browned in a frying pan or roasted at 325°F/165°C for 10 minutes, cut in chunks

½ pound/225 grams escarole/Batavian endive, cut crosswise into ½-inch/12-millimeter ribbons

2 plum tomatoes, seeded and diced

1 tablespoon fish sauce

2 teaspoons lemon juice or white wine vinegar, or as needed

Cayenne pepper (optional)

1 baguette, whole or split, toasted

Olive oil

In a large saucepan, sweat the onion and garlic in just enough canola oil to coat them. Season with a three-finger pinch of salt. When the vegetables have softened, add the stock and bring to a simmer. Add the sausage, greens, tomatoes, fish sauce, and lemon juice and cook just until the greens are wilted. Taste and adjust the seasonings with lemon, salt, or fish sauce, and some cayenne, if you wish.

Brush the toasted baguette with olive oil and lightly sprinkle with salt. Serve the soup with the baguette.

CREAM OF CELERY ROOT SOUP/SERVES 4

Traditional thick, creamy soups like this one use a roux-thickened base of stock or milk (a béchamel) and are flavored by the main ingredient, which can be anything from broccoli to celery root to pumpkin. These soups are economical, easy, and enormously satisfying. Following the method here, you can replace the celery root with cauliflower, potato, parsnip, turnip, or carrot. To make a creamy green vegetable soup, use asparagus, broccoli, or another vegetable and substitute chicken or vegetable stock for the milk, creating what's called a velouté (vuh-LOO-tay) rather than a béchamel.

3 tablespoons all-purpose/plain flour

5 tablespoons/70 grams butter

1 medium onion, cut into small dice

3 cups/720 milliliters milk

Kosher salt

1 pound/455 grams celery root, three-fourths cut into a large dice, the remainder cut into a small dice for garnish

⅓ cup/75 milliliters heavy/double cream

Lemon juice or white wine vinegar

Optional garnishes: fresh parsley, Brown Butter (page 146)

In a large saucepan, cook the flour and butter over medium heat until the flour takes on lightly baked aroma. Add the onion and cook until soft. Add the milk and bring to a simmer, whisking to disperse the flour. Season with a three-finger pinch of salt. When the béchamel has thickened, add the large pieces of celery root and cook until tender, 10 to 15 minutes.

Purée the soup in a blender, leaving the blender cap off and covering the blender with a kitchen towel. Otherwise the soup can explode out of the blender and make a scalding mess. Pour the soup through a fine-mesh strainer into a clean saucepan. Taste and add more salt if needed. The soup can be refrigerated for up to 2 days.

In a small saucepan, simmer the small pieces of celery root in water to cover until tender, 3 to 4 minutes. Drain and put on paper towels/absorbent paper.

Return the soup to a simmer. Stir in the cream. Add 1 teaspoon lemon juice. Stir and taste, then add more if necessary.

Reheat the celery root garnish in a pan or in a microwave. Divide the garnish among bowls. Ladle the soup over the garnish, top with the optional garnishes if desired, and serve.

COLD SNAP PEA SOUP WITH MINT AND HONEY/SERVES 4

Boiling and shocking green vegetables is a great way to ensure they have vivid color and are perfectly cooked when you need them. Purée those perfectly cooked and chilled vegetables until they can pass through a strainer, and you've got a delicious soup. This is a wonderful summer soup to serve when snap peas are hanging on the vine. In the winter, use the same technique to make warm broccoli soup. Reheat the soup and whisk a little butter into it, season with lemon, and garnish with blanched broccoli florets.

8 cups/2 liters water

¼ cup/55 grams kosher salt, plus ½ teaspoon and more as needed

1 pound/455 grams snap peas

12 large mint leaves

Ice cubes

1 tablespoon honey

Lemon juice

Optional garnishes: 1 cup/ 115 grams blanched and shocked peas, dollops of crème fraîche, a few drops of truffle oil

In a large pot, combine the water and the ¼ cup/ 55 grams salt and bring to a boil. Boil the snap peas until tender, 2 to 3 minutes. Stir in the mint leaves and immediately drain the peas. Transfer the peas and mint to an ice bath (see page 49) and stir occasionally until thoroughly chilled. Drain.

Put the peas and mint in a blender with a few ice cubes, the honey, ½ teaspoon salt, and a squeeze of lemon and purée until smooth. Pass the soup through a fine-mesh strainer into a clean bowl, pressing down on the thick purée with a ladle or spatula to pass it through the strainer. Taste for seasoning, and adjust with honey, salt, and lemon as necessary. Ladle into bowls, top with one of the garnishes if desired, and serve.

SWEET BELL PEPPER SOUP/SERVES 8

Want to impress your nearest and dearest with a truly soigné soup? This easy, rich cream soup is straight out of The French Laundry kitchen and yet would not make Rachael Ray feel that she's overcomplicating her food. The key is a tool, a fine-mesh strainer, which creates a voluptuous texture. The bell peppers/capsicums are steeped in cream, then the mixture is blended until smooth and strained. It's a lovely way to prepare a soup. The result is so rich that I only recommend serving a small amount as a canapé or starter, which makes it all the more enticing. The soup, which has an appealing pastel color, can be served hot or cold. If you serve it cold, be sure to taste it for seasoning when it's cold (cold food usually needs more aggressive seasoning than hot food).

The same method works with nearly any vegetable, but the best choices are nongreen vegetables such as root vegetables, fennel, cauliflower, and mushrooms. The recipe makes the most heavenly mushroom soup you've ever tasted. Unlike the other vegetables, mushrooms should be seared (see page 201) and seasoned with freshly ground pepper and perhaps a pinch of curry.

1 pound/455 grams red, orange, and/or yellow bell peppers/capsicums, seeded and cut into 2-inch/5-centimeter pieces

1 cup/240 milliliters heavy/double cream

Kosher salt

Lemon juice

Combine the vegetables and cream in a saucepan and bring the cream to a simmer over high heat. Reduce the heat to low and cook the vegetables until tender, about 5 minutes. Purée, adding a three-finger pinch of salt and leaving the blender cap off and covering the blender with a kitchen towel, until the contents are thoroughly puréed, about 2 minutes. Taste and add more salt if needed. Add a squeeze of lemon. Pass the soup through a fine-mesh strainer into a clean pan or bowl. Taste again for seasoning and adjust if necessary. Serve in ¼-cup/60-milliliter portions.

Preparation photographs begin on the following page.

1/Start with bell peppers/capsicums in cream over high heat.

2/Bring to a simmer.

3/The cream will bubble and reduce.

4/Pour into the blender.

5/Instead of capping the blender, cover the mouth with a towel.

6/Purée thoroughly.

7/Strain through a fine-mesh strainer into a clean pan.

8/Serve this soup in cups to sip.

14

SAUTÉ:
The Hot Seat

"SAUTÉ," CHEF PARDUS SAID TO MY class at the Culinary Institute to begin that day's lecture, "is a *blast*. Sauté is where the action is on a Saturday night. Sauté is where you guys all want to be in about three years, right? Sauté is the next step to sous chef. Sauté is the guy who's juggling eight or ten pans at a time, makin' flames, makin' things jump. Sauté is the hot seat."

But then he paused. The eloquent, excitable chef transformed into donnish professor, turning to an easel with the lesson's talking bullets, his wooden spoon a pointer: "Sauté *is*: a rapid, *à la minute* cooking technique. It has no tenderizing effect, so the product has to be tender. You cannot *sauté* a lamb shank. The cooking is fast. That's why it's so much fun. Bing bang boom, it goes out the door. In a small amount of oil. Over high heat."

That was my introduction to this particular cooking technique, in the bold strokes that begin any education. And as time went on, as should happen in any education, my understanding deepened, increment by increment, by sautéing and paying attention, and thinking about it and asking people questions. Shortly before I left the Culinary Institute of America to write *The Making of a Chef*, I interviewed its president at the time, 1996, Ferdinand Metz. We were discussing what a culinary education was all about, what defined it.

Ultimately, he said, it was about the basics. "Do I understand the basics?" he said.

"So in sautéing," he went on immediately, "you could say, my God, there are probably ten different temperature levels of sautéing. Some things need a very harsh level; others need a very soft level that almost generates moisture. Whether it's chicken or bacon, all those things require different levels."

It was that moment, there in an office, that I took another step forward. I'd never considered that we sauté bacon. It may be a matter of semantics, but the truth is, words do matter and we do need to know varying levels of heat when we sauté. I sauté steak at a different temperature than I sauté julienned zucchini/courgettes. And this is why sauté is one of the most difficult, if not the most difficult, of the techniques to master. Sautéing requires more judgment, is dependent on more nuance, than any of the other techniques in this section.

Chef Pardus was right in all that he said, but nothing in cooking is absolute. Learning the varying heat levels of sauté is critical, as are other factors such as the material on which you're sautéing, the size of the pan you're using, and the state of whatever it is you're sautéing: Is it straight from the refrigerator or has it tempered? Has it been salted? Is it moist or dry?

The word itself comes from the French verb *sauter*, "to jump," and referred to what chefs do when they're cooking a lot of small items in a pan: they toss them into the air and catch them in the pan as an easy way of stirring. We now refer to anything cooked in a pan on the stove top using a small amount of oil or butter as being sautéed. We sauté a chicken breast even though we're not jumping it.

But *sauté* is a good word. It connotes movement, action, speed. We often use the word *fry* as a synonym for sauté, which is acceptable, I suppose, but I prefer to use the word *fry* to denote plenty of oil at high heat (see technique #19). Frying is always done at a high temperature and uses plenty of fat. Sauté can be done at many temperatures and uses minimal fat.

Also, frying can be done in a pan with straight or sloping sides, but usually straight sides. Sautéing is done in a pan with sloping sides. (Pan nomenclature is inconsistent from company to company. All-Clad, for instance, calls a pan with sloping sides a frying pan; I call it a sauté pan. In culinary school we were taught that a pan with sloping sides, a sauté pan, is a *sauteuse*, and a shallow pan with straight sides is a *sautoire*. It's a useful distinction.) Use clean stainless-steel pans for almost all sautéing (see page 346 for more on pans). Sloping sides not only allow for the cook to jump sautéed peas in the pan, but also allow for circulation around what's being cooked, which carries the cooling moisture away. When using a small amount of oil for high-heat cooking, use a pan with sloping sides. This is less critical with lower temperature sautés.

While the venerable Mr. Metz suggested there were ten temperature levels, I think it's most useful to break them down into three levels.

The first and most common level is high heat. The reason for sautéing at a high temperature is to create flavor in the form of a good seared exterior, a crust. To do this, we want the fat as hot as it can get before it starts to smoke, between 350° and 450°F/180° and 230°C, depending on the fat you're using. Vegetable oils get hotter than animal fat (lard, clarified butter, or chicken fat, for instance). The smoke point, when fat begins to smoke, is the point at which it starts to break down; the oil degrades and begins to release flammable fumes, and any food cooked in that fat will taste acrid. This is bad for the food, and it is dangerous if the fat ignites (if this happens to you, don't panic; just put a lid on the pan).

For this last reason, it's a good idea to heat your clean, dry pan first, then add your oil. You can add your oil to a cold pan, but this increases the chance that you will become distracted by other kitchen work and forget about the pan on the stove until you see or smell the smoke or, worse, a pan aflame. When you add oil to a hot pan, the oil heats very quickly. You don't want to add too much oil, but you don't want to add too little, either. If you add too little oil, the meat can cool the oil and pan down so much that the meat will stick.

The next stage of good high-heat sautéing is knowing when to put the food into the pan. If you haven't heated the pan and the oil enough, the food can stick to the pan. More important, the food can steam rather than brown, and browning is the main reason for high-heat sautéing.

Learn to gauge the heat of the oil by sight. How does it behave when it hits the pan? Is it slow and viscous (if so, the pan is not that hot)? Does it immediately begin moving quickly and fluidly in the pan (indicating it is very hot)? Or does it immediately start smoking (it's too hot!)? High-heat sautéing should be done when the oil is very hot. It shouldn't start smoking on contact with the pan, but instead should begin to ripple and wave in perceptible currents.

The next phase of good high-heat sautéing is putting the meat in the pan. The meat should already have been taken from the refrigerator and seasoned with salt at least a half hour earlier so that it can absorb the salt and also temper, that is, have a chance to warm up a little to ensure more even cooking. Look at the meat. Is it dry or is it sitting in a puddle of juices? This is very important. If wet meat goes into the hot oil, the moisture will drop the temperature of the oil immediately, preventing browning and potentially causing the meat to stick to the pan. If it's damp, pat it dry before putting it into the pan. Some chefs even like to give the meat a very fine dusting of flour to ensure that the surface is completely dry and to give the browning a little more complexity. Don't use too much; if flour falls off the meat into the oil, it can burn.

Lay the meat gently into the pan. Don't be afraid of the heat and the oil; don't throw the meat. Let your hand get close to the surface and allow the meat to fall away from you. The hot fat shouldn't splash, but if it does, it will splash away from you.

Once the meat is in the pan, the next most important thing to do is this: *nothing*. Don't touch it; don't move it; don't shake the pan. Let it cook.

If you've heated your pan and allowed the oil to get hot, you shouldn't have a problem with sticking. The meat may stick at the beginning; if so, it's especially important not to move it and risk tearing the flesh. If the pan is hot, it will give the meat a good sear, and the meat will pull easily away from the pan.

When you turn the meat, consider the heat level. If what you're cooking is very thin, you may want that high heat. If what you're cooking is a little thicker or requires a little more time to cook through (chicken, for instance), you may want to reduce the heat so that the exterior doesn't overcook (or you may want to turn the meat and put it in a hot oven, a technique called pan roasting; see page 253). The point is that once you've got a flavorful sear, what you're concerned with next is cooking the food through.

The final critical moment in sautéing is knowing when to remove the meat from the pan. This is only accomplished with practice and by paying attention. The best way to judge doneness is by touch. Learn touch. Press a finger into the raw meat and pay attention to how it feels. Press a finger into it while it's cooking. Press a finger into it when it has cooked for too long and note the difference. By practicing and paying attention, you can teach yourself how done a piece of meat is by touch. The more cooked the meat gets, the firmer it becomes. Another way to gauge doneness is with an instant-read thermometer, but this is impractical when we sauté, especially for very thin cuts. A piece of meat and some fish will begin to get squishy and grow increasingly stiff as they become hot inside. Again, learning the distinctions is a matter of practice and paying attention.

After you remove the meat from the pan, let it rest for about half as long as it took to cook in the pan. It's good form to let it rest on a paper towel/absorbent paper, which will absorb residual cooking fat. Resting meat is the final stage of its cooking. The heat, concentrated at the exterior, needs time to equalize throughout the meat. When you're determining how long to leave meat in the pan, keep in mind that the food continues to cook even after it's out of the pan. This resting period conveniently gives you time to finish anything else you might be serving.

For medium- and low-heat sautéing, you have even more control. Use lower temperatures when you don't need to develop flavors through browning, when you simply want to heat something through (blanched vegetables, for instance) or to render fat (the duck breast on page 100, for example). Tender, lean cuts benefit from a tasty browned crust—this requires high heat. But not everything does. The way we chose the level of heat to use is by evaluating what it is we're sautéing and the effects we want to bring to it.

The recipes in this chapter feature the sauté technique and differing heat levels:

HIGH-HEAT SAUTÉS

- Sautéed Chicken Breasts with Tarragon Butter Sauce
- Sautéed Scallops with Asparagus
- Sautéed Mushrooms

STIR-FRY

- Spicy Beef with Bell Peppers

MEDIUM- AND LOW-HEAT SAUTÉS

- Sautéed Summer Squash
- Brussels Sprouts Sautéed in Spicy Bacon Fat
- The Way to Sauté Bacon

SAUTÉED CHICKEN BREASTS WITH TARRAGON BUTTER SAUCE/SERVES 4

This preparation is straight out of culinary school 101. While I'm wary of using solitary chicken breasts, when they're properly cooked and served with a delicious sauce, they're a delight—economical, tasty, and satisfying.

I like what's called a supreme, sometimes referred to as an airline breast or Statler breast—half of a chicken breast with the wing joint attached. You can make the breast more attractive by cutting off the joint end of the wing and scraping the wing bone clean. This recipe works fine whether or not the chicken breasts have the wing joints attached, but the breasts with the joints will take a couple of minutes longer to cook.

You can order supremes, or you can cut your own. For this recipe, buy two chickens. With the tail away from you, run the blade of your knife along the keel bone, beneath each breast and over the ribs, to remove the breast and tender in one piece. When you reach the front of the chicken, follow the wishbone straight down and through the joint where the wing connects to the body. Remove the second wing joint. To french the wing joint, chop off the joint end of the wing and scrape the bone clean, freeing any tendons still sticking to the bone. (Save the legs and wings for the fried chicken on page 307, and use the carcass for the Easy Chicken Stock, page 65.)

Because the breast is so lean, I like to serve it with a simple butter sauce flavored with fresh herbs, shallot, and wine. It couldn't be easier, but if you're serving company, or simply feel like putting on airs in the middle of the week, call it a *beurre blanc*, which it is.

4 skin-on boneless chicken breasts or 4 skin-on boneless breasts with the wing joint attached

Kosher salt

Canola or other vegetable oil

Simple Butter Sauce (page 200), made with tarragon

At least a half hour before you intend to cook the chicken breasts, remove them from the refrigerator. Rinse the breasts, pat dry, and give them a liberal salting on both sides. Set them on a plate lined with paper towels/absorbent paper and allow them to come to room temperature.

Put a baking sheet/tray in the oven and preheat to 200°F/95°C/gas ¼. The cooked chicken can be kept warm in the oven while you make the sauce using the pan in which the chicken is sautéed. Or you can make the sauce ahead in a separate pan, and keep it on the stove top until you're ready to reheat and serve it.

Heat a large sauté pan over high heat for several minutes until it's hot. Check the heat level by holding your hand above the surface. While the pan is heating, pat the chicken breasts dry. Add enough oil to cover the bottom of the pan. A depth of ³⁄₁₆ inch/5 millimeters is ideal, but gauge the depth by eye. It is better to err on the side of too much oil. You're not eating the oil, just cooking in it. When the oil is hot, showing visible convection currents, lay each chicken breast skin-side down in the oil. Don't move them, but let them cook and brown. After they've cooked for a minute, you can lift them to be sure they're not sticking and that all the skin has been in contact with the oil. After a couple of minutes, once the skin is golden brown, reduce the heat to medium. Turn the chicken breasts when they've cooked halfway through, about 4 minutes if they've tempered completely. Cook for another 5 minutes or so. The breasts will need 10 to 12 minutes total if the wing joints are attached. Remove the breasts to the baking sheet/tray in the oven.

Pour off any excess fat in the sauté pan and make the butter sauce as directed. Serve it spooned over the sautéed chicken.

SAUTÉED SCALLOPS WITH ASPARAGUS/SERVES 4

I first saw a variation of this recipe at The French Laundry where the *poissonnier* at the time, Grant Achatz, put it over the top with truffles and asparagus tied in a cute little bundle with a chive, additional chlorophyll keeping the sauce intensely green. And it was fabulous, but the main reason it was so good was that scallops and asparagus are an unparalleled pair on every level: contrasting colors and textures, and a wonderful mix of flavors.

The main critical points are to cook and shock the asparagus properly and to get a good colorful crust on the scallops. The hardest part is finding good scallops. Try to find a good fishmonger who can offer large dry-packed scallops in the fall and winter when they are primarily harvested. The larger they are, the better the dish will be, and the easier it will be to prepare.

1½ pounds/680 grams asparagus, boiled and shocked

1½ pounds/680 grams scallops

¾ cup/170 grams butter, cut into 3 equal pieces

Fine sea salt

Canola oil

Kosher salt

About 2 tablespoons lemon juice

Finely chopped lemon zest for garnish

Remove the tips from the asparagus and reserve for garnish. Cut the stalks into pieces and purée in a blender until completely smooth. You may need to add a little water, ¼ cup/60 millieters or so, to ensure they're completely puréed. You can also use a food processor; if you do, pass the purée through a basket strainer to remove any long fibers. The asparagus can be prepared up to 24 hours before serving and stored in the refrigerator.

Remove the scallops from the refrigerator 1 hour before cooking and place them on a plate lined with paper towels/absorbent paper. They usually have a little nib of connective tissue on their side; remove and discard this.

Just before cooking the scallops, put the puréed asparagus in a saucepan over low heat. Put the asparagus tips and 1 piece of the butter in a sauté pan over low heat.

Season the scallops on both sides with fine sea salt. Heat a large sauté pan over high heat. It needs to be large enough that the scallops aren't crowded, or you won't get a good sear, one of the pleasures of this dish. Add enough oil to cover the bottom of the pan. A depth of ³⁄₁₆ inch/5 millimeters is ideal, but gauge the depth by eye. It is better to err on the side of too much oil. You're not eating the oil, just cooking in it. When it's very hot, just before it smokes, add the scallops and cook until they are beautifully seared, about 2 minutes. Turn and continue cooking just until the scallops are warm in the middle and medium-rare, about 2 minutes more. With scallops, it's better to err by undercooking them; raw scallops are delicious, but overcooked scallops are rubbery. Remove the scallops to paper towels/absorbent paper to drain.

While the scallops are cooking, raise the heat on both pans with asparagus to medium. Warm the tips in the butter. Bring the puréed asparagus to a simmer and season with kosher salt, then whisk in the remaining butter.

Immediately before serving, add the lemon juice to the asparagus sauce. Divide the sauce among plates or large bowls. Place the scallops on the sauce and garnish with the warmed asparagus tips and lemon zest.

Preparation photographs begin on the next page.

1/To blanch, your water should boil aggressively.

2/Remove immediately to an ice bath to shock.

3/The ice bath sets the vivid color.

4/Remove the tips and save for garnish.

5/Add the chopped stalks to a blender.

6/Add a little water if necessary.

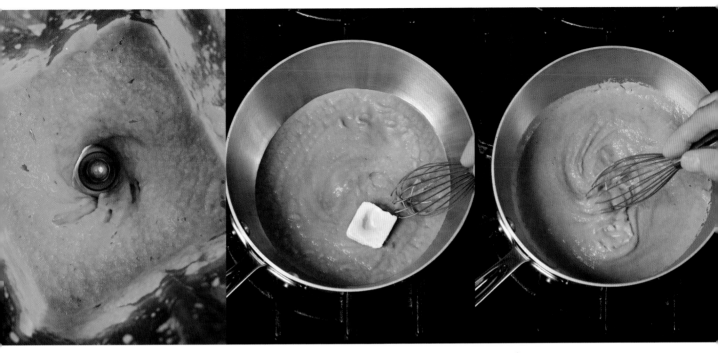

7/The longer you purée, the finer the sauce will be.

8/Add butter to finish the sauce.

9/Whisk to emulsify.

10/Currents in the oil will tell you your pan is properly heated.

11/Add the scallops to the hot oil.

12/After the scallops are seared, flip them to finish cooking. Cook the scallops to medium-rare to keep them tender, a couple of minutes per side.

SAUTÉED MUSHROOMS/SERVES 4 AS A SIDE DISH OR MAIN-DISH COMPONENT

Unless you have access to a variety of wild mushrooms, which can have great texture and flavor no matter how you cook them, the mushrooms available to you will need to be properly cooked in order to wrest flavor from them. White and brown button mushrooms, portobellos, shiitakes, and even oyster mushrooms benefit from being seared, which triples their flavor. For this, you need a very hot pan. Making your work more difficult is the fact that mushrooms contain abundant water. If the mushrooms begin releasing the water before they are properly seared, you are doomed to serving steamed mushrooms.

To sauté mushrooms properly, you need a large pan and a generous film of oil just at the smoking point. Add only enough mushrooms to cover the bottom of the pan without crowding them. And they should be left alone, not moved in the pan, until they are seared.

Mushrooms cooked this way are delicious on their own, served as a side dish. You can also add them to stews, sauces, soups, risottos, and pastas. To enhance their flavor, always use a generous amount of salt after they've seared (salting too early can encourage them to release water) and a generous amount of freshly ground pepper. Minced shallot never hurt mushrooms. You can deglaze with some white wine for even more complexity. If you don't add wine, use a few drops of lemon juice to bring out their flavor. A pinch of curry powder has a wonderful flavor impact, too. I cut the mushrooms in large pieces for stews and stand-alone side dishes, and into slices for sauces and garnish. The seared mushrooms can be transferred to a plate to cool and used a day later. To finish the mushrooms, reheat them gently in a bit of butter and adjust the seasoning.

Mushrooms add depth of flavor and enhance the savoriness of countless dishes. To make a great steak sauce, combine them with an equal amount of caramelized onion and a little butter or cream, and something acidic such as wine or cognac. To make an easy, excellent soup, reheat the mushrooms in cream and purée them, and season with lemon or curry. Or add them at the end of cooking coq au vin or beef similarly simmered in wine. And they make a juicy stuffing for meats and pastas. Duxelles, mushrooms that are finely chopped or diced and then sautéed, can be used in innumerable ways, including a versatile sauce (see page 201).

SIMPLE SAUTÉED MUSHROOMS

Canola oil (about ¼ cup/60 milliliters for a 12-inch/30.5-centimeter sauté pan)

1 pound/455 grams white mushrooms, quartered or cut into slices ¼ inch/6 millimeters thick

Kosher salt

Freshly ground black pepper

ENHANCED SAUTÉED MUSHROOMS

Canola oil for sautéing (you'll need about ¼ cup for a 12-inch/30.5-centimeter sauté pan)

1 pound white mushrooms, quartered or cut into slices ¼ inch/6 millimeters thick

2 tablespoons minced shallot

Kosher salt

Freshly ground black pepper

¼ teaspoon curry powder

½ cup/120 milliliters white wine

MAKE THE SIMPLE SAUTÉED MUSHROOMS:
Heat a sauté pan on high heat for 3 to 5 minutes. Add enough oil to completely coat the bottom. Allow the oil to get up to smoking temperature. Add enough mushrooms to cover the bottom of the pan in one loose layer. You'll probably need cook them in two batches. Sear the mushrooms for 1 minute. You can press down on them with a spatula to intensify the sear. Turn or toss the mushrooms to sear them on the other sides. Season the mushrooms with salt and pepper. Transfer to a plate or bowl. Wipe the pan clean and repeat with the second batch if necessary.

MAKE ENHANCED SAUTÉED MUSHROOMS: Heat the sauté pan on high heat for 3 to 5 minutes. Add enough oil to completely coat the bottom. Allow the oil to get up to smoking temperature. Add enough mushrooms to cover the bottom of the pan in one loose layer. You'll probably need to cook them in two batches. Sear the mushrooms for 1 minute. You can press down on them with a spatula to intensify the sear. Turn or toss the mushrooms to sear them on the other sides.

Add the shallot and stir to combine with the mushrooms. Season with salt and pepper and half of the curry powder if cooking the mushrooms in two batches. Cook for 30 seconds, stirring to distribute the shallot and seasonings. Add ¼ cup/ 60 milliliters of the wine (add all the wine if cooking the mushrooms in one batch). Transfer to a plate or bowl. Wipe the pan clean and repeat with the second batch if necessary.

THE STIR-FRY

Stir-frying, a variation on sautéing rather than on frying, involves high heat, a small amount of oil, and tender ingredients rapidly cooked. True stir-frying requires mortifyingly high heat, a surface so hot that the food shouldn't stand still or it will burn. Rather, the food is danced over the surface. This intense heat and speed account for much of the distinctive flavor of great stir-fries. That same flavor is difficult to replicate because no home kitchen has the kind of BTUs required to maintain this much heat in a pan after the food is added to it.

But there are several techniques you can use to elevate the level of your stir-fries and strengthen all your cooking muscles in the process. First, be sure to use a heavy-duty steel surface, whether a wok or sauté pan. Second, have all your ingredients cut and ready by the stove. Third, put your pan on the heat and keep it there until it's so hot that a teaspoon of water will form a mercury-like ball and race on the hot surface. Fourth, add your meat first. It should be patted dry if it's moist; the drier it is, the better—moisture will drop the temperature fast. Fifth, spread the meat over the surface so that as much of the meat is touching the surface as possible. Sixth, don't touch the meat for 20 seconds or so. Then carry on with the rest of the ingredients, adding fragrant aromatic vegetables and seasonings next (scallions, ginger, garlic, in most cases).

For those who insist on attaining the heat required for authentic stir-frying, my chef instructor, Michael Pardus, recommends buying a turkey deep-fry kit and rigging a wok over the propane flame. Short of that, the above techniques work fine and result in excellent stir-fries, such as the one here.

SPICY BEEF WITH BELL PEPPERS / SERVES 4 TO 6

I make this stir-fry weekly for my daughter, who also loves it cold the next day. A basic all-purpose stir-fry, it works well with sliced skinless, boneless chicken thighs or thinly cut pork shoulder. If you like very spicy dishes, I highly recommend using the whole dried chiles; they have a nutty flavor when cooked this way, but they're very hot. The cooking chiles give off strong smoke, so it's best to have an exhaust fan running full speed. The chiles can be cooked hours or days in advance and added later along with the bell peppers/capsicums. There should be plenty of sauce; I like to thicken it at the end with a slurry, a mixture of cornstarch/cornflour and water, so that the sauce coats the ingredients.

SAUCE

2 tablespoons hoisin sauce

1 tablespoon black bean sauce

1 tablespoon chili sauce with garlic

1 tablespoon peanut butter

1 tablespoon dark soy sauce

1 tablespoon lime juice

1 tablespoon fish sauce

½ cup/120 milliliters water

2 pounds/910 grams beef flank, cut across the grain into thin strips

Kosher salt

1 bunch scallions, ratty ends removed and white and green parts thinly sliced on a bias

5 garlic cloves, thinly sliced

One 1-inch/2.5-centimeter piece fresh ginger, grated and roughly chopped

¼ cup/60 milliliters canola oil

5 to 10 whole dried red chiles (optional, depending how hot you want the stir-fry)

3 bell peppers/capsicums, preferably green, red, and yellow, seeded and cut into thin strips

¾ cup/110 grams peanuts

2 teaspoons cornstarch/cornflour mixed into 1 tablespoon of water

2 teaspoons Asian sesame oil (optional)

2 tablespoons toasted sesame seeds (optional)

MAKE THE SAUCE: In a bowl, combine all the ingredients.

Place the beef in a medium bowl and season with two three-finger pinches of salt. Add the scallions, garlic, and ginger. This can be done up to a day ahead of cooking.

Heat a wok or large, heavy-bottomed sauté pan over high heat for 5 minutes. Add the oil and then the chiles (if using). Cook, stirring, until the chiles are black, 30 to 60 seconds. Add the beef mixture and spread it as evenly as possible across the surface of the pan. If your pan isn't big enough to spread the meat in one layer, cook the beef in two batches. Let it cook for 1 minute or so without stirring it, then toss and stir for about 1 minute to cook the meat evenly.

Make a well in the center of the beef mixture and pour the sauce into it. Stir the sauce well to make sure the peanut butter melts into the sauce. When the sauce has started to simmer, add the bell peppers/capsicums and return the liquid to a simmer. If you wish, you can cover the pan for 1 minute until the liquid comes back up to heat. Add the peanuts and cook for about 2 minutes until the vegetables are tender. Stir in the cornstarch/cornflour mixture. Remove from the heat. Season with the sesame oil and garnish with the sesame seeds, if desired, and serve.

SAUTÉED SUMMER SQUASH/SERVES 4 AS A SIDE DISH

This easy, refreshing, and colorful side dish is especially suited to white meats and fish. It uses medium rather than high heat and finishes in a couple of minutes. The squash and carrots can be julienned by hand, but it's far easier to use a Japanese mandoline if you have one. It's a tool I recommend for numerous cutting jobs.

1 medium zucchini/courgette

1 medium yellow squash

1 large carrot, peeled

2 tablespoons butter

Kosher salt

Freshly ground black pepper

¼ lemon

If cutting the vegetables by hand, julienne the squashes and carrot into pieces as thin and long as possible. Use only the exterior flesh of the squashes; discard the interior seeds. If using a mandoline, fit it with the julienne blade. Work from the sides of the squashes until you reach the seeds; discard the seeds. The vegetables can be cut up to 4 hours in advance and refrigerated, covered with a damp towel.

Heat a sauté pan over medium heat. Add the butter. When the butter has melted, add the squashes and carrot and cook just until softened. Season liberally with salt and pepper, and with a squeeze of lemon. Serve immediately.

BRUSSELS SPROUTS SAUTÉED IN SPICY BACON FAT/SERVES 4

Sautéing cooked green vegetables is a great strategy for transforming the commonplace into the dramatically delicious. The method here can be followed for any green vegetable—beans, peas, spinach, celery—but something about brussels sprouts goes especially well with bacon and hot pepper flakes. The technique is to boil and shock the sprouts, then reheat them gently in the bacon fat. Rather than halve the sprouts, you could shave them on a Japanese mandoline; the raw shaved leaves sauté very quickly.

½ pound/225 grams bacon, cut into ¼-inch/6-millimeter lardons, cooked (see facing page), fat reserved

1 teaspoon red pepper flakes

1 pound/450 grams brussels sprouts, halved, boiled until tender, then shocked in ice water

Kosher salt

In a large sauté pan, reheat the bacon and its fat over medium heat. Add the red pepper flakes and cook for 30 to 60 seconds. Add the brussels sprouts and cook, stirring to coat them with the spicy bacon fat, until heated all the way through, 3 to 4 minutes. Taste and season with salt if needed. Serve immediately.

THE WAY TO SAUTÉ BACON

This technique could very easily have gone in the water chapter, because it takes advantage of water's consistent low-heat capacity to begin cooking the bacon and rendering the fat. I first saw this method done when spending time in the kitchen of Primo, Melissa Kelly and Price Kushner's restaurant in Rockport, Maine. One of the chefs told me to cook the bacon by first covering it with water. It seemed almost counterintuitive, given that water leaches out flavor and salt. But it's a brilliant method.

The water cooks the bacon at 212°F/100°C or so, tenderizing the tough muscle and starting to render the fat. This is the chief benefit, the tenderizing effect, so it's especially apt with lardons or larger chunks of bacon. Also, you don't have to pay attention to the pan until the water is gone and the bacon is calling you with a noisy crackling. Yes, the water pulls out the flavor and salt, but once it cooks off, the bacon sautés in all that flavorful fat.

Because bacon freezes so well, I keep thick slabs in the freezer, so any time I need lardons, for a salad or stew, they can quickly be ready to go. Starting the bacon in water is the perfect way to cook it when it's frozen.

"It was taught to me when I was at An American Place, Larry Forgione's restaurant in New York City, by chef Rich D'Orazi," Kelly told me. "Since then I have never cooked lardons any other way."

Neither have I.

Bacon as desired (strips, lardons, slabs)

Choose a sauté pan in which the bacon will fit snugly in one layer. Put the bacon in the pan and add cold water to cover. Bring to a boil over high heat. When the water has almost cooked off, you'll begin to hear a noisy crackle and popping. Reduce the heat to medium low and sauté the bacon until nicely browned and crisp on the outside and tender and chewy inside. Serve immediately.

15

ROAST:
High and Low

LIKE SAUTÉ, "ROAST" IS DEFINED BY WHAT instructors in culinary schools call dry heat—that is, cooking without the cooling, moderating effects of water. It can be divided into two sub-techniques: high-heat roasting and low-heat roasting.

Terminology about roasting is erratic given that there's no difference between roasting and baking. Roasting may once have referred solely to meats cooked over an open flame, whereas baking referred to anything cooked in an enclosed oven. Today we typically say we roast meats and we bake doughs and batters. That will be the distinction here (even though we do bake ham, we don't roast meat loaf, and we both bake and roast potatoes).

High heat is used to develop flavor. Browning the skin of fowl and the exterior of meats makes it taste delicious. We use low heat for cooking larger items uniformly. Thus, we roast a chicken in a very hot oven to develop flavor, and we roast a big prime rib in a low oven to cook the center before the exterior is overcooked.

Because roasting does not involve water, and water is required for dissolving the connective tissue that makes meats tough, we usually don't roast tough cuts of meat. You would not roast a pot roast because it would go from tough to dry. I do roast a leg of lamb, on the other hand, for flavor; after being cooked, the tough collection of muscles is tenderized by being cut into thin slices.

That's really all there is to know about roasting. It's one of the simplest, most common, and best methods of cooking. It also fills up the kitchen with irresistible aromas. When you are determining how to roast something, think about its qualities. Is it naturally tender? How big is it? Does it have skin (which is mostly water that needs to cook off before browning happens)? Is your goal to make the exterior tasty or to have the item cook uniformly all the way

through? To put it generally, use high heat to develop flavors of what we call *caramelization* (though you're not actually caramelizing anything unless you're baking a tarte Tatin). Caramelization, the sweet, savory complexity of roasted things, only starts to happen at temperatures of 300°F/150°C and higher. If you only want to cook something through without developing additional flavors, and without overcooking the outside while keeping the inside rare, use temperatures well under 300°F/150°C.

I almost always do high-heat roasting at 425°F/220°C/gas 7 to 450°F/230°C/gas 8. At the higher end, all fats begin to smoke, so you need a clean oven and a ventilation fan for the most efficient roasting temperatures. For large cuts such as a big roast, I use a low oven, 225°F/110°C/gas ¼ or so, which is virtually a poaching temperature, especially given that moisture evaporating off the surface of the food has a cooling effect on the food.

Vegetables are delicious roasted. The flavors developed in vegetables cooked at high heat are so distinct from the flavor of the same vegetables boiled that they almost ought to have different names. Roasted asparagus spears are more complex in flavor than boiled asparagus. Roasted brussels sprouts are a dream, roasted broccoli a revelation.

There are only a few matters of finesse in roasting. They apply to other forms of cooking and are mainly common sense. Let your food come to room temperature before roasting it. The food also should be relatively dry; any moisture has to cook off before the good roasted flavors can develop. And always preheat the oven.

Many ovens come with a convection feature, meaning a fan in the oven can be activated to continuously circulate the air. Convection is especially helpful in achieving a crispy skin on poultry because the moisture cooking out of the skin is carried away from the bird. Convection also prevents hot and cool spots in your oven. I recommend convection cooking for most high-heat roasting. Because the circulation makes the heat more efficient, acting as a kind of turbo-charger, convection cooking can be faster than cooking without convection. Pay attention to how your convection works and adjust your cooking times accordingly.

Try to avoid roasting in a vessel with very high sides, which prevent hot air from circulating around the food you're cooking. My favorite vessel for roasting is an ovenproof sauté pan or a cast-iron frying pan.

Don't cover food that you're roasting. Covering food will result in steamed food rather than roasted food. Putting a top on a pan or covering it with aluminum foil is a method more like a braise than a roast because it turns what would be dry heat into moist heat. This can be used to your advantage if what you're roasting is tough. You might first cook a pork shoulder roast at a low temperature covered, allowing the steamy heat to work on the connective tissue, then, when the roast is tender, uncover it and develop the exterior color.

I'm starting with roasted vegetables because they're so delicious and because my sense is we don't roast them often enough. Also, when they're roasted, they become a bigger aspect of the meal because of the increased complexity of the flavors. Boiled cauliflower is fine, but you need a decent sauce, in my opinion, or a garnish to make it interesting. Roasted cauliflower can almost be the centerpiece of a meal the way a beef or pork roast would be.

The only vegetables not suitable for roasting are leafy vegetables. You wouldn't roast spinach, as it would dry out, and you wouldn't roast kale, because it would never become tender (though you can bake this green into wholesome "chips"). All other vegetables are suitable for roasting— green and root vegetables alike. Because vegetables are almost entirely water, some care must be taken to prevent them from drying out. I like to coat most vegetables in a little oil before putting them in a hot oven. The oil also helps deliver the heat evenly over their surface. And when you're roasting, pay attention to the moisture level. Some vegetables that you might prefer crispy, such as broccoli, and others, such as root vegetables, are best when their exterior is nicely browned but their interior is moist.

ROASTED CAULIFLOWER WITH BROWN BUTTER/SERVES 4 TO 6

(DEPENDING HOW BIG THE CAULIFLOWER IS AND HOW YOU'RE SERVING IT)

When you roast a cauliflower, it develops caramel-nutty flavors that are beautifully enhanced by the flavor of the browned butter. This robust dish can be the centerpiece of a vegetarian meal or a side for roasted meat. It's also a good substitute for roasted potatoes if you're looking to reduce your carb intake. The cauliflower needs to cook for more than an hour, with the butter added toward the end of the cooking and used as a finishing baste.

1 cauliflower

1 tablespoon canola oil

6 tablespoons/85 grams butter, at room temperature or softened

Kosher salt

Preheat the oven to 450°F/230°C/gas 8 or 425°F/220°C/gas 7 if you're concerned about smoke.

Cut off the stem of the cauliflower as close to the base as possible and remove any leaves that may still be attached. Rub the oil over the cauliflower.

Put the cauliflower in an appropriately sized ovenproof sauté pan or frying pan. Slide the pan into the oven and roast the cauliflower for 45 minutes. Remove the cauliflower from the oven and smear the butter over the surface. Sprinkle with a three-finger pinch of salt and return to the oven. Roast for another 30 minutes, basting the cauliflower a couple of times with the melted butter, until the cauliflower is well caramelized and tender; a knife inserted should meet no resistance. Slice and serve from the pan.

LEG OF LAMB WITH MINT YOGURT SAUCE/SERVES 8

Leg of lamb is an interesting cut to roast because it's composed of several different muscles that are fairly tender on their own but are bound to one another by tough connective tissue. This calls for moderate roasting so that you get some tenderizing from the cooking yet don't cook the lamb so hard that the exterior is overdone while the meat is still cold at the bone. As with pan-roasted pork tenderloin (see page 255), I prefer a healthy coating of crushed coriander seeds and black pepper and add garlic and thyme to the pan. The simple sauce is mint based, traditional with lamb; but cilantro/fresh coriander also works well if you want something a little less traditional. Roasted potatoes with onion make a great accompaniment. They can be cooked along with the lamb, then crisped in the oven while the lamb rests.

Roasted leg of lamb is a festive offering for a group, and because the roasting results in varying levels of doneness, it can satisfy a variety of palates.

1 garlic head

4- to 6-pound/1.8- to 2.7-kilogram leg of lamb

Kosher salt

2 teaspoons coriander seeds

2 teaspoons black peppercorns

3 tablespoons canola oil

4 to 6 stems fresh thyme

1 to 2 teaspoons lemon juice

1 cup/240 milliliters Greek yogurt

¼ cup/20 grams minced mint

About 2 hours or as many as 2 days before cooking the lamb, peel 3 garlic cloves and cut them into large slivers. Insert a paring knife into the lamb and slide a sliver of garlic down the blade into the meat. Repeat until the leg is uniformly studded with garlic. If you are preparing the lamb well in advance, give the lamb an aggressive salting, about 1 tablespoon's worth, then refrigerate until 2 hours before cooking it.

Preheat the oven to 350°F/180°C/gas 4.

Place the coriander seeds and peppercorns on a cutting board and crush with the bottom of a pan. Rub the lamb with 1 tablespoon of the oil. Sprinkle with the coriander and pepper and with salt if you haven't already salted the meat.

In a large ovenproof sauté pan or heavy-gauge roasting pan/tray, heat the remaining 2 tablespoons oil over high heat. Add all but 1 large clove of the remaining garlic, unpeeled, to the pan along with the thyme and stir to coat. Add the lamb and sear on all sides (the shape of the leg may prevent you from searing every bit of surface), 3 to 4 minutes per side. As you sear the leg, baste it with the oil. Put the pan in the oven and roast the lamb to an internal temperature of 130°F/57°C, about 1½ hours.

At least 20 minutes before serving the lamb, peel the remaining garlic clove and crush, mash, or mince it. In a small bowl combine the garlic, 1 teaspoon of the lemon juice, and ½ teaspoon salt and let sit for a few minutes. Add the yogurt and stir. Set aside.

Remove the lamb to a carving board (plenty of juice will be released as you carve), and let rest for 20 to 30 minutes. Taste the sauce and add more lemon juice if you wish. Stir in the mint. Slice the leg of lamb vertically, parallel with the bone, into thin slices. After the lamb is carved, spoon the accumulated juices over the slices. Serve with the yogurt sauce.

The Generosity of the Roasted Chicken

There is no more iconic home-cooked meal than a roasted chicken. I believe that just about any book addressing home cooking ought to include a recipe for roasted chicken, even though all the recipes are practically the same.

You can vary this recipe any way you wish—rub butter and herbs beneath the skin, roast the bird on a bed of vegetables, stuff it with aromatic vegetables and herbs, flavor it with a green Thai curry paste or a mix of cumin and dried chiles. In the end, roast chicken is roast chicken, and for that we should be grateful. Few things are more economical and soul satisfying to cook and to share at the table than a beautifully roasted chicken.

There may be no food more generous than roasted chicken. The aroma fills a kitchen. That's a pleasure, even if you're not aware of it. When the bird comes out of the oven, it must rest in its cooking vessel or on a cutting board, and it's something to behold while the rest of the meal is completed. It's gorgeous and enticing (cut off a wing or the butt to taste immediately, just to make sure it's delicious). If you wish, use some of the fat and the juices and browned skin stuck to the pan to make a sauce (see page 195). Separating the legs from the bird releases juices, ready to be taken advantage of.

All the preparations lead up to the eating. In our house, there are four of us, and the sharing of a single bird with its various parts is, to me, if not my kids, a spiritual satisfaction. We usually have leftovers, and the carcass and bones can be transformed into stock (see page 65), the backbone of yet another meal a day or two later, such as chicken and dumplings or any number of soups.

PERFECT ROASTED CHICKEN/SERVES 4

There are three finesse points to a perfect roasted chicken. Though infinite variables make one roasted chicken different from another (the quality of the chicken, the seasonings used, how long you cook the bird), three main goals are essential if you want to wind up with a perfect roasted chicken. They concern seasoning, oven temperature, and—the most talked-about issue but rarely addressed practically—the maintenance of a juicy breast and fully cooked thighs.

Seasoning in this case is salt. A chicken should be liberally salted. It should have a visible coating of salt, not just a fey sprinkle. As Thomas Keller put it to me, "I like it to rain down on the chicken." An aggressive use of salt not only seasons the exterior so the chicken tastes delicious, it also helps dehydrate the skin so that you wind up with a crisp brown skin and not a pale soggy one.

Chickens should be roasted in a very hot oven, as hot as your stove and kitchen can take. A hot oven—ideally 450°F/230°C/gas 8 but at least 425°F/220°C/gas 7—accomplishes two important feats: it browns the skin, and it cooks the leg and thigh fast, giving the breast less opportunity to dry out.

The most common reason people end up with a dry and flavorless breast is that they fail to address what is happening in the cavity of the bird. If the ends of the legs are not tied together in front of the cavity or if the cavity is empty, hot air swirls around the cavity of the bird, cooking the breast from the inside out. To prevent this, you must truss the chicken, which I think is part of the pleasure of roasting a chicken, but most home cooks don't want to bother with it. If you count yourself among the latter, simply put something into the cavity, preferably something tasty—lemon, onion, garlic, herbs. I repeat: if you don't want to truss the chicken, stick a lemon in it.

Of course, you don't want to under- or overcook the bird. My experience of roasting a chicken most weeks of the year for the past twenty years is that 1 hour at 450°F/230°C is perfectly sufficient for a 4-pound/1.8-kilogram bird (50 minutes for a bird under that). But as a rule of thumb, you should use the cavity juices to judge doneness. After 45 minutes, if you tilt the bird so that the juices spill cracklingly into the rendered fat, you will notice that they are red. When you tilt the chicken and the juices that stream out are clear, it's safe to take the bird out of the oven.

Finally, a chicken ought to rest a good 15 minutes before you cut into it. Don't worry about the chicken getting cold. It won't. It's a big, solid bird that retains heat well (touch it after 10 minutes and see for yourself).

Continued on the next page.

One 3- to 4-pound/1.4- to 1.8-kilogram chicken

1 lemon and/or 1 medium onion, quartered (optional)

Kosher salt

About 1 hour before cooking the chicken, remove it from the refrigerator, and rinse it. If you intend to make a pan sauce (see page 195), cut off the wing tips and add them, along with the neck if you have it, to the pan in which you will roast the bird. Truss the chicken or stuff it with the lemon or onion, or both. Salt it and set it on a plate lined with paper towels/absorbent paper.

Preheat the oven to 450°F/230°C/gas 8 or to 425°F/220°C/gas 7 if you're concerned about smoke. Set the oven on convection if that's an option. Put the chicken in an oven-proof frying pan and slide it into the oven.

After 1 hour, check the color of the juices. If they run red, return the chicken to the oven and check it again in 5 minutes. Remove the chicken from the oven and let rest for 15 minutes before carving it.

Carve the chicken and serve.

1/A roast chicken benefits from an aggressive coating of salt.

2/Truss your chicken to prevent the breast from overcooking.

3/Roasting in a skillet encourages good air circulation.

SPICY ROASTED GREEN BEANS WITH CUMIN/SERVES 4

In the summer I boil green beans. In the winter, I roast them. Here, I add red pepper flakes and cumin. If I have some bacon fat on hand, I use that as the cooking fat, which adds another dimension.

3 tablespoons canola oil or rendered bacon fat

1 to 2 teaspoons red pepper flakes

2 teaspoons cumin seeds

5 or 6 garlic cloves, smashed with the flat side of a knife

1 pound/455 grams green beans, stem ends removed

Kosher salt

Preheat the oven to 450°F/230°C/gas 8 or to 425°F/220°C/gas 7 if you're concerned about smoke.

Set an ovenproof frying pan over high heat, and add the oil, red pepper flakes, cumin seeds, and garlic. When the cumin and pepper flakes begin to sizzle, add the green beans and toss them with the oil so that they're nicely coated.

Slide the pan into the oven and cook the green beans, removing them once or twice to stir them, until they are nicely colored and tender, about 20 minutes. Season with a three-finger pinch of salt midway through the cooking. Serve hot from the pan.

SUBTECHNIQUE: **PAN ROASTING**

An important cooking technique to hold in your arsenal is the pan roast. The name alone conjures a sense of deliciousness even without any food in the title. The technique simplifies cooking, gives you flexibility and control over your food, and frees up the stove top so you can work on other parts of your meal while the main course finishes cooking.

The pan roast is simply the combination of two dry-heat techniques: sauté and roast. Meat is first seared on the stove top in a sauté pan, then is turned and put in the oven to finish cooking. In other words, first you develop the flavor on the exterior of the meat on a very hot surface, and then you cook the interior by putting it in an environment where it's surrounded by heat.

Any meat can be pan roasted if it's thick enough and is naturally tender. Very thin, lean cuts of meat and thin fillets of fish don't benefit from pan roasting, but thicker cuts of meat and more muscular fish are perfect candidates. Beef tenderloin, steaks, veal chops, chicken breasts with the wing joint attached, and fish such as cod, monkfish, or grouper pan roast beautifully.

All you need is a pan that you can put into the oven, a heavy-duty stainless-steel sauté pan with a metal handle or a cast-iron frying pan. When you've finished pan roasting, you're going to have a pan with a very hot handle. I use heavy-duty side towels for grabbing hot pans. Whenever I take a pan out of the oven, I leave a side towel on the handle so that I or someone else at the stove doesn't grab it and get burned.

The pan roast is used all the time in the restaurant kitchen. It ought to find its way into more homes. Of the many ways that we combine cooking techniques to our great advantage, the pan roast is among the most versatile.

PAN-ROASTED COD WITH CHORIZO VINAIGRETTE/SERVES 4

Cod is a hearty fish that carries the big flavor of the chorizo and the acidity of the vinaigrette well. Because it's a meaty fish, it can be roasted with great results. First the fillets are seared in hot oil, then they are turned and finished in the oven while you prepare any other dishes you're serving.

**4 skinless cod fillets, about 6 ounces/
170 grams each**

Canola oil

Fine sea salt

Chorizo Vinaigrette (page 213)

Preheat the oven to 350°F/180°C/gas 4.

Rub the cod fillets with oil and sprinkle with salt.

Put an ovenproof, nonstick pan over high heat. When it's hot, add enough oil to cover the bottom of the pan to a depth of ⅛ inch/3 millimeters. Allow the oil to get hot. Lay the cod fillets in the pan and cook until golden brown, about 2 minutes.

Turn the fillets and slide the pan into the oven. Cook until the center of the cod is warm, 4 to 5 minutes. Test a fillet by inserting a paring knife or cake tester, then holding the metal to the skin below your lower lip; if it's cool, return the cod to the oven for a few more minutes.

Drain the fillets on paper towels/absorbent paper and serve topped with the vinaigrette.

PAN-ROASTED PORK TENDERLOIN WITH GARLIC, CORIANDER, AND THYME/SERVES 4

One of the advantages of the pan roast is that it gives you the opportunity to add flavor to what you're cooking through basting. Here, after a whole pork tenderloin is seared on the stove top, garlic and fresh herbs are added to the pan along with a little butter, which picks up the flavor of the aromatics and delivers them to the pork as a baste. Basting also coats the surface with hot fat that helps cook the meat more quickly and evenly. Any of the roasted vegetables in this chapter makes an excellent accompaniment.

One 1¼-pound/570-gram pork tenderloin

Kosher salt

Freshly ground black pepper

1 teaspoon coriander seeds, lightly toasted and crushed in a mortar with pestle or on a cutting board with a pan, or roughly chopped with a knife

1 teaspoon canola oil

4 tablespoons/55 grams butter

3 garlic cloves, partly smashed with the flat side of a knife to open them up but not flatten them

3 or 4 sprigs fresh thyme, plus ½ teaspoon picked thyme

Zest from 1 orange

About 1 hour before cooking the pork, remove it from the refrigerator and season it with salt and pepper and the coriander seeds. Pork tenderloins have one end that tapers. Consider folding the tapered end over onto the meat and tying it with butcher's string so that the tenderloin has a uniform thickness. Alternatively, you can leave it as is (it will be medium-well done by the time the tenderloin is medium-rare), or you can cut off the end and save it for another use.

Preheat the oven to 350°F/180°C/gas 4.

Put an ovenproof sauté pan that's large enough to contain the tenderloin over high heat. When the pan is hot, add the oil. When the oil is hot, lay the tenderloin top-side down in the pan. Let cook, without moving it, until it is nicely browned, 1 to 2 minutes. Add the butter, garlic, and thyme sprigs to the pan. Turn the tenderloin. When the butter has melted, spoon it all over the tenderloin and slide the pan into the oven. After several minutes, remove the pan and baste the tenderloin. Squeeze it. It should still be fairly squishy (rare). Return it to the oven for another few minutes. Baste again if you wish.

Remove the tenderloin from the oven. The total cooking time should be about 10 minutes. The tenderloin should still be somewhat pliable but beginning to show signs of firmness. If you must, check the internal temperature with an instant-read thermometer; it should be between 130° and 135°F/54° and 57°C. Baste the tenderloin again, add the thyme leaves to the butter in the pan, and set the pan aside for 10 minutes.

To serve, cut the tenderloin crosswise into slices about ½ inch/12 millimeters thick. Drizzle some of the herbed basting fat over the slices and sprinkle some orange zest over the top before serving.

16

BRAISE:

The Alchemy of Moist Heat

BRAISE IS NOT ONLY ONE OF THE MOST
valuable techniques in the kitchen, it is a kind
of emblem of the true cook. More than any other
technique, it is what cooking is all about: transformation, turning raw, tough, inexpensive
ingredients into hot, tender, delectable dishes.
When we braise, we are realizing our abilities
as cooks in ways that are richer, more fulfilling,
and more illuminating than when we employ
any other single technique.

Braise is also one of the most generous
techniques: it fills the kitchen.

A decade ago, deep in a Cleveland, Ohio,
winter, with nothing but blackness by 6 P.M.,
I was addressing bills I didn't quite have the funds
to pay, and I wondered why I wasn't nearly as
miserable as I ought to be. It was the short ribs
braising in the oven, the kitchen windows
steamed from the heat, my wife Donna reading the New York Times while the water for egg
noodles came to a boil. Braised beef short ribs
with buttered egg noodles. So simple. Braising
sets the tone of warmth and satisfaction and
fullness in your home, even when your bank
account isn't any of those things. But short ribs
can help that situation, too, because their price
is half that of tenderloin or strip steak. We
braise the most inexpensive cuts, turning them
into treasures.

Another reason braises are great is that
they get better over time. You can make them
one, two, or three days ahead, and the flavors
only deepen.

These qualities—inexpensive dishes that
are treasures and are best when made days in
advance—also make braises the perfect entertaining food.

Even the way we describe the process is
tantalizing: floured meat sizzling in hot fat, golden
brown crust on those fatty short ribs, simmered
gently in rich stock until meltingly tender.

Another great facet of braising is that it's
easy. Anyone can do it and do it well. It's not like
decorating a cake or boning a chicken in one
piece. Everyone can get a pan hot, get a good sear
on a piece of meat, add some liquid to the pan,
slip it in the oven, and then find something else
to do for hours.

Before I get into the specifics of the technique, what exactly does *braise* mean?

There is no definitive consensus among
texts or chefs. The word originates from a French
term for putting live or glowing coals under,
around, and on top of a cooking vessel. Some
believe it designates that the meat is only partially submerged; others say that doesn't matter.
Some say browning the meat first should be part
of the definition. Others say a braise is anything
cooked in liquid in the oven, meat or vegetable,
until tender.

Braise is defined by several factors: what
we braise is tough, usually a heavily worked muscle, which is why we need to braise it. The food is
usually seared to add flavor to the finished dish
and, important with meat, to set the exterior so
that when you add the liquid, the meat doesn't
release a lot of blood, which would coagulate and
rise to the surface. Liquid, usually stock, is added
to the pot, along with any other ingredients, such
as aromatic vegetables and seasonings, and the
contents are brought to a simmer and then put in
the oven, usually covered or partially covered.

Of course, there are infinite variations.
Sometimes you don't want to sear the food
first. Sometimes you cover the pot, sometimes
not. Sometimes the meat is submerged; other
times it's only partially covered. Braise usually
indicates a single large item or several large
items—a pot roast, lamb, veal shanks. Stew,
a form of braise, is usually composed of an abun-
dance of ingredients or ingredients that are cut

up into smaller pieces. The word *braise* has broadened to include cooking even tender ingredients, braised fish and braised vegetables. But the term always indicates that liquid is involved, and thus braise is considered moist heat cooking, as opposed to dry heat techniques such as roast and sauté.

One of the most important steps in braising is choosing the right vessel. You can braise in a shallow sauté pan (the coq au vin on page 51 is an example of this) or in a deep pot, but the material should be heavy and a good heat conductor. Without question, my favorite type of vessel for braising is made of enameled cast iron. Such vessels are very heavy and can be used on the stove top and in the oven. The enamel is a low-stick surface that also gives you good browning, and the vessels are easy to clean. Of the various brands available, Le Creuset is the best known and is the industry standard. The cookware is expensive but worth the investment. It's good to have a large pot and a smaller pot because the other important factor is size. A small item is difficult to braise in a large pot. That would require too much liquid. Choose a pot in which the ingredients fit snugly; this allows you the most efficient use of liquid and delivers to it the maximum amount of flavor.

How much liquid you put in the pot depends on what you're after. If you want your meat cooked uniformly, you'll need to submerge it. If you want to develop more flavor on the exterior, submerge it halfway so that the exposed part browns.

If you cover the pot, the liquid will boil. An uncovered pot, or one that's only partially covered—by leaving the lid ajar or by cutting a parchment/baking paper lid—will cook the food more gently and reduce the cooking liquid, thus intensifying the flavor.

Moisture is the key. When you harness the power of moist heat to break down the tough foods, you can focus your energies on flavor. For instance, you don't need to submerge something in liquid to make it tender. You can simply wrap it in aluminum foil with a couple tablespoons of water and get the same effect, without losing the flavor of the meat to the cooking liquid.

Generally speaking, the optimal braising temperature never goes above 300°F/150°C; again, it depends on what you're cooking and how you're cooking it. You can braise at 225° or 325°F/110° or 165°C, but in my experience, the more gently you cook the food, the better it tastes. If you're covering the pot and the food is submerged, the temperature will be 212°F/100°C, regardless of the oven temperature. Just remember that the harder and more vigorously the liquid boils, the more fat will be emulsified into the liquid, and the more the vegetables will disintegrate.

But, nothing in cooking is absolute. A preparation popular in France calls for braising a leg of lamb at high roasting temperatures, 425° to 450°F/220° to 230°C for 6 or 7 hours.

When you pay attention to the two simple parts of the braise—tenderizing the meat and flavoring the dish—it's difficult to go wrong.

Finessing the braise is part of the fun and distinguishes one braise from another. There are countless touches that can be applied or ignored. Braises can be simple one-pot meals, or you can take time to refine them and make them very clean and flavorful.

The liquid you choose can be homemade stock. Veal stock is the best stock for braising because it tends to take on the flavor of what you're braising, and it's rich in gelatin, which gives the sauce body. But stock is not imperative. Because you're cooking the ingredients for a long time, you can make your stock at the same time as you're braising. In these cases, water is fine. You can also use other flavorful liquids. The Braised Pork Belly with Caramel-Miso Glaze (page 269) is braised in freshly squeezed orange juice, the Red Wine–Braised Short Ribs (page 270) in wine. You can braise in canned puréed or crushed tomatoes.

To cover or not to cover? Most braises should be covered. Uncovered pots will be much cooler than the covered pots due to the evaporation, which will also reduce the quantity of the sauce you end up with. If you want something to cook hard in a simmering liquid, something that needs a lot of tenderizing, then cover the pot. If you want some reduction, but not a lot, and gentle cooking, cover the pot with the lid ajar or make a parchment round and press this down on top of your braise.

Almost always you'll want to remove the fat rendered into the sauce, which can make braises feel greasy. To do this, let the braise sit so that the fat rises to the top, then spoon it off. If you're not serving the braise right away, chill it; the fat will harden and be easy to remove. When you do this, always let the meat chill in the liquid, or it can dry out and become stringy and flavorless. If you need to cool the meat outside the sauce, be sure to cover it with plastic wrap/cling film.

When a braise is done, the cooking liquid will have absorbed most of the flavors of the meat. The vegetables, however, will be over-cooked. This is fine for a weekday stew, but if you want to raise the braise a level, strain the cooking liquid, add new vegetables, perhaps adjust the consistency with a roux or slurry, cook the vegetables just until done, and add the meat to heat through (see the short ribs for an example).

BRAISED FENNEL WITH THYME/SERVES 4 TO 8

Fennel is an aromatic vegetable that works beautifully as a braise, becoming very flavorful and tender. I like to serve this with whole roasted or grilled/barbecued fish such as the branzino on page 300, using the fennel tops to stuff the fish cavities.

Plain/all-purpose flour

2 fennel bulbs, each quartered lengthwise

3 tablespoons canola oil

4 or 5 sprigs fresh thyme

2 tablespoons butter

Kosher salt

Preheat oven to 325°F/165°C/gas 3.

Put some flour on a plate. Dredge the cut sides of the fennel quarters in the flour. In an ovenproof pot just large enough to contain the fennel, heat the oil over medium-high to high heat. You want the oil to be hot, but you don't want to burn the flour. Add the fennel and cook the floured sides until nicely browned. Add enough water to come ½ inch/12 millimeters up the sides of the fennel, then add the thyme, the butter, and a three-finger pinch of salt. Bring the water to a simmer.

Cover the pot and slide it into the oven. Cook until the fennel is tender (a knife inserted should meet no resistance), 20 to 30 minutes. Serve immediately.

p. 262/twenty

BRAISED LAMB SHANKS WITH LEMON CONFIT/SERVES 4

Few other braised meats can achieve the richness and depth of braised lamb shanks. This recipe seasons the braising liquid with spices associated with Moroccan cooking. Try to find the *ras-el-hanout*, a North African spice blend that is like curry. It adds extra depth of flavor, but the recipe is delicious without it. If you can't find it, it's easy to make; there are a number of recipes online.

Like most braised meats, the shanks are best cooked one to three days before serving. If you serve them on the same day, be sure to spoon off the rendered fat. I like to accompany the lamb and tomato-based sauce with curried couscous and sautéed red peppers, but basmati rice or boiled potatoes would work well, too.

4 lamb shanks

Kosher salt

All-purpose/plain flour

Canola oil for sautéing

1 large onion, cut into medium dice

5 garlic cloves, smashed with the flat side of a knife

1 tablespoon ground cumin

1 tablespoon ground coriander

½ teaspoon cayenne pepper

2 teaspoons *ras-el-hanout* or curry powder

1 cinnamon stick

Lemon Confit (page 33), 1 lemon scraped of pulp and pith, julienned or finely chopped

One 28-ounce/800-gram can whole peeled tomatoes, puréed in a blender or with a hand blender with their juices

1 tablespoon minced fresh parsley or cilantro/fresh coriander (optional)

Season the lamb shanks liberally with salt and set aside long enough for the salt to dissolve, at least 15 minutes or as many as 2 days. Put enough flour for dredging the shanks into a plastic bag. Add the shanks and coat with the flour.

In a Dutch oven or other heavy ovenproof pot, add enough oil to reach ¼ inch/6 millimeters up the sides and heat over high heat. When the oil is hot but not yet smoking, shake any residual flour off the lamb shanks and sear them until they have a nice crust. Remove to paper towels/absorbent paper.

Preheat the oven to 300°F/150°C/gas 2.

Wipe out the pot, add a thin film of oil, place over medium-high heat, and sauté the onion and garlic until the onion develops some color, about 10 minutes. Add the cumin, ground coriander, cayenne, *ras-el-hanout*, cinnamon, and three-quarters of the lemon, and stir to cook the spices and coat the onion, about 1 minute.

Nestle the shanks in the pan, add the tomatoes with their juices, and bring to a simmer. Cut out a round of parchment/baking paper that will fit your pot (see page 170). Press this paper lid onto the shanks or cover the pot with a lid, placing the lid slightly ajar. Set the pot in the oven. Cook the shanks until they are fork tender, about 3 hours.

Remove the pot from the oven and let the shanks cool to room temperature. Refrigerate until thoroughly chilled.

Remove the congealed fat on the surface and discard. Reheat the shanks over medium-low heat or in a 300°F/150°C/gas 2 oven, just until heated through. While the lamb is reheating, soak the remaining preserved lemon in water for 5 to 10 minutes. Serve the lamb with the sauce and garnish with the lemon and the parsley, if desired.

Preparation photographs begin on the next page.

1/Flour the meat you are braising.

2/Add the meat to the hot fat.

3/The flour gives the meat a dry surface for better searing.

4/The flour will brown and add flavor.

5/The seared meat will have a nice crust.

6/Drain the excess oil from the meat.

7/Sweat the onions first, then add your dry seasonings.

8/Stir the spices to coat the onion.

9/Nestle the shanks in the pan.

10/Add the braising liquid. Here it's puréed tomatoes.

11/Add the preserved lemon.

12/Make a parchment lid.

Continued on the next page.

13/Measure the circle by placing the tip at the center of the pot and cutting the triangle at the edge of the pot.

14/Cover with the parchment round.

15/Press the paper lid into the shanks. The paper will keep in heat and allow evaporation.

16/The lamb shanks after cooking.

17/Chill with the lid on, then remove the paper.

18/Scrape off and discard the congealed fat before reheating and serving.

BRAISED DUCK LEGS/SERVES 4

If there's a single preparation of duck that under-scores that it ought to be more prominent in our kitchens, it's braised duck legs. They are relatively inexpensive, easy to prepare, and deeply delicious. This braise uses only water and aromatic vegetables, which flavor the liquid, as does the duck. You could also use homemade chicken or vegetable stock. This dish is fabulous with mashed potatoes (see page 146, use the sauce in the place of the browned butter), couscous, or egg noodles. The legs are served whole, but the meat can be removed from the bone and served with a salad or open-faced on a baguette, or tossed with diced roasted potatoes as a fancy duck hash.

4 duck legs

Kosher salt

1 tablespoon canola oil

1 large onion, sliced

2 carrots, cut into 1-inch/2.5-centimeter pieces

4 garlic cloves, smashed with the side of a knife

1 tablespoon tomato paste/purée

1 to 1½ cups/240 to 355 milliliters white wine

7 to 10 stems fresh thyme, tied together

1 to 1½ cups/240 to 355 milliliters water

1 tablespoon fish sauce

1 tablespoon sherry vinegar

Freshly ground black pepper

2 teaspoons cornstarch/cornflour dissolved in 1 tablespoon of water

Season the duck legs aggressively with salt 30 to 90 minutes, or up to 2 days, before cooking.

Preheat the oven to 300°F/150°C/gas 2.

In a pot just large enough to contain the legs, lidded, heat the oil over medium heat. Add the onion and cook, seasoning with a three-finger pinch of salt, until the onion is softened and translucent, 3 to 4 minutes. Add the carrots, garlic, and tomato paste/purée and cook for 1 or 2 minutes. Nestle the duck legs in the pan, and add the wine, thyme, and enough water so that the liquid just covers the duck. Raise the heat to high and bring to a simmer. Cover and simmer for about 30 seconds, then slip the pot into the oven. Cook, covered, for 3 hours.

The duck will be done but can sit until you're ready to serve it. Just before serving, turn on the broiler/grill. Remove the duck legs from the pot and broil/grill until the skin is crispy. Strain the cooking liquid into a small saucepan (discard the aromatics). Bring to a simmer, spoon off the fat that rises to the top (if you wish), and reduce by about a quarter. Add the fish sauce and sherry vinegar and season with pepper. Taste and add more vinegar if you wish. Add the cornstarch/cornflour and water to thicken the sauce. Serve the duck with the sauce.

BRAISED PORK BELLY WITH CARAMEL-MISO GLAZE/SERVES 6

Pork belly, the cut from which we get bacon, is my favorite part of the pig. It's got succulent meat and plenty of fat, and can be used in many different preparations, from the Chinese char sui (barbecue) to bacon and pancetta to braises like the one here. You need to make this dish at least a day ahead of serving it, or as much as a five days ahead, because the pork needs to chill in its cooking liquid, which can be water, pork or chicken stock, or, as here, orange juice.

I recommend that the pork be finished with caramel-miso glaze and garnished with scallions and red chiles, but the basic braised pork is a great base and can be flavored in any way desired. The pork could be used with beans in a stir-fry or be sautéed until crispy and served with a salad and red wine vinaigrette (see page 211). You could sauté it and make a pork sandwich with nothing more than bread and a good mustard. Few meats match the glory of pork belly.

1½ teaspoons coriander seeds

1½ teaspoons black peppercorns

3 pounds/1.4 kilograms pork belly

Kosher salt

2 bay leaves

1 large onion, sliced

5 garlic cloves, smashed with the flat side of a knife

1 cup/240 milliliters freshly squeezed orange juice

Canola oil

Caramel-Miso Glaze (page 181)

2 tablespoons seeded and minced red chiles

2 scallions, white and pale green parts only, finely sliced on a bias

Combine the coriander seeds and peppercorns in a sauté pan and toast over medium-high heat until fragrant, 2 minutes. Transfer to a cutting board and crush with the bottom of a pan.

Preheat the oven to 250°F/120°C/gas ½.

Season the pork liberally on all sides with salt. Place it fat-side up in a baking dish. The more snugly it fits, the better. Scatter the crushed spices, bay leaves, onion, and garlic over the pork. Add the orange juice and cover the dish tightly with aluminum foil. (You can also wrap the pork along with the other ingredients, using only ¼ cup/60 milliliters juice, in aluminum foil; be sure to seal it tightly.) Put the dish in the oven and cook the pork until fork tender, about 6 hours. Allow it to cool in the cooking juices, then cover and refrigerate until thoroughly chilled, overnight or for up to 5 days.

Remove the pork from the dish, scraping off the seasonings (all of which you can discard, though the cooking liquid can be strained and used in the Caramel-Miso Glaze). Cut the pork into 12 equal cubes.

Coat the bottom of a nonstick pan with canola oil and put it over medium-high heat. Sear the pieces of pork on all sides, then add the glaze to reheat it and coat the pork. When the pork is heated through and nicely glazed, arrange on plates. Spoon the glaze over the pork, and garnish with the chiles and scallions.

RED WINE–BRAISED SHORT RIBS/SERVES 4

Short ribs are the go-to ingredient when I entertain in the winter. They're relatively inexpensive but are enormously satisfying. If you make a little extra effort to refine the sauce, the ribs are worthy of the finest table. This recipe serves four but can easily be scaled up as needed, using two short ribs per person. The ribs are best and easiest to prepare a day or two in advance. Serve them on buttered egg noodles.

Canola oil

All-purpose/plain flour

8 beef short ribs

2 large onions, cut into large dice

Kosher salt

4 carrots, cut into bite-size pieces

2 celery stalks, cut into 1-inch/
2.5-centimeter pieces

2 tablespoons tomato paste/purée

3 cups/720 milliliters Zinfandel or other
fruit-heavy red wine

1 garlic head, halved horizontally

One 1-inch/2.5-centimeter piece of fresh ginger

2 bay leaves

⅓ cup/75 milliliters honey

1 teaspoon peppercorns, cracked beneath a
sauté pan

1 tablespoon butter

1 pound/455 grams mushrooms, seared
(see page 201)

GREMOLATA
2 tablespoons minced fresh parsley

1 tablespoon minced garlic

1 tablespoon grated or minced lemon zest

In a Dutch oven or other heavy ovenproof pot, add enough oil to reach ¼ inch/6 millimeters up the sides and heat over high heat. Put some flour on a plate. Dredge the short ribs in the flour, shaking off the excess. When the oil is hot, add the ribs and brown on all sides. You may need to do this in batches; you don't want to crowd the pan, or the ribs won't brown. Remove the ribs to a plate lined with paper towels/absorbent paper. (This can be done a day before cooking the ribs; cover them and refrigerate until you're ready to proceed.)

Preheat the oven to 250°F/120°C/gas ½.

Wipe the pot clean and sauté half of the onions in a film of oil over medium heat until softened. (Refrigerate the remaining onions until needed.) Add a four-finger pinch of salt and stir. Add the half of the carrots (refrigerate the remaining carrots until needed) and the celery and cook for about 4 minutes longer. The longer you cook the vegetables, the deeper the flavor of the sauce will be. For intensely deep flavor, cook until the carrots and onions are browned. Add the tomato paste/purée and cook to heat it.

Nestle the ribs in the pot. Add the wine (it should come three-fourths of the way up the ribs), garlic, ginger, and bay leaves. Season with a three-finger pinch of salt and add the honey and peppercorns. Bring to a simmer, cover the pot with a parchment round (see page 170) or a lid set ajar, and slide into the oven. Cook the ribs for 4 hours.

Remove the pot from the oven and allow the ribs to cool, covered. When the ribs are cool enough to handle, put them on a plate, cover with plastic wrap/cling film, and refrigerate. Strain the cooking liquid into a tall vessel (a 4-cup/960-milliliter glass measuring cup is best), cover, and refrigerate. When the liquid has chilled, remove the congealed fat and discard.

Melt the butter in your braising pot. Add the reserved onions and carrots and sauté until softened, 3 to 4 minutes. Return the ribs to the pot and add the seared mushrooms. Add the reserved cooking liquid. Bring to a simmer, cover, and cook over medium-low heat until the carrots are tender and the ribs are heated through, about 15 minutes.

MAKE THE GREMOLATA: In a small bowl, stir the parsley, garlic, and lemon zest until evenly distributed.

Serve the short ribs with the carrots, onions, mushrooms, and sauce. Garnish with the gremolata.

17

POACH:
Gentle Heat

WE USE THE POACH TECHNIQUE FOR ITS gentleness and for its impact on the moistness of the finished dish. Fish or meat that might dry out or seize up in the high dry heat of a sauté pan or oven can remain tender and succulent when poached. Shrimp/prawns and lobster, which can become tough when cooked over high heat, emerge tender when cooked at poaching temperatures (see Butter-Poached Shrimp, page 141).

When we use the term *poach*, we almost always refer to cooking something that's already tender. I think it's a meaningful distinction. You can poach a brisket in stock for hours and hours until it becomes tender, but I like to reserve the terms *braising* and *stewing* for this kind of long, slow, moist cooking meant to tenderize. With one exception, I will only use the term *poach* here, in basic techniques, as a method to cook tender foods or foods without abundant connective tissue: fish, tender meat and sausage, root vegetables, legumes/pulses, and eggs.

Also, when we use the term *poach*, we mean temperatures below simmering. Since there are few tender foods you want become hotter than 185°F/85°C, there's no reason that poaching temperatures should be above that. Poaching is best accomplished between 160° and 180°F/71° and 82°C, below simmering. Water only begins to bubble at about 190°F/88°C.

The most commonly poached food is fish. Poaching is probably the easiest way to cook fish well for those less experienced with fish or cooking generally, especially thick, rich varieties such as salmon and halibut. I prefer poaching fish to sautéing it—sautéing or roasting fish at high heat tends to bring out the oils in fish that can make it taste "fishy."

We also poach some delicate sausages, seafood, or chicken mousselines, for instance, to ensure that the fat stays bound within the food. Quenelles, mousselline dropped off a spoon, are always poached. Tender meat, such as beef tenderloin, can be poached to good effect (see page 277). Boneless chicken breast can be poached, but that strikes me as something you'd need to make if you're cooking for the infirm. Root vegetables are best poached, rather than boiled, so that their interior cooks before their exterior begins to disintegrate. Similarly, legumes, dried beans, are best cooked at poaching temperatures for the same reason, so that they don't start falling apart before they're cooked.

The temperature is the defining attribute of poaching, as it has a highly controlled and uniform impact on the food. The second attribute is the liquid itself. It can be water alone. It can be water flavored with aromatics, in effect, a quick vegetable stock—thus the French *court bouillon*, literally "short broth" or quick stock. This stock, a preparation most commonly used for fish, usually includes something acidic, such as vinegar, wine, or citrus. The poaching liquid also can be a traditional stock or any flavorful liquid, such as tomato water. However your liquid is flavored, so too will be your food. Water is very dense and so is an excellent transmitter of heat to the food. Salmon poached in 180°F/82°C water will cook twice as fast as salmon in a 175°F/80°C oven. Another advantage of water is that it retains heat well—when you get it to the right temperature, it stays there.

The other option for poaching liquid is fat. Halibut in olive oil or duck fat is heavenly. The richness of the oil that coats the fish when you serve it makes oil a superb poaching medium. You can poach duck legs in duck fat or pork belly in lard (or olive oil) to make a confit (see page 286), my one exception to the only-poach-tender-meats rule. Confit is more a subtechnique of poach than of braise. Fat has the advantage over water of keeping more of the flavor in the food. Water pulls the flavor out of the food, but oil doesn't extract flavor as much. Yes, juices are squeezed out of the flesh as it cooks, but meat tends to retain more of its flavor when cooked in fat as opposed to water. The main thing you need to be careful about when you prepare a confit is oil temperature; oil can get much hotter than water, and if you let it get too hot, the meat can become tough and stringy, rather than meltingly tender.

A final category of poach is called shallow poach. Though used seldom at home, it is simple and is a great example of a technique that creates its own sauce (see page 284).

The Importance of Crunch

Contrasting textures are an important part of composing any dish. Keep in mind that poached foods are always soft and delicate. Always try to serve something crunchy along with them, whether crackers, a toasted baguette, or a crunchy vegetable.

SALMON POACHED IN COURT BOUILLON/SERVES 4

Poaching salmon, or poaching most any fish, is an easy way to ensure perfect cooking. The gentle heat, the low temperature, and the fluid environment are a perfect match for the way that fish, delicate by composition, respond to heat. By deep poaching the salmon, you're less likely to overcook it or dry it out. The fish that respond best to poaching are the fattier fish with tightly bound muscle fibers, the strong-swimming and meaty fish: salmon, halibut, pike, snapper, and grouper.

Salmon is commonly poached because it responds so well to the technique. Good salmon properly poached will become almost buttery in flavor and texture. Always flavor the poaching water, or court bouillon, to enhance the flavor of the fish. I like roughly a two-to-one ratio of water to wine if using wine, and a ten-to-one ratio of water to vinegar if using vinegar (though you can make the liquid even more acidic if you wish). Aromatics standard in stock are added to the liquid.

This method works with salmon of any size, such as two fillets or a whole side. Use a pan that just fits the salmon so that you use as little court bouillon as possible. You may need to double the bouillon, depending on the size of your salmon and the size of your pan. It's best to portion the salmon before cooking so that all pieces cook evenly. I prefer to remove the skin beforehand, but you may find it easier to remove it after cooking. The following quantities should be enough for four pieces of salmon fit snugly in a pot. If you're unsure how much to make, put your salmon in the pot and cover with cold water, then measure that quantity of water and make that much court bouillon.

I would serve the salmon with Hollandaise (page 199), a traditional sauce for salmon, or simply with a squeeze of lemon.

VINEGAR COURT BOUILLON
6 cups/1.4 liters water
1 Spanish onion, thinly sliced
2 carrots, thinly sliced
2 bay leaves
Small bunch fresh thyme (optional)
½ to ¾ cup/120 to 180 milliliters white wine vinegar or lemon juice

WINE COURT BOUILLON
4 cups/960 milliliters water
1 Spanish onion, thinly sliced
2 carrots, thinly sliced
2 bay leaves
Small bunch fresh thyme (optional)
2 cups/480 milliliters white wine

One 24-ounce/630-gram side of salmon, pin bones and skin removed

MAKE THE COURT BOUILLON: Combine the water, onion, carrots, bay leaves, and thyme (if using) in a pan just large enough to contain the salmon. Bring the water to a simmer, reduce the heat to low, and cook for 20 to 30 minutes. Raise the heat to high and add the vinegar or wine.

Bring the liquid to 180°F/82°C. Slide the salmon into the pan; it should be completely submerged in the liquid. Cook the salmon until medium-rare, an internal temperature of 135° to 140°F/57° to 60°C, about 10 minutes, depending on the salmon, or longer if you like it completely cooked through. Use a slotted spatula to remove the salmon from the court bouillon and serve.

BEEF TENDERLOIN POACHED IN BEEF STOCK WITH ROOT VEGETABLES/SERVES 4

This is a fancier take on pot-au-feu, the French boiled beef dish, but what makes it special is the lemon vinaigrette, seasoned with garlic, cracked coriander seeds (it's fine to leave some seeds whole, as they give an intriguing crunch and flavor burst), and the amazing umami ingredient, fish sauce. I began making a version of this in the early 1990s after reading a similar recipe in the *New York Times*, but I can't seem to find it. I include the recipe because I like the nature of the poached beef, which we don't normally think of poaching. It's important to use fresh beef stock; anything else would ruin the elegant flavor and texture of the meat. The stock, which should be good to begin with, picks up the flavor of the beef and celery root and leeks to become an intensely flavorful broth served with the finished dish.

This is a wonderful winter dish. It calls for sliced tenderloin, but if you buy a whole tenderloin and trim it yourself, you're left with abundant trim, irregular-shaped pieces that would work beautifully here.

VINAIGRETTE

2 tablespoons lemon juice

2 teaspoons finely minced garlic

2 teaspoons fish sauce

3 tablespoons olive oil

2 teaspoons coriander seeds, toasted and lightly cracked

1 teaspoon butter or oil

2 fat leeks, trimmed, halved, thoroughly rinsed, and thinly sliced in 1-inch/2.5-centimeter pieces

Kosher salt

4 cups/960 milliliters fresh beef stock

2 carrots, sliced or cut on the diagonal

1 large potato, peeled and cut into large slices

1 celery root, cut into large batons (like big french fries)

Freshly ground black pepper

12 slices beef tenderloin, each about ½ inch/ 12 millimeters thick, seasoned with salt and freshly ground black pepper (See the head note about using trim from a whole tenderloin; plan on 6 ounces/170 grams of meat per portion.)

1 tablespoon minced cilantro/fresh coriander

Recipe continues on page 279.
Preparation photographs begin on page 280.

MAKE THE VINAIGRETTE: In a small bowl, combine the lemon juice, garlic, and fish sauce. Let sit for a few minutes so that the garlic has time to give up some of its strength. Whisk in the oil, then add the coriander seeds.

Melt the butter in a 5-quart/4.7-liter pot over medium heat and sweat the leeks, adding a four-finger pinch of salt. Add the stock and bring to a simmer, then reduce the heat to low. Add the carrots and potato and simmer gently for 5 minutes or so. Add the celery root and continue to cook until the vegetables are tender. Taste and adjust the seasoning with salt and pepper.

Add the beef, pressing it down into the stock so that it's submerged. Raise the heat to medium-high and cook the beef just until rare, 1 to 2 minutes. Divide the leeks among 4 warm bowls. Distribute the root vegetables evenly, and top each serving with 3 pieces of beef. Pour the stock over the beef. Stir the vinaigrette and spoon over the beef and vegetables. Garnish with the cilantro/fresh coriander and serve.

1/Bring the beef to room temperature and sweat the leeks with salt.

2/Add the stock.

3/Add the root vegetables.

4/Add the beef.

5/The beef will cook gently.

6/The coriander vinaigrette.

7/Spoon the coriander vinaigrette over the finished dish.

The Best Way to Poach Eggs

Poached eggs are one of many favorite foods to cook. Simple, healthful, and inexpensive, they can be a main ingredient or a substantial garnish on anything from a salad to a soup.

More people than not, it seems, advise adding vinegar to the poaching water, believing that the acidity helps more of the egg white to congeal. I'm not going to say that this is nonsense, since acid does affect protein, but I will argue that adding vinegar to poaching water has no noticeable effect on the egg white, other than that it can make the egg taste sour. Therefore, I do not recommend putting vinegar in poaching water. I poach in plain water. If you want beautiful eggs, understand that an egg white is composed of several different proteins that coagulate at different temperatures and that there is a thin, watery part of an egg white and a thick, viscous part. The thin part is what flies away in wisps and makes the poached egg messy and ill shaped.

For gorgeous poached eggs, follow this method, which I first read about in Harold McGee's invaluable *On Food and Cooking*. Crack each egg into a small ramekin or bowl. Pour the egg into a large perforated spoon and leave it there for a second or two to allow the thin white to fall through the holes, then tilt the spoon to return the egg and thick white to the ramekin.

My only technique is to poach eggs in water that is not boiling or simmering. Bring a pot of water to a boil, reduce the heat to low, and then, when all bubbling subsides, add the eggs. Cook them just long enough for all the egg white to congeal, 3 to 4 minutes. Remove each egg from the water with a perforated or slotted spoon, holding a folded towel beneath the spoon so that the water drains off the egg before you serve it.

WARM ARUGULA SALAD WITH BACON AND POACHED EGGS/SERVES 2

This is my favorite lunch to make for my wife and myself when we can carve out some child-free hours in the middle of the week. It's more than a salad—it's an occasion, a time when Donna and I can focus on each other, alone in a quiet house and are not exhausted from the day as we can be by the time dinner is done and the dishes are clean. I highly recommend that all couples with school-age kids make time for lunch at home, during the week, once or twice a month. Relationships are stronger when people cook together. This salad is so easy to prepare that there's plenty of time to talk. I always serve it with a warm baguette and a Pinot Noir or Shiraz.

4 ounces/115 grams arugula/rocket

4 ounces/115 grams thick bacon, cut into lardons

1 large shallot, sliced

2 large eggs

Red wine vinegar

Balsamic vinegar

Kosher salt

Freshly ground black pepper

Bring a pot of water to a boil for poaching the eggs. Put the arugula in a salad bowl.

Sauté the bacon until crisp on the outside and tender on the inside (see page 241). Add the shallot and cook until wilted and transparent. Spoon the bacon and shallot and as much bacon fat as desired over the arugula. Toss the greens so they are evenly coated with the fat.

Turn the heat under the boiling water to low and add the eggs (see facing page for technique).

Sprinkle the greens with red wine vinegar to taste, 1 to 2 tablespoons. Add a few drops of balsamic vinegar. Season with salt and pepper and divide among plates or large bowls. When the eggs are done, top each salad with a poached egg and serve.

SHALLOW-POACHED WALLEYE WITH WHITE WINE–SHALLOT SAUCE/SERVES 4

Shallow poaching means poaching fish in just a little liquid, so that it's not submerged. This recipe and technique can be used with any fish, but it's best with dense fish that have tightly bundled muscles, such as walleye, grouper, snapper, or halibut, which will retain some bite when cooked.

This is a healthful way to prepare fish, a way to cook it just right, then make a quick sauce in the pan with the liquid that the fish has flavored. Serve the fish and sauce with sautéed zucchini/courgette (see page 240) or roasted cauliflower (see page 246).

2½ tablespoons butter

1 tablespoon all-purpose/plain flour

1 large shallot, minced

1 cup/240 milliliters dry white wine

3 or 4 sprigs fresh thyme (optional but recommended)

4 walleye fillets, about 6 ounces/170 grams each, skin removed

Fine sea salt

¼ lemon

1 tablespoon chopped fresh parsley

In a small bowl, combine 1½ tablespoons of the butter and the flour and knead until the flour is completely incorporated into the butter, to make *beurre manié* (kneaded butter).

In a sauté pan over medium heat, sweat the shallot in the remaining 1 tablespoon butter. Add the wine, ½ cup/120 milliliters water, and the thyme (if using). Bring to a simmer. Lay the fillets in the pan and cover with a lid—preferably a parchment/baking paper lid (see page 170), which allows for some reduction—and poach the fish until just cooked through, 3 to 4 minutes. The liquid should only come halfway up the fish.

Remove the fish to a platter and keep warm in a warm oven or covered with plastic wrap/cling film. Raise the heat to high, swirl in the beurre manié, and cook until it has melted and the sauce has thickened. Taste the sauce and adjust the seasoning with salt or a squeeze of lemon. Serve the fish, spooning some of the sauce over each fillet and sprinkling with parsley.

HALIBUT POACHED IN OLIVE OIL/SERVES 4

I like poaching in olive oil because the results are invariably tasty. Remember that the oil doesn't penetrate the muscle, but only coats the fish, so you're not eating all the oil. The oil helps retain flavors that would be lost if poaching in water. To avoid using too much oil, choose a pan in which the fillets will fit snugly. If you have duck or goose fat on hand, that would make an awesome variation.

Halibut is a wonderful, meaty, flaky fish that goes well with any number of side dishes, including sautéed mushrooms, corn, asparagus, or new potatoes.

4 halibut fillets, about 6 ounces/170 grams each

Olive oil

Fine sea salt

Lemon juice

Choose a pan appropriate for the amount of fish. Fill the pan with enough oil to submerge the fillets. Bring the oil to 150°F/65°C. Submerge the fillets in the oil. Monitor the oil temperature to make sure it stays between 145°F and 155°F/63° and 68°C (it will drop when you put the fillets in). Poach the fillets until heated through to the center, 10 to 15 minutes. As long as you keep the temperature low, you shouldn't need to worry about overcooking the fish.

Remove the fish with a slotted spatula to a rack to drain or to a plate lined with paper towels/absorbent paper. Season with salt and lemon juice and serve.

DUCK LEGS CONFIT/MAKES 8 DUCK LEGS

Simple to prepare and fantastically flavorful, duck confit is one of my all-time favorite preparations. Most important is that a big batch can be prepared ahead. Since the duck will keep in the refrigerator for six months or longer, I always have some on hand for making an excellent last-minute canapé, lunch, or dinner. For instance, duck can replace the bacon in the arugula/rocket salad on page 283.

    The confit method is simple: season the duck legs a day before cooking them; poach them in fat until they are fork tender; allow them to cool submerged in the fat. Confits are traditionally made with the fat of the animal being cooked—duck in duck fat, pork in pork fat—but that's not strictly necessary. At home, where we tend not to keep vats of duck fat, an inexpensive olive oil is a flavorful alternative.

    This recipe is for eight legs, but you can use as many or as few as you wish. I give two ways to season the duck, depending on your preference and the time you want to spend.

SEASONING 1

2 tablespoons kosher salt

2 teaspoons granulated sugar

1 teaspoon freshly cracked black pepper

SEASONING 2

2 tablespoons kosher salt

1 teaspoon freshly cracked black pepper

Pinch of ground cloves

2 pinches of ground cinnamon

4 garlic cloves, smashed with the flat side of a knife

1 tablespoon brown sugar

4 to 8 sprigs fresh thyme

3 bay leaves, broken up

8 duck legs

Olive oil

MAKE THE SEASONING: Combine all the ingredients in a small bowl and stir to distribute evenly.

Place the duck legs in a baking dish or a large plastic bag. Sprinkle with the seasoning to coat the legs evenly, rubbing the seasoning into them. Cover and refrigerate for 18 to 36 hours; halfway through, rub the legs once to redistribute the seasoning.

Preheat the oven to 175° to 200°F/80° to 95°C.

Rinse the seasoning off the duck legs and pat dry. Lay them in an appropriately sized ovenproof pan or dish, and add olive oil to cover. Heat over high heat until the oil reaches 180°F/82°C. Put the pan in the oven, uncovered, and cook the legs for 8 to 12 hours. When the duck legs are fully cooked, they will have sunk to the bottom of the pan and the oil will be clear.

Allow the duck to cool in the pan. Transfer the legs to a container in which they can be covered with the oil. Pour the oil over them.

(Reserve the concentrated meat juices at the bottom of the pan for another use if you wish.) The legs should be completely submerged in oil if you intend to store them for more than a week. Refrigerate until ready to use.

To finish the duck, remove the legs from the oil, being careful not to tear the flesh or skin, which will be fairly delicate. Reheat them, skin-side down, in a nonstick pan until the skin has begun to crisp, then turn and finish cooking until the legs are completely heated through. You can also reheat the legs in a 425°F/220°C/gas 7 oven until completely heated through. The legs are best when the skin is crisp. To ensure crispy skin, deep-fry the legs for 1 to 2 minutes. You can also remove the meat from the bones and sauté it for serving on a salad, croutons, or risotto, with roasted potatoes, or any way you wish.

18

GRILL:
The Flavor of Fire

WE GRILL FOOD OVER OPEN FLAME because fire makes food taste so good. It's not the only reason we grill. We grill because it's too hot in the kitchen to cook. We grill because the power's out, and it's the only way to get heat into the food. Grilling can be a communal act and so we grill to entertain and to share the cooking. We grill because it's fun. But mainly, we grill for flavor.

The key to successful grilling, like all of cooking, is heat management. Grilling is different from other forms of cooking in that the heat is alive. Unlike a 300°F/150°C oven or a medium-high burner, the heat is in continuous flux. Moreover, we don't usually have a temperature gauge, so grilling engages our senses in ways that other forms of cooking don't. We sense how hot a fire is by standing near it, holding a hand over the coals, or sensing the heat on our face (that's a hot fire!). We think ahead about how the food is going to change the fire—whether rendering fat will generate smoke and flames.

The smells of grilling food satisfy us in ways that smells generated by other forms of cooking don't. The smell of chicken being sautéed doesn't come close to delivering the aromatic happiness of chicken on the grill. The smell of hamburgers grilling at a summer barbecue is relaxing.

All this is why grilling can be so much fun—because it engages our bodies and minds more than any other form of cooking.

And this accounts for half the reason I don't like gas grills. When we trade the act of lighting natural materials and waiting for them to become hot embers for the convenience of turning a knob, we're preventing some of those bodily and sensory pleasures available to us when we build and cook over a live fire. The other reason is that we have less control over the cooking when we cook on a gas grill—in fact, when we use a gas grill we give away more control over our cooking than when we use any other kind of heat. We have less control of the direct heat—it tends to be low or high—and we have less control over the ambient heat—the grill is either open or covered, but with large holes that can't be sealed off. Imagine driving a car with only two speeds— would you feel comfortable doing that? It would be a nightmare. That's what cooking on a gas grill is, for me, except I'm not going to kill anyone.

Some preparations, such as a whole grilled chicken, I can't recommend cooking on a gas grill. It's kind of like upside-down broiling in the oven, with all the fat falling on the heating element. Frankly, I don't *always* mind giving up the sensory engagement of a live fire, and am grateful sometimes for the immediate heat of a gas grill. If you do a lot of grilling, gas can't be beat for mid-week, bang-it-out cooking. But I hate the control I relinquish when I cook over gas. There's nothing wrong with gas grills, as long as you recognize that a gas flame below ceramic briquettes is a different kind of heat than live embers, so much so that I almost think of them as separate kinds of cooking.

What I have to say about grill technique applies to gas flames and natural coals alike, but they differ so much that the lessons we learn from grilling over gas are only half as many and half as deep as those we learn when we cook over live coals. Here, I focus on cooking over live coals. Much of this chapter will apply to gas grills, but not all.

The Basics: Three Kinds of Heat

When we grill, we use two categories of heat: direct and indirect—and with indirect, we typically put ambient heat, a subcategory, into play.

Direct means the food is cooked directly over coals. The temperature is hot, and the food is dripping liquid onto the coals, which return flavorful smoke.

Indirect means the food is not directly over hot coals. The side of the food that's on the grill is not getting appreciably more heat than the side away from the heat. It's receiving a gentler, more uniform heat than were it to be directly over coals.

Almost always when we use indirect heat, we cover the grill to take advantage of the strong ambient heat contained in a covered grill. When we use direct heat, we usually don't. We cover food over direct heat to prevent flames and to increase the heat on the top and sides of the food.

How and when to use which? Understand what you're trying to accomplish—think. We grill for two reasons, to cook the food and to flavor the food, and each reason requires a distinct strategy depending on what you're cooking and flavoring. If you're cooking something tender, you don't need to cook it for long, so you usually cook it over direct heat for high flavor (lamb chops). If you're cooking something that you need to make tender, you need to use indirect heat. Most often, because direct heat generates the flavor and indirect heat achieves tenderness, you can use both (see the butterflied/spatchcocked chicken on page 295). Think of your covered grill as a smoke roaster or simply as a really hot oven with smoke in it. Smoke clings to the meat, cooks there, and deepens in flavor.

The last thing you want to consider is how hot you make your fire. Do you want it really hot (resulting in a flavorful crust, desirable for a strip steak)? Or do you want it gentle (so that your food becomes thoroughly tender, desirable for spareribs)?

A number of smaller issues make grilling more or less successful. When you spread out the coals and put the grill rack over it, allow it to get hot before putting food on it (just as you would let a sauté pan get hot), which will help prevent sticking. It's helpful also to coat the rack with

some oil, which prevents sticking. Spray it with vegetable oil or rub it with a vegetable-oil-soaked cloth. Some food benefits from being rubbed with oil first, which helps heat transmission to the food. I rarely use wood chips in normal grilling; I think food gets plenty of flavor from the coals. I prefer regular charcoal briquettes to other fuel sources, but that's a matter of preference. I usually use a charcoal chimney and newspaper to start a fire, but that's a cost issue rather than a flavor issue, as far as I'm concerned. Most grill aficionados think using lighter fluid gives the food a bad flavor, but I grew up with a dad who only used lighter fluid and grilled a lot, so I have a nostalgic fondness for it. I prefer using a chimney, but if I need a large fire—more coals than will fit in a chimney—or am in a hurry, I use lighter fluid.

USEFUL COOKING TOOL: The Cable Thermometer

One of the most useful tools I have for roasting or grilling large cuts of meat is a cable probe thermometer. It gives you certainty in your cooking, whether for a big prime rib or a whole pork loin or even a big loaf of bread. The thermometer is also a terrific tool for monitoring the temperature of a stock you may be slow cooking in your oven. Most cable thermometers come with an alarm that sounds when a desired temperature is reached. It allows me to monitor the temperature of something in my oven from a remote on my desk. It's convenient, but not necessary. The important thing is the probe, which monitors the internal temperature continuously.

But again, the primary concerns when grilling are flavor and texture. Anything that can be sautéed, poached, or roasted can be grilled, including virtually any meat and fish. Fruits such as pears and peaches are excellent grilled. Most vegetables, even lettuces, can be grilled to great effects; the only issue here is whether or not the vegetable would fall through the rack. We grill for flavor, and as you're developing that flavor, you also need to be cooking the food properly, that is, quickly for tender food, slowly for tougher food.

The Sausage Exception:
Tender Food That Needs Indirect Heat

Sausage, one of the most commonly grilled items, is also one of the most difficult to do perfectly. The flavor of smoke goes really well with sausage, so grilling is the best possible way to cook most sausages, but they require special attention. You need to flavor sausages with the fire, but also cook them gently enough that the interior cooks through before the exterior is overcooked. The worst that can happen over live flames is that the sausage cooks too quickly and the expanding air and juices split the casing open, causing all the fat and flavor to fall onto the fire, and generating bitter, unhealthy smoke residue. The result is overcooked dry sausage, or sausage that's overcooked on the outside and raw at the center. Sausage, meat tenderized from the grinding, nevertheless requires some indirect heat, or very low direct heat. To cook sausages, start them over a medium-high flame to get some color on them, and finish them in indirect heat, inside a covered grill.

Creating Indirect Heat:
Setting Up Your Grill

Unless I've got to grill a lot of items at once, I almost always give myself a good amount of cool space on the grill if I need to slow down the cooking—or, more accurately, let the cool interior catch up to the hot exterior of the food.

All this means is that I put enough coals in the grill to cover half the bottom when I spread them out. This gives me a hot area and a cool area, and when I put food onto the cool area and cover the grill, such as for the chicken on page 295, I cook that food in what amounts to a 450°F/230°C smoky oven.

Grilling is all about heat management, so be sure to give yourself options. Build a fire on one half of your grill so that your food can be in any of three different temperature zones: hot direct heat, hot indirect heat, and warm indirect heat (on the cool side of an uncovered grill).

Combination Grilling:
Grill to Start, Finish in the Oven

This is one of the most useful grilling techniques I know. I use it when I want to grill a large piece of meat, one that benefits from the flavor of the grill but also needs a lot of time to cook all the way through. The pork shoulder for the Carolina barbecue on page 97 is a perfect example. So is the grilled prime rib on page 296. The method is also great for cooking a whole beef tenderloin and full pork loin.

The method and the idea are simple. Build a very hot fire (for flavor). Grill the meat over direct heat until it is well seared, and has begun to drip juices and fat that result in smoky heat. Remove it from the grill, place it in a low oven, and cook it until it reaches the desired internal temperature. The flavor of the fire stays on the meat, and even seems to bake in and develop a deeper smoke flavor from the extra time in the heat.

This is an ideal method for entertaining. Often, I'll grill the meat early in the day and finish it later in the oven. You can even grill it a day ahead and keep it chilled in the refrigerator, finishing it when you need it. If you chill the meat, it's important to take it out of the refrigerator long before you need it so that it can come to room temperature before you put it in a low oven.

The Truth About Marinades

They don't tenderize meat, they don't penetrate the meat to any meaningful degree, and alcohol and acids can harm the meat more than they help it. What then do marinades do? They flavor the outside of the meat—at this, they are excellent.

The only way we truly tenderize meat is by pounding it or by cooking it. True, some enzymes and acids can denature protein and penetrate the meat, but what they primarily do to the meat is make the exterior mushy.

Yes, marinades can penetrate the meat over time to some extent, but not very far or efficiently. If you want flavors to penetrate the meat, your best strategy is to use a brine or a salty rub, or include a healthy amount of salt in your marinade.

The alcohol in a marinade in effect cooks the exterior of the meat, and not in a good way. But alcohol can add great flavor to a marinade, so if you want to make a wine marinade, I recommend cooking the wine first to get rid of the alcohol and intensify the flavor of the wine. A white wine marinade is an effective way to flavor the ubiquitous, boneless, skinless chicken breast, the skim milk of the protein world. Red wine makes a great flavoring for beef. Simply cook the wine with some aromatic vegetables and herbs, allow it to cool, and combine it with the meat you're grilling.

When you marinate meat, understand what you're after. Marinades attach themselves to the meat and cook with it, so that when we eat the meat, we eat some of the marinade.

RIP'S OWN MARINADE FOR LONDON BROIL OR FLANK STEAK/MAKES ABOUT 1½ CUPS/360 MILLILITERS MARINADE

My dad's dear friend Peter Zacher claims to have met Don the Beachcomber, originator of the tiki bar, on a beach in Hawaii and secured the famed restaurateur's recipe for the ribs served at his eponymous bar-restaurant. He gave it to my father and called it Peter's Own. My dad fussed with it some and made it his own. The sugar in the marinade gives the beef a flavorful charred crust; the soy balances the sweetness. It's a great example of a marinade flavoring the exterior of the meat. My dad used this for London broil, but it's great with flank or sirloin, ribs, or even chicken. The meat should be marinated for at least 6 hours and may be marinated for up to 3 days.

½ cup/120 milliliters soy sauce

½ cup/120 milliliters ketchup/tomato sauce

¼ cup/50 grams firmly packed brown sugar

4 to 5 garlic cloves, minced or smashed with the flat side of a knife

1 tablespoon Worcestershire sauce

1 tablespoon ginger powder

½ tablespoon onion powder

In a small bowl, combine all the ingredients.

BASIC WHITE WINE MARINADE FOR CHICKEN AND FISH
MAKES 1½ CUPS/360 MILLILITERS MARINADE

The key here is to cook the alcohol out of the wine so it doesn't denature the exterior of the meat. Use this marinade for grilled chicken or for the Sautéed Chicken Breasts with Tarragon Butter on page 231. Marinate the chicken for 6 to 8 hours, fish for 2 to 4 hours. If the chicken must be marinated longer, halve the amount of salt.

1½ cups/360 milliliters good white wine

2 garlic cloves, smashed with the flat side of a knife

¼ onion, sliced

1 teaspoon black peppercorns, crushed on a cutting board with a pan

1 tablespoon tarragon leaves

Kosher salt

Ice or cold water

In a saucepan over high heat, combine the wine, garlic, onion, peppercorns, and tarragon. Season with 1 tablespoon salt. Simmer for 5 minutes. Hold a lit match over the mixture to ignite the remaining alcohol. Continue to simmer until no flames remain, and you can't ignite any alcohol.

Strain the marinade into a measuring cup and add enough ice or cold water to bring the level to 1½ cups/360 milliliters. Return the strained ingredients to the liquid.

BUTTERFLIED CHICKEN WITH LEMON-TARRAGON BUTTER BASTE/SERVES 4

This is a summertime staple in our house that begins in the spring, as welcome as spring after countless roasted chickens throughout the winter. My father, who taught me the pleasures of grilling all the way through the harsh Cleveland winters of my childhood, created the baste, and I've never found a better one. This recipe may be the one instance where I prefer dried tarragon to fresh tarragon—the heat from the fire would kill the fresh. Dad would simply melt the butter and didn't mind that it separated. I use the *beurre monté* technique to keep the butter whole, swirling chunks of butter into the heating lemon juice, then adding the remaining ingredients, because the baste adheres to the chicken better.

The chicken is cooked first over direct heat to give it some immediate color and get the skin rendering some of its fat. Don't walk away for too long, or you're likely to return to find the chicken engulfed in flames. (I don't recommend cooking this or any whole chicken preparation in a gas grill because flaming can be an unavoidable problem.) Please cover the grill if you intend to leave it, to minimize the chance of flames and burnt chicken. After 10 minutes, you turn the bird onto the other side of the grill, skin-side up, and cover to finish cooking over indirect heat, basting frequently so that the smoke from the butter solids and shallot roast into the chicken.

You can reserve the bones for Easy Chicken Stock (page 65) if you wish—they make it deliciously smoky.

One 3- to 4-pound/1.4- to 1.8-kilogram chicken

Kosher salt

Juice from 1 lemon

½ cup/115 grams butter, cut in 4 or 5 chunks

2 tablespoons minced shallot

1 tablespoon dried tarragon

2 tablespoons dry mustard

Rinse the chicken and pat it dry. Remove the wing tips and discard or save for stock. Stand the chicken on its neck and breast, butt-end up. Use a chef's knife to slice down through the ribs on either side of the backbone to remove the backbone. Open up the chicken, and press the breast down to flatten it. Fold the legs in so that the drumsticks run parallel down the center of the chicken. Tie the ends of the drumsticks together with butcher's string. Liberally sprinkle the chicken on both sides with salt.

Build a hot fire large enough to fill half of a grill with a dense layer of coals.

In a small saucepan over medium-high heat, combine the lemon juice and 1 chunk of butter. Swirl or whisk the butter continuously until it's half melted. Add another chunk of butter and keep swirling the butter, adding the remaining chunks as the others melt. When the butter is completely melted, reduce the heat to low and add the shallot, tarragon, and mustard, stirring to combine. Turn the heat off and cover the pan to keep the butter warm.

Spread the coals evenly on one side of the grill. Put the grill rack on to preheat. When it's hot, put the chicken skin-side down over the coals and cook for 10 minutes. Cover the grill if flames begin to flare. Flip the chicken and continue to cook for another 10 minutes. Turn the chicken again so it is skin-side up, and move it to the cool side of the grill. Cover and continue to cook for a total time of about 50 minutes. Turn the chicken and baste the bony side once, and allow the baste to cook on the chicken. Turn the chicken again, baste the skin, and cover the grill. Save one last brushing for after you've taken the chicken off the grill. Allow the chicken to rest for 10 to 20 minutes before carving and serving.

GRILL-ROASTED PRIME RIB/SERVES 6 WITH LEFTOVERS

I don't think there's a better way to cook a rack of beef or a whole beef tenderloin than this combination grill-roast method. It gives the meat great grilled flavor and allows you perfect control of temperatures and timing. I use the method in summer and in winter, during holidays, to serve beef tenderloin sandwiches on a buffet or a rack of beef for a large group of people.

The ribs themselves are an added benefit. You can serve them immediately, but I like to save them, for a second leftover meal the next day. They're delicious spread with some Dijon mustard and bread crumbs, and cayenne if you like the meat hot, then broiled. I buy 1 pound/455 grams per person, which is usually enough to have leftovers.

If you want to do a tenderloin instead of a prime rib, sear the tenderloin on all sides, about 3 minutes per side. Leave at room temperature until you're ready to finish it, or refrigerate it and remove it 3 hours before you want to begin cooking it. Tenderloins will take about 15 minutes per pound to reach rare.

If you want to concentrate the flavors, start preparing this dish 2 to 4 days before you want to serve it by salting the meat and leaving it to dry, uncovered, in the refrigerator.

Serve with Brown Butter Mashed Potatoes (page 146) or Make-Ahead Mushroom Risotto (page 328).

One 6-pound/2.7-kilogram rack of beef

2 to 5 tablespoons kosher salt

2 tablespoons canola or olive oil

2 teaspoons coarsely cracked or chopped black pepper

2 teaspoons coarsely cracked coriander seeds

Rinse the beef and pat it dry. Line an appropriately sized baking sheet/tray or platter with paper towels/absorbent paper. Liberally sprinkle the beef all over with the salt. You should have a nice crust of salt on the exterior. This is best done several days before cooking; refrigerate the beef, uncovered, until the day you cook it.

Remove the beef from the refrigerator 3 to 4 hours before grilling. Rub the beef with the oil and sprinkle all sides with the pepper and the coriander seeds.

Build a hot fire on half of a grill (you'll be searing all sides of the rack of beef). Spread the coals out, put an oiled grill rack over them, and allow it to get hot. Put the beef on the rack over the coals, and cover the grill. Sear the beef on all sides, 3 to 4 minutes per side (covering will keep more smoke on the meat and reduce the flames from the rendering fat). When all sides are seared, move the meat to the cool side of the grill, cover, and cook for another 10 minutes.

If you're serving the beef immediately, preheat the oven to 250°F/120°C/gas ½. Put the beef, ribs-down, in a roasting pan/tray and roast it to an internal temperature of 125°F/52°C for rare or 130°F/54°C for medium-rare. This will take about 15 to 20 minutes per pound, but can vary depending on the internal temperature of the meat when you began cooking it.

(If you're serving the beef the following day, refrigerate it, covered with plastic wrap/cling film. Remove it about 4 hours before you want to cook it, and proceed as directed.)

Allow the meat to rest for 15 to 25 minutes after you remove it from the oven. Remove the beef loin from the ribs, slicing along the ribs downward to remove the loin in one piece. It's best to do this on a carving board with a moat, or channel, around the periphery. The beef will release a lot of juice, which can be spooned over the meat when serving. Slice the meat as desired. If you wish to serve whole pieces on the bone, simply slice them whole and serve with the juices.

GRILLED SPRING VEGETABLES WITH
BALSAMIC VINAIGRETTE/SERVES 4

Grilling vegetables makes them satisfying and complex. So when the first vegetables of the season arrive along with warming weather, I make whole meals out of grilled vegetables. A platter of grilled vegetables and a small side of risotto (see page 328) are a perfect spring meal.

When grilling a variety of vegetables, it's important to build a hot fire on only one side of the grill, leaving plenty of space to hold the cooked vegetables where they'll stay warm but won't overcook. The vegetables here are suggestions. You are limited only by the availability of good produce.

The vinaigrette is flavored with balsamic vinegar because the sweetness pairs beautifully with the charred flavors of the vegetables.

1 summer squash, quartered lengthwise

1 zucchini/courgette, quartered lengthwise

1 sweet onion such as Vidalia, quartered lengthwise through the root end so the wedges stay together on the grill

4 ripe plum tomatoes, halved lengthwise

1 head radicchio, halved lengthwise

12 to 20 asparagus spears (3 to 5 per serving, depending on their size)

Olive oil

BALSAMIC VINAIGRETTE
1½ tablespoons red wine vinegar

1½ tablespoons balsamic vinegar

1 tablespoon minced shallot

½ teaspoon Dijon mustard

Kosher salt

¼ cup/60 milliliters olive oil or canola oil

Build a hot fire on half of a grill.

Rub the vegetables with oil. Spread the coals out over half the grill and cover with the grill rack. Put the squash, zucchini/courgette, and onion over direct heat and sear, 3 to 4 minutes on each side. Move both squash to the cool side of the grill and move the onion to the edge of the heat (they can take a little more cooking). Sear the tomatoes and radicchio, 3 to 4 minutes on each side, then move to the cool side of the grill. Put the asparagus over direct heat and cover the grill. Cook the asparagus for about 2 minutes, then turn the spears. When the spears are tender, remove all the vegetables to a platter.

MAKE THE VINAIGRETTE: In a small bowl, combine the vinegars, shallot, and mustard. Season with a two-finger pinch of salt. Whisk the oil into the vinegar.

Spoon the vinaigrette over the vegetables and serve.

GRILLED PEAR SALAD WITH HONEY-WALNUT VINAIGRETTE/SERVES 4

Grilling fruit is a wonderful preparation. Pineapple, peaches, melon—all are enhanced by the charred flavor. Here, pears are grilled for a summer salad with prosciutto and nuts.

VINAIGRETTE

2 tablespoons lemon juice

2 tablespoons honey

Pinch of cayenne pepper

Kosher salt

2 tablespoons walnut oil or canola oil

¼ lemon

3 pears

Canola oil

4 slices of baguette or good-quality bread

Olive oil

½ pound/225 grams arugula/rocket

4 ounces/115 grams prosciutto, julienned

½ cup/55 grams walnuts, lightly roasted

½ cup/60 grams coarsely grated Parmigiano-Reggiano

Freshly ground black pepper

MAKE THE VINAIGRETTE: In a small bowl, combine the lemon juice, honey, and cayenne. Season with a two-finger pinch of salt. Slowly whisk in the oil.

Build a hot fire on one side of a grill. When it's ready, squeeze the ¼ lemon into a bowl of cold water. Quarter the pears and cut out the cores, keeping the pears in the water as you work. When you're ready to cook the pears, remove them from the water, pat dry, and rub with canola oil. Grill the pears over direct heat until they are nicely marked on the cut sides and are tender. Move the pears to the cool side of the grill (or to a plate, as they don't need to be piping hot). Toast the baguette slices on both sides over the coals. Remove from the grill and brush with olive oil.

In a salad bowl, toss the arugula/rocket with the vinaigrette, reserving 1 to 2 tablespoons. Divide among plates, and garnish with the prosciutto, walnuts, and Parmigiano. Cut each pear wedge in half lengthwise. Arrange the slices on the salad. Drizzle with the remaining vinaigrette and season with pepper. Serve with the baguette slices.

GRILLED BRANZINO WITH FENNEL, LEMON, AND SHALLOT/SERVES 4

Grilling is a great technique for whole fish and fish on the bone. The bone keeps the meat very moist and succulent. The high heat of the grill dehydrates the skin, crisping and browning it, and the fruit and vegetables stuffed in the fish help, along with the bones, to keep the flesh moist.

I recommend serving the fish with the Sautéed Summer Squash on page 240, including in the mix the fennel not used for stuffing the fish. Or accompany the fish with potatoes poached until tender, halved, and stirred with fresh thyme, parsley, and chives and plenty of butter, plus a shaved fennel salad. It's a good idea to serve a wedge of lemon on the side as well. For those who don't like skin, consider setting out a bowl for the skin and bones; most of the bones in this mild, flavorful fish peel right out.

Branzino, a European sea bass, is also an excellent fish to roast whole in a very hot oven, 450°F/230°C/gas 8 (convection if you have it), prepared as below but simply set on a preheated baking sheet/tray.

1 fennel bulb with fronds

Fine sea salt

4 branzino, scales, gills, and pectoral fins removed (Each will be 10 to 12 inches/25 to 30.5 centimeters long and a little under 1 pound/455 grams.)

8 thin lemon slices

1 shallot, thinly sliced

Olive oil

Prepare a very hot fire in a grill, using enough coals to grill all the fish over direct heat.

Remove the fronds from the fennel to use for stuffing the fish. Halve the bulb and cut eight thin slices, also for stuffing the cavity. Lightly salt the fish cavities. Stuff two lemon slices, two fennel slices, the fennel fronds, and some shallot in each fish. (If you're concerned about the garnish falling out when you turn the fish, secure it with two toothpicks.) Rub both sides of the fish with olive oil. Sprinkle both sides with salt.

Rub the grill rack with oil and lay the fish on the rack. Cook until the skin is browned, about 4 minutes. Turn the fish, being careful not to let the stuffing fall out. Cover the grill and cook until the fish is warm in the center. An instant-read thermometer inserted high into the cavity against the spine should read about 140°F/60°C. (The fish, thanks to the bones, can rest for 5 minutes or so while you finish any side dishes, and will remain hot and moist.) Remove and discard the stuffing before serving the fish.

1/*Mise-en-place* for branzino.

2/Stuff the fish with aromatics.

3/When browned on one side, flip the fish.

4/Remove and discard the stuffing before serving the fish.

19

FRY:
The Hottest Heat

BOILING FOOD IN OIL IS ONE OF THE MOST flavorful methods of cooking food and perhaps the most misunderstood and least used at home. We tend to think of fried foods as high in calories, and while there's no denying that deep-fried foods retain some of the calorie-dense oil they're cooked in, when you fry properly, the food should not be overly oily. The oil is not penetrating the dense muscle of a chicken drumstick undergoing deep-frying. Rather, the oil is cooking the water out of the skin and batter and turning them a flavorful, crisp, golden brown as it heats the meat through. When you drop batons of potato into hot oil, the water in the potato boils and vaporizes in countless bubbles, pushing the oil away from the potato.

As my friend Russ Parsons, food editor of the *Los Angeles Times*, writes in his book *How to Read a French Fry*, "At a certain point, depending on the temperature and the food being fried, the exiting steam and the penetrating oil collide and reach an uneasy balance. That is why food that is properly fried has a crisp exterior but a very delicate interior. In reality, the outside is fried, but the inside is steamed."

The high heat is responsible for the flavorful browning, but adding to its benefits is the impact of the density of the oil, which makes the oil an extraordinarily efficient heat transferer. A chicken leg in 350°F/180°C oil cooks two or three times faster than a chicken leg cooked in a 350°F/180°C/gas 4 oven. The density of the oil may also help prevent flavor from being squeezed out of the meat along with the vaporizing water, another reason fried chicken may be more chickeny than roasted chicken.

Although deep-frying food is an efficient technique for making food delicious, a drawback is the cost. Oil is more expensive than the inexpensive hot air of your oven. But frying oil can be strained into a pot or back into the oil container and used again.

To mitigate expense, we can use a second fry technique, called panfrying. Panfrying means cooking food in a shallow amount of oil, not the thin layer used for sautéing, but enough oil so that about half of what you're panfrying is submerged. We use this technique for thinner items such as pork chops or chicken, which we often bread (see page 306). Anything you can panfry—that breaded pork chop, for instance—can be deep-fried, but in most cases this would be a waste of oil, since the basically same effect can be achieved through panfrying.

Both panfrying and deep-frying cook food at very high temperatures uniformly and efficiently. In addition to the added expense of oil, many people avoid deep-frying because they're afraid. Others avoid it because they associate it with high calories, others because of the way the house smells the next day (an exhaust fan really helps!), and still others because they don't like the cleanup.

Why, then, deep-fry? Because deep-fried food is so tasty! If you love to make food delicious, there may be no tastier way of cooking. It's not an everyday technique, but for special occasions, there may be nothing better than fried chicken (see page 307) or Apple-Cinnamon Doughnuts (page 317).

Three Rules for Deep-frying

1/ Always use a large pot, at least 7 quarts/ 6.6 liters, and only fill it a third of the way (you'll need ½ to 3 quarts/2.4 to 2.8 liters oil). The release of voluminous bubbles causes the oil to rise in the pot to as much as twice its volume. Putting too much oil in too small a pot can result in overflowing oil, making a mess or, worse, igniting.

2/Use a thermometer to ensure that you are cooking at the right temperature (usually 350° to 375°F/180° to 190°C) and are not letting the oil get too hot.

3/Don't leave a pot of oil over flame unattended.

That's all there is to it. The biggest safety issue is simply not letting the oil get too hot. Oil should not smoke. When it smokes, it has begun to break down, and the fumes it releases can ignite. Add a little more oil to cool it. If the oil ignites, don't freak out. Simply put a lid on the pot and turn off the burner until the oil has cooled.

There are a few less critical considerations. Peanut/groundnut oil is the best oil for deep frying—it is flavorful and has a high smoke temperature. Canola, corn, and other vegetable oils are fine to use and less expensive than peanut oil.

Don't crowd your pot. Putting in too much food can drop the temperature to the point that your food is not cooking but soaking in oil. Cooking food in plenty of oil also ensures even, thorough cooking and a uniformly crisp exterior.

Perfect French Fries

Potatoes are one of the best reasons to go to the trouble of deep-frying. They are an exception to the practice that almost all foods should be deep-fried at 350° to 375°F/180° to 190°C. To ensure crispy french fries/chips, first blanch them in 275°F/135°C oil for 10 minutes or until tender. Remove them to a rack and allow them to cool (they can be refrigerated or even frozen at this point). When you're ready to complete cooking them, bring the oil to 350° to 375°F/ 180° to 190°C and fry them until golden and crisp. Remove them from the oil, allow the oil to drain off, and then put the fries in a large bowl lined with paper towels/absorbent paper. Flip and toss the fries in the bowl while raining fine grain sea salt down on them. Serve immediately.

Awesome Potato Chips

You need a mandoline or some way of cutting the potatoes uniformly. I use a Benriner mandoline, also called a Japanese mandoline. The key is not to crowd the chips/crisps in the oil, so I do them in one-potato batches.

Bring the oil to 350°F/180°C. Slice the first potato. Working quickly, slip each slice into the oil individually as if you were dealing cards. Have someone join you if possible—the faster you get the slices into the oil, the more evenly they'll cook. Stir them with a spider or basket strainer (I use a big basket strainer, commonly available at Asian markets). While they're cooking, cut the next potato. When the first batch is golden brown, remove the chips from the oil, shaking off the excess, and put in a bowl lined with paper towels/absorbent paper. Shake the bowl aggressively as you salt the chips with fine sea salt. You can keep them warm in a 200°F/ 95°C oven while you make successive batches.

How to Panfry

Pour ¼ to ⅓ inch/6 to 8 millimeters of oil into a pan over high heat. When the oil begins to get wavy and shimmery, it should be hot enough to cook in. If you're unsure, dip a wood chopstick into the oil; it should start bubbling instantly. If it doesn't, the oil is not hot enough. When the oil is hot, add the items you're panfrying. Cook until the underside is golden brown, then turn the food and continue cooking until the second side is golden brown.

Holding Fried Food

One of the advantages of serving fried food is that it holds well in a hot oven. If you've given it a nice protective crust, the interior will stay hot and moist in a warm oven. This is especially valuable when frying tough cuts, or cuts that can take extended heat such as chicken legs. I often put fried foods on a rack and hold them in a

250°F/120°C/gas ½ oven, which is hot enough to keep the exterior crisp and to allow the meat to finish cooking. Steam released by the food can make the exterior soft, so use the convection feature if your oven has it.

Standard Breading Procedure

One of the ways to create a crispy crust on food that doesn't already have one is to bread it. The standard method is to use a flour, egg, and bread crumb trio.

Set up three dishes, the first with flour, and the second with 1 or 2 eggs beaten to uniformity, and the third with bread crumbs. I prefer panko, Japanese bread crumbs that are good for frying because they stay especially dry and crisp. Dip the food in the flour to give it a dry surface. Then dip it in the egg, which will adhere to the dry flour. Next dredge the food in the bread crumbs, which will adhere to the wet egg.

If you'd like an extra-thick crust, or you want to prevent something liquid from leaking out (butter in chicken Kiev, for example, or to make fried ice cream), repeat the process as needed.

Adding seasoning to the flour or the egg is a good way to flavor the crust. Try stirring plenty of black pepper or paprika or onion and garlic powder into the flour, or Sriracha or other hot sauce into the egg, or fresh herbs, depending on what you're cooking.

Reusing and Discarding Oil

Oil you've used for deep-frying can be reused. If you fry often, you may want to designate a pot with a lid as your frying pot and store the oil, covered, in the pot in your pantry. Otherwise, you can strain the oil and store it in its container. If you cook potatoes, oil can be reused numerous times. Oil used for batter-fried foods, especially meats, breaks down very quickly; this oil can only be used once or twice.

It's best not to dump used oil down your drain. Over time, oil can solidify in the pipes and build up to the point that you may require plumbing intervention. Allow spent fry oil to cool and return it to an empty oil container and discard. Some cities have oil disposal or recycling programs.

ROSEMARY-BRINED, BUTTERMILK FRIED CHICKEN

This is the best fried chicken, ever. There, I said it. If it's not, then I want to try yours.

I started paying attention to fried chicken in a serious way when I began work on the book *Ad Hoc at Home*. Ad Hoc is Thomas Keller's Napa Valley restaurant devoted to family meals. It offers one family meal each night, and everyone eats it. The fried chicken is so popular that it is served twice a week. Chefs Jeff Cerciello and Dave Cruz have tried all kinds of methods, mainly centering on the best crust. They decided that the trio of flour, buttermilk, and flour is best, and I agree. But the key here is the brine. Salt keeps the chicken juicy and seasoned, and also helps pull the rosemary deep into the flesh. So even after the rapture from eating the crust has passed, the flavor of the chicken holds you.

This brine, like all brines flavored with aromatics, is best when you bring the ingredients to a simmer in all the water. But if you're like me, sometimes you'll be caught short and need to hurry things along. If you have a scale, you can bring half the water to a simmer with the other brine ingredients, and let the aromatics steep for 20 minutes. Measure the remaining water as ice and pour the brine over the ice. Or simply combine the brine with cold water.

Because so few people make fried chicken at home, I like to serve it to friends. Happily, it's a great do-ahead dish; the chicken will keep well for a couple of hours. You can fry it and then keep it on a rack in a 250°F/120°C/gas ½ oven until you need it. If you have a convection oven, use that feature to keep the crust crisp. The thighs will become delectably tender given the extra time in the low heat. Serve on a platter garnished with branches of deep-fried rosemary and grated lemon zest.

BRINE

1 small onion, thinly sliced

4 garlic cloves, smashed with the flat side of a knife

1 teaspoon vegetable oil

Kosher salt

5 or 6 branches rosemary, each 4 to 5 inches/ 10 to 12 centimeters long

4½ cups/1 liter water

1 lemon, quartered

8 chicken legs, drumsticks and thighs separated

8 chicken wings, wing tips removed

3 cups/420 grams all-purpose/plain flour

3 tablespoons freshly ground black pepper

2 tablespoons paprika

2 tablespoons fine sea salt

2 teaspoons cayenne pepper

2 tablespoons baking powder

2 cups/480 milliliters buttermilk

Oil for deep-frying

Recipe continues on page 309.
Preparation photographs on page 310.

MAKE THE BRINE: In a medium saucepan over medium-high heat, sauté the onion and garlic in the oil until translucent (see sweating, page 69), 3 to 4 minutes. Add 3 tablespoons salt after the onion and garlic have cooked for 30 seconds or so. Add the rosemary and cook to heat it, 30 seconds or so. Add the water and lemon, squeezing the juice from the wedges into the water and removing any seeds. Bring the water to a simmer, stirring to dissolve the salt. Remove from the heat and allow the brine to cool. Refrigerate until chilled.

Place all the chicken pieces in a large, sturdy plastic bag. Set the bag in a large bowl for support. Pour the cooled brine and aromatics into the bag. Seal the bag so that you remove as much air as possible and the chicken is submerged in the brine. Refrigerate for 8 to 24 hours, agitating the bag occasionally to redistribute the brine and the chicken.

Remove the chicken from the brine, rinse under cold water, pat dry, and set on a rack or on paper towels/absorbent paper. The chicken can be refrigerated for up to 3 days before you cook it, or it can be cooked immediately. Ideally, it should be refrigerated, uncovered, for a day to dry out the skin, but usually I can't wait to start cooking it.

Combine the flour, black pepper, paprika, sea salt, cayenne, and baking powder in a bowl. Whisk to distribute the ingredients. Divide this mixture between two bowls. Pour the buttermilk into a third bowl. Set a rack on a baking sheet/tray. Dredge the chicken in the flour, shake off the excess, and set the dusted pieces on the rack. Dip the pieces in the buttermilk, then dredge them aggressively in the second bowl of flour and return them to the rack.

Heat oil in a pan for deep-frying to 350°F/ 180°C. Add as many chicken pieces as you can without crowding the pan. Cook the chicken, turning the pieces occasionally, until they are cooked through, 12 to 15 minutes depending on their size. Remove to a clean rack and allow them to rest for 5 to 10 minutes before serving.

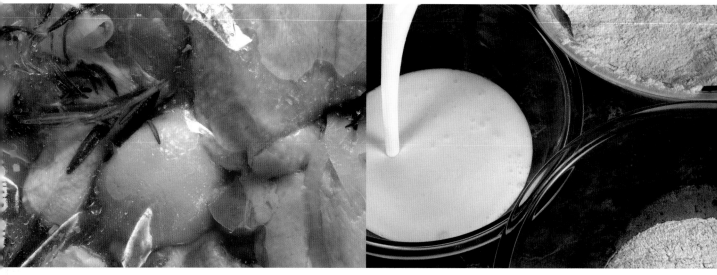

1/Brine the chicken with aromatics.

2/Have the buttermilk and two bowls of flour ready.

3/Use one bowl for plain chicken.

4/Cover thoroughly with flour.

5/Submerge the chicken in the buttermilk.

6/Dredge in the second bowl of flour.

7/Shake loose excess flour.

8/Place on a rack.

FISH TACOS WITH GUACAMOLE AND FRESH SALSA/SERVES 6

Deep-frying battered foods is a commitment, so it's best to save it for special preparations like these fish tacos. My friend and fellow cook Sandy Bergsten, a devotee of the fish taco, puts it best: "I always order them and am downright thrilled when they are the perfect combination of light crispy fish, crunchy lettuce, a dollop of creamy avocado, and just the right drizzle of sauce—it should all come together almost like a vacation in the Caribbean in your mouth. Couple with a cold Corona with a lime and a little sunburn, and they can't be beat."

You can take these to any level you wish. You could use store-bought guacamole and salsa, but both are fairly easy to make and worth the effort. You can also make your own corn tortillas, but if you don't want to do that, I recommend using flour tortillas, which will allow the flavors of the fish and salsa to come through better than store-bought corn tortillas.

The batons of light fish are coated in a tempura batter before they are deep-fried. The fish is cut into thick strips because the idea is to have a good amount of surface area for the batter and crunch but not so much that you lose the flavor of the fish.

FRESH SALSA

3 ripe plum tomatoes, cut into small dice

1 small onion, finely chopped (ideally about half the amount of diced tomato)

1 small jalapeño chile, seeded and finely chopped

1 small garlic clove, minced (about 1 teaspoon)

Kosher salt

Pinch of ground cumin

Fresh lime juice

1 tablespoon roughly chopped cilantro/fresh coriander

GUACAMOLE

1 tablespoon minced shallot

1 tablespoon lime juice

2 ripe avocados

Kosher salt

¾ cup/105 grams cake/soft-wheat flour

¼ cup/35 grams cornstarch/cornflour

1 teaspoon baking powder

1½ pounds/680 grams white fish such as halibut, cod, rockfish, flounder, haddock, hake, or orange roughy, cut into large strips about ¾ by ¾ inch/2 by 2 centimeters

Fine sea salt

Oil for deep-frying

About 1 cup/240 milliliters sparkling water

6 medium tortillas, warmed

1 cup/50 grams julienned iceberg lettuce

½ cup/40 grams torn cilantro/fresh coriander

6 lime wedges

MAKE THE SALSA: At least 30 minutes before you cook the fish, combine the tomatoes, onion, chile, and garlic in a small bowl. Season with a three-finger pinch of salt, the cumin, and lime juice. Toss to combine. Before serving, toss again, add the cilantro/fresh coriander, and toss to combine.

MAKE THE GUACAMOLE: In a small bowl, combine the shallot and lime juice and allow the shallot to macerate for 5 to 10 minutes. Put the avocado flesh in a bowl, discarding the skin and pits. Using a fork or potato masher, mash the avocado until creamy. Season with a good three-finger pinch of salt. Add the shallot mixture and stir to combine. Cover with plastic wrap/cling film, pressing it onto the guacamole if you're making it more than a few hours in advance.

In a bowl large enough to dip the fish, combine the flour, cornstarch/cornflour, and baking powder.

Season the fish with salt. Ready a platter with paper towels/absorbent paper on which to drain the fish.

Heat the oil in a pan for deep-frying to 350°F/180°C.

When the oil is hot, add the sparkling water to the flour mixture and stir with a fork or two chopsticks to form a light batter. The batter should coat the fish lightly, not heavily, but not so lightly that it runs off the fish. If it's too heavy, add a little more water. If you overdid the water, stir in a little more flour. Add the fish strips to the bowl and gently toss to coat them evenly. Lift out the strips, allowing the excess batter to drip for a moment. Lay each strip in the oil. Stir gently to ensure even cooking, turning as necessary. When the strips are a nice even brown, after 2 minutes or so, remove to the platter.

Set a tortilla on each plate. Divide the fish evenly among the tortillas. Garnish each serving with a heaping tablespoon of guacamole, some lettuce, a heaping tablespoon of salsa, and some torn cilantro/fresh coriander. Roll up the tortillas and serve with the lime wedges.

CHIPOTLE-CORN FRITTERS WITH CILANTRO-LIME DIPPING SAUCE/MAKES 15 TO 20 FRITTERS

I was reminded how much I like fritters when I was working on my book *Ratio*. Fritters are fruits or vegetables held together by what is essentially a pancake batter. All I've done here is add some new flavors to the batter. You don't want to use too much batter, as it expands when cooked and the fritters can become heavy and cakey.

DIPPING SAUCE

1 tablespoon minced shallot

1 tablespoon lime juice

1 cup/240 milliliters Mayonnaise (page 119)

¼ cup/20 grams roughly chopped cilantro/ fresh coriander

½ cup/70 grams cake/soft-wheat flour

1 teaspoon baking powder

2 teaspoons ground cumin

Kosher salt

⅓ cup/75 milliliters milk

1 large egg

2 garlic cloves, minced

2 chipotle chiles in adobo sauce, seeded and finely chopped

1 tablespoon adobo sauce

2 cups/300 grams fresh corn kernels

½ cup/50 grams chopped onion

Oil for panfrying

Torn cilantro/fresh coriander

Lime wedges

MAKE THE DIPPING SAUCE: In a small bowl, combine the shallot and lime juice and allow the shallot to macerate for 5 to 10 minutes. Add the mayonnaise and stir to mix. Stir in the cilantro/ fresh coriander.

In a large bowl, combine the flour, baking powder, cumin, and a three-finger pinch of salt. In a small bowl, combine the milk, egg, garlic, chipotle chiles, and adobo sauce and whisk until uniformly mixed. Pour over the flour mixture and whisk just to combine. Put the corn and onion in a separate bowl and add enough batter to just cover.

Heat ½ inch/12 millimeters of oil in a large frying pan. When it's hot and ripply, spoon in the batter, about 2 tablespoons at a time. Cook, turning as needed, until the fritters are golden brown and crisp on the outside and cooked through, 5 to 7 minutes. Remove to a paper towel–/absorbent paper–lined platter and sprinkle with salt.

Serve the fritters garnished with torn cilantro/fresh coriander and accompanied with lime wedges and the dipping sauce.

PANFRIED PORK CHOPS WITH LEMON-CAPER SAUCE

SERVES 4

The best way, to my taste, to cook a pork chop is panfrying. The method here somehow brings out its porkiness. Try to find a local source for pork. Your efforts will be repaid with superior flavor. Otherwise, try to find a store that sources humanely raised pork, such as Whole Foods. The generic grocery store pork often has very little flavor. But if that's the only option, this is definitely the way to cook it. The breading adds flavor and crunch and serves as a barrier to the pork loin, which will dry out if overcooked. I recommend using pork chops that are between 1 and 1½ inches/2.5 to 4 centimeters thick. If they're too thin, they will overcook before a good crust develops.

For even better pork chops, brine them ahead with the sage-garlic brine on page 29. Brining adds flavor and makes the pork juicier. The chops are complemented with a simple sauce.

4 bone-in pork chops

Kosher salt

Freshly ground black pepper

About 1 cup/140 grams all-purpose/plain flour

1 large egg, beaten with a couple of tablespoons of water

1½ cup/175 grams panko bread crumbs

Oil for panfrying

LEMON-CAPER SAUCE

6 tablespoons/85 grams butter

4 lemon slices, each about ⅛ inch/ 3 millimeters thick

3 tablespoons capers

1 tablespoon finely chopped fresh parsley

About 1 hour before cooking the pork chops, remove them from the refrigerator and season liberally on both sides with salt and pepper.

Put the flour, beaten egg, and panko in separate dishes. Dredge each chop in the flour and shake off any excess. Dip in the egg and then dredge in the panko.

Heat ¼ to ½ inch/6 to 12 millimeters oil in a pan over high heat. When the oil is hot and ripply, lay the pork chops in the pan and cook until golden brown, 3 to 4 minutes. Turn the pork chops and cook until golden brown, about 3 to 4 more minutes. Remove to a rack while you make the sauce. (The chops can be put in a 200°F/95°C/ gas ¼ oven for 30 minutes if you want to hold them or need to cook them in batches; if holding them for this long, cook them rare to medium-rare, so that they finish in the oven.)

MAKE THE SAUCE: Put the butter in a small sauté pan over low heat. When it begins to melt, add the lemon slices in a single layer and the capers. Raise the heat to medium-high and swirl the ingredients in the pan. When the butter is piping hot and frothing, add the parsley. Remove from the heat and stir.

Serve the pork chops, topping each with some of the sauce, including a lemon slice, and some capers.

APPLE-CINNAMON DOUGHNUTS/MAKES ABOUT **30** DOUGHNUTS

This is a very easy preparation for what I find to be an addictive pleasure. A quickly made dough called *pâte à choux* (paht ah SHOO)—the dough used to make cream puffs—is loaded with diced apple, fried, and rolled in cinnamon sugar. The doughnuts make a wickedly good start to the day and also a surprisingly easy and impressive passed dessert after dinner.

4 tablespoons/55 grams butter

½ cup/70 grams all-purpose/plain flour

2 large eggs

1 to 1½ cups/120 to 180 grams finely diced, peeled Granny Smith apples (1 to 2 apples)

1½ cups/300 grams sugar

1¼ teaspoons ground cinnamon

Oil for deep-frying

In small saucepan over high heat, combine the butter and ½ cup/120 milliliters water. When the butter has melted and the water comes to a boil, reduce the heat to medium and add the flour. Stir until the flour absorbs the water and becomes a paste. Continue cooking the flour for another 30 seconds or so. Remove from the heat. Stirring rapidly, add the eggs one at a time, and stir until completely incorporated. Let the dough cool enough to handle.

Add the apples to the dough and stir until well combined. Invert a large plastic bag over your hand and scoop out the apple dough. Cut a ½-inch/12-millimeter hole in the corner of the bag.

In a bowl large enough to toss doughnuts, combine the sugar and cinnamon and stir to mix.

Heat oil in a pan for deep-frying to 350°F/180°C. Pipe the dough into the oil, cutting the dough off at roughly 2-inch/5-centimeter intervals, or as desired. (Or shape them using two spoons and drop them into the oil off the spoons.) Cook until golden brown and cooked through, about 3 minutes; remove a doughnut, cut it open, and see if the center is set and warm. Remove the doughnuts from the oil to a bowl lined with paper towels/absorbent paper to drain them, then roll them in the cinnamon sugar. Serve immediately.

Preparation photographs begin on the next page.

1/A basic pâte à choux begins with water and butter.

2/Add the flour.

3/The flour will absorb the water.

4/The paste will pull away from the pan.

5/Beat in the eggs one at a time.

6/Stir until the eggs are completely incorporated.

7/Add the apples.

8/Scoop out the dough with a plastic bag.

9/Slice a corner from the bag.

10/Pipe the dough into the oil.

11/Fry until golden brown.

20

CHILL:
Heat Extraction

WHEN WE DEFINE COOKING, WE ALMOST always do so in terms of applying heat to food. Rarely do we recognize that part of cooking is often taking the heat away. Yes, we take things out of the oven or out of the pan. Anyone can put food into heat. The real skill is the awareness of when to take the heat away from it.

Moreover, few skills teach us as much about the way food and cooking work than understanding the power of stopping or reversing the application of heat. It forces us to pay attention to the stages of cooking—learning how a vegetable goes from hard to tender to soft helps us stop its march to mush. We learn to envision a steak as it goes from soft to firm on the outside and soft on the inside to firm throughout and therefore overcooked. We learn to see and understand the power of "carryover cooking": that food continues to cook well after it's removed from the oven or pan, whether a leg of lamb or a custard. Ultimately we learn to have greater control over our food so that we're more agile in the kitchen.

Restaurant kitchens have mastered heat removal by necessity. If restaurants cooked the way most people do at home, by making a dish from start to finish when it's needed, they would be out of business in days because getting all the food out of the kitchen would take too long. Restaurants function only by cooking much of the food ahead, then cooling it. They're not precooking tender meat and fish, but soups and sauces, vegetables and starches, absolutely. Sometimes a restaurant kitchen will start meat to get a good sear, then finish it in half the time when the order is called.

In a sense, restaurants exist by serving really good leftovers. There's no reason why home cooks can't benefit from the restaurant tactic of precooking food. This will give you more time to spend with your guests at a dinner party or to prepare a nutritious and tasty meal for your family midweek.

The chilling-cooling technique can be divided into two categories: simply removing food from the heat or plunging food into coldness—in other words, gentle, gradual cooling or abrupt cooling.

The gentle or gradual cooling is the inevitable result of serving what you're cooking, but paying attention to it as part of the cooking process makes you a better cook. We know that a blueberry pie has to cool before you can cut into it, and that you don't want to let eggs get cold or they won't be as delicious to eat. We also need to be aware that a chicken or leg of lamb, when pulled from the oven, is like a little heat bomb. It's filled with heat, and it doesn't release this heat quickly. Items that are high in fat tend to hang on to heat as well. Items that have a lot of surface area, a batch of green vegetables, say, or pasta, release their heat quickly.

Usually, when we want to arrest the cooking of something, we put it into a very cold environment, a refrigerator, a freezer, a bowl set in ice, or a bowl of ice water. More times than not, the item we're chilling this way will be heated later. Tender green vegetables are perfect to shock and reheat—they may be better that way, more vividly colored, more precisely cooked.

Pasta can be cooked in advance and shocked in ice water, drained, and tossed with oil. Hard-cooked eggs must be shocked to prevent the exterior of the yolks from turning green from the iron and sulfur in the egg. Large cuts of tender meat can be seared or grilled, then chilled and finished when needed. Vanilla sauce and other custards must be chilled by straining them into a bowl set in ice so that the eggs don't overcook.

Many things shouldn't be cooked and chilled. Fish is not good reheated; most don't even benefit from resting. The same goes for thin, tender cuts of meat, such as veal scaloppine. But generally speaking, most food can be partially cooked, chilled, and reheated with good results.

Carryover Cooking

Carryover cooking is the term used for the impact of the latent heat remaining within cooked food. Food keeps cooking after you take it out of the pan, off the heat, or out of the oven. While many factors determine how long carryover cooking goes on and how many degrees the food will go up, the general rule of thumb is 10°F/5°C. If you are cooking a leg of lamb to 140°F/60°C, for example, remove it from the oven when the internal temperature is 130°F/54°C. The presence of latent heat is also why you don't need to worry that cooked meat allowed to rest will cool too quickly. The bigger the item of food, the more its temperature will rise during carryover cooking, and the longer the heat will remain in that item.

Learning how to shock and reheat is a restaurant kitchen skill that is enormously useful at home.

What Foods Can I Cook in Advance?

Almost all foods can be cooked in advance and reheated, except for those that would dry out or those that rely on a crisp crust—such as lean meat and fish and many fried foods. Some things cook so quickly that even if you wanted to cook them ahead, it's not practical (fresh corn, for example). Also, the faster you cool the food, the better it will reheat.

FRUITS: Any fruit that you would cook—from apples and stone fruits to peppers/capsicums and eggplant/aubergine—can be cooked ahead, chilled, and reheated as needed.

GREEN VEGETABLES: All green vegetables can be cooked in advance, shocked in an ice bath, and reheated. Tender green vegetables (peas, beans, broccoli) that are boiled should be shocked the moment they're done, drained, and stored, covered, on paper towels/absorbent paper. Leafy green vegetables can be cooked and cooled the same way. They can be sautéed and allowed to cool, then refrigerated and later reheated. The same goes for roasted green vegetables. Braising greens, such as kale and collards, can be cooked and reheated.

NONGREEN VEGETABLES: Onions can be cooked in advance. If root vegetables such as carrots or potatoes are to be served hot, it's usually better to keep them warm until you need them rather than refrigerating them. Mushrooms can be cooked in advance, usually over very, very high heat, then gently reheated. Cauliflower and cabbage can be cooked ahead.

GRAINS AND GRAIN PRODUCTS: Just about all foods in this category can be cooked in advance. I routinely cook pasta ahead of time. Rice reheats very well.

DRIED BEANS: All dried beans can be cooked in advance.

MEAT: Thick, tender cuts of meat can be cooked to flavor the exterior, then refrigerated and reheated when needed. Thick, tough cuts of meat are usually improved by being braised, chilled, and reheated.

FISH: As a rule, fish should not be cooked in advance. Shellfish can be cooked, chilled, and eaten cold, but if you want to serve it hot, it's best to cook it when you want to serve it.

Freezing

When we remove heat drastically from food, it freezes. We use freezing to turn a delicious sauce into an even more delicious ice cream. Or we add sugar to a fruit juice and freeze it into sorbet.

Freezing food to preserve it is part of our routine cooking. We once relied on canning and curing to preserve food; now we put it in

Continued on page 326.

1/When using a large volume of salt, weigh it.

2/Your water should be brine strength.

3/Use a lot of water relative to the amount of vegetables you are cooking.

4/The water should maintain a boil when you add the vegetables.

5/Remove the vegetables immediately to an ice bath.

6/The ice bath is equal parts ice and water.

7/For faster chilling, move the vegetables around.

8/Perfect pre-cooked (and shocked) beans—still bright green.

the freezer. We freeze food so routinely that we scarcely think about what a wonderful luxury it is. As happens with most things we take for granted, we forget that freezing can be done well, or done poorly. It's a skill like any other in the kitchen.

There are two parts to thoughtful freezing. The first is to recognize that air is food's enemy in the freezer. Food exposed to air dehydrates and gets freezer burn. Therefore, the better food is wrapped, the less its surface is exposed to air, the longer it will keep in the freezer. The best way to store food in the freezer is by sealing it with a vacuum sealer. A vacuum sealer forces a layer of plastic against the entire surface of the food so that the water stays in the food. If you are not using a vacuum sealer, wrap the food tightly in plastic wrap/cling film and then wrap it a second time or put the wrapped food in a plastic bag. The extra layer will further protect the food from air and also from odors that can creep into the food.

COOKING TIP:

Adding salt to an ice bath lowers the temperature well below freezing. Need to chill a warm bottle of white wine fast? A salt and ice water bath will chill it in 5 minutes.

The second part of thoughtful freezing is not to neglect the food and let it go to waste. How many of us put things in the freezer, forget about them, and let them go bad? I'm a huge offender. Always label food before committing it to the freezer. Organize your freezer regularly to make sure you're using the food you've taken time to wrap and label.

CRISPY BRAISED VEAL BREAST/SERVES 4 TO 6

You often see veal breast stuffed, but I like to braise it until the meat is tender, chill it, then coat it in bread crumbs and fry it until crispy on the outside but still tender and succulent inside. The long braising process results in a heavenly sauce that completes the dish. Some veal breasts are sold boneless; others have the bone and cartilage. If you cook a bone-in cut, remove the bone and cartilage after the breast has been cooked and is cool enough to handle, but is not chilled. I prefer veal breast for its marbling, and I try to buy it bone-in for the richness that the bones add to the finished sauce, but you can substitute veal brisket or even beef brisket if this is all that's available to you. This same technique also works very well with osso bucco.

One 5- to 7-pound/2.3- to 3.2-kilogram veal breast

Kosher salt

Canola oil

1 large Spanish onion, sliced

4 or 5 garlic cloves

1 tablespoon tomato paste/purée

2 bay leaves

2 or 3 carrots, or as needed

4 cups/960 milliliters beef stock, chicken stock, vegetable stock, or water

2 tablespoons butter mixed with 2 tablespoons all-purpose/plain flour

Freshly ground black pepper

About ¼ cup/60 milliliters Dijon mustard

Panko bread crumbs

Gremolata (page 271)

Rinse the veal and pat dry. Sprinkle all over with salt.

Pour ¼ inch/6 millimeters of oil into a Dutch oven or other heavy ovenproof pot just large enough to accommodate the veal. Heat the oil over high heat. When the oil is very hot, sear the veal on all sides. Remove the veal and pour off the oil. Return the veal to the pot. Pack the onion slices beside the veal. Add the garlic, tomato paste/purée, and bay leaves. Pack any open areas around the veal with carrots. Add as little stock as possible but still submerge the veal completely.

Preheat the oven to 275°F/135°C /gas 1.

Bring the liquid to a simmer over medium-high heat. Cover the pot, slide it into the oven, and cook until the veal is fork tender, about 4 hours.

Allow the veal to cool, covered, at room temperature. Carefully remove it from the pot to a cutting board. Remove the bones and cartilage if there are any, then return the veal to the braising liquid and refrigerate it, covered, for 1 to 3 days.

To complete the dish, discard the congealed fat on the surface. Carefully remove the veal breast to a cutting board. Reheat the liquid until it is steaming hot. Strain through a fine-mesh strainer into a small saucepan. Cook the liquid over medium-low heat until reduced by half. Keep over low heat. Just before serving, whisk in the butter-flour paste, and continue to whisk until the sauce has thickened.

Cut the veal breast into four to six rectangular pieces. Season with salt and pepper. Brush the top and bottom of each piece with the Dijon mustard. Press the top and bottom in the panko. Pour ¼ inch/6 millimeters of oil into a sauté pan large enough to contain the veal. Heat over medium-high heat. Add the veal pieces and cook until nicely browned on top and bottom and hot inside, 3 to 4 minutes per side.

Put some of the sauce on each plate and set a piece of veal on top. Garnish with the gremolata and serve.

MAKE-AHEAD MUSHROOM RISOTTO/SERVES 6

Truly great, ethereal risotto typically happens when you make it from start to finish and you have a long history of practicing it and understanding its nuances. This may be why risotto has a reputation for being difficult, or that it requires laborious and painstaking attention. That said, even the most inexperienced cook can make *fantastic* risotto. Moreover, you can start it hours or even a day or two before you need it, and finish it in about 10 minutes. For this reason, risotto is the ideal dish for entertaining. An impressive side dish or vegetarian main course, risotto is truly elegant comfort food.

There's only one risotto dogma I adhere to: fresh stock. Because the process of making risotto involves plenty of liquid that is reduced and absorbed by the rice, whatever you use will be concentrated in the rice and be the dominant color on the canvas. When you concentrate store-bought broths, the worst of their characteristics, especially saltiness, is magnified. When you use fresh stock, all its good characteristics are concentrated. This, more than your skill at the stove, is the secret to excellent risotto. Happily, great stock is easy—see page 65 for Easy Chicken Stock.

This recipe provides the quantities for making risotto for four, but it's best to cook risotto by eye. You don't even need to measure the rice— I simply make one handful of uncooked rice per person. For a lighter, springtime version, replace the mushrooms with diced zucchini/courgette, yellow squash, and red bell pepper/capsicum.

6 tablespoons/85 grams butter

1 medium onion, cut into small dice

Kosher salt

¾ cup/150 grams Arborio or Carnaroli rice

1 cup/240 milliliters dry white wine

3½ cups/840 milliliters chicken or vegetable stock, or as needed

Sautéed Mushrooms (page 236) and any liquid they may have released

¼ cup/60 milliliters heavy/double cream

½ cup/60 grams freshly grated Parmigiano-Reggiano

¼ cup/20 grams minced fresh parsley (optional)

Grated zest of 1 lemon (optional)

In a large sauté pan over medium-high heat, melt 2 tablespoons of the butter. Add the onion and cook, stirring in a three-finger pinch of salt, until the onion is soft and translucent, 1 minute or so. Add the rice and stir. Cook the rice for 2 minutes or so, allowing it to toast. Add the wine and stir continually as it reduces. Raise the heat to high if you wish. Continue stirring after the wine has cooked off. All stirring should be done vigorously to help the rice release its starch, which makes the dish creamy.

Add 1 cup/240 milliliters of the stock and continue stirring until the stock has cooked off and the rice begins to take on a creamy appearance. Add another 1 cup stock and repeat the process. When the stock has cooked off, remove the rice to a plate or a container that will allow it to cool quickly. The edges of the rice kernels should be pale, and the centers should be white; the rice should have a slight crunch. When the rice has cooled, cover it with plastic wrap/cling film and refrigerate it for up to 2 days (though it will be best if used that day).

To finish the risotto, return it to the sauté pan with the remaining stock. Place over high heat and stir until the stock comes to a simmer. Add the mushrooms and stir. When the stock has cooked off, taste the risotto and adjust the seasoning. If the rice is still too al dente, add water or more stock and cook until the rice is soft and creamy but not mushy. Reduce the heat to low and stir in the remaining butter. Add the cream and continue to stir until incorporated. Stir in the Parmigiano-Reggiano. Serve immediately, garnished with the parsley and grated lemon zest, if desired.

DEVILED EGGS/MAKES 48 DEVILED EGG QUARTERS

A deviled egg is one of those items that, whenever I'm offered one, I accept. As soon as I eat it, I think, "Why don't I have these more *often*?" Deviled eggs make a fantastic canapé—satisfying, simple to prepare ahead, and unbeatably affordable. I will take a deviled egg over belabored smoked salmon and caviar on a blini every time. This is more proof that the expense of ingredients doesn't necessarily correlate with a dish's deliciousness.

If there's a problem with deviled eggs, it's that they're customarily served halved, and that's a big portion. How many can you eat? Combine that with their richness, and they can easily be too filling for you and your guests. So I like to quarter them and pipe or spoon the yolk mixture onto the quarters. They make for much more neatly consumed bites. Piping the mixture into the whites is less messy and tedious than using a spoon.

The garnish is up to the cook. I'm happy with some sweet paprika sprinkled on top. If it's holiday time, use some minced parsley. You might add a leaf of tarragon in the summer, or put a crisp delicate crouton on top. You might fold something into the yolk mixture, what chefs call *interior garnish*—macerated minced shallot, or finely diced celery or red onion. Or, if you want to make the eggs fancy (and extend the egg motif), garnish each serving with a small dollop of sevruga caviar or a few salmon eggs.

12 large eggs, preferably at least 1 week old

1 to 1½ tablespoons Dijon mustard

¼ cup/60 milliliters Mayonnaise (page 119)

1½ tablespoons finely minced shallot, macerated in lemon juice (see page 84)

Kosher salt

Freshly ground black pepper

Optional garnishes: 2 teaspoons finely chopped celery, tarragon leaves, small delicate croutons

Cayenne pepper or sweet paprika

Place the eggs in a pan that will hold them in a single layer, but is not so big that the eggs roll around the bottom. Add enough water to cover the eggs by about 1 inch/2.5 centimeters. Bring the water to a boil over high heat. When the water reaches a full boil, take the pan off the heat and cover it. Let the eggs sit in the hot water for 13 minutes if they were at room temperature to begin with or 15 minutes if they were cold.

Lower the eggs into an ice bath (see page 49) and allow them to chill thoroughly, at least 10 minutes. Chilling the eggs is especially critical, as it prevents the yolks from turning green and sulfurish.

Peel the eggs. I like to crack them in the ice bath, because sometimes that makes them easier to peel; very fresh eggs can be difficult. Halve the eggs lengthwise, and scoop the yolks into a bowl, then cut the halves into quarters.

Add the mustard, mayonnaise, and shallot to the yolks and season with ¼ teaspoon salt and several fine grinds of black pepper, and mix until all the ingredients are evenly dispersed and the yolks are creamy. If adding an interior garnish, such as chopped celery, fold it in here.

Put the yolk mixture into a plastic bag. Cut a ¼- to ⅜-inch/6-millimeter to 1-centimeter hole in one corner of the bag. If you have a fluted pastry tip, insert it into the hole. (For making deviled eggs occasionally, this method suffices, but if you prepare them often, you will want to acquire a pastry/piping bag and tips.)

Pipe filling onto each egg quarter. Garnish with a sprinkle of cayenne or sweet paprika, or as desired, and serve.

DEVILED EGGS WITH BLUE CHEESE AND BACON

MAKES 12 DEVILED EGG HALVES

This recipe is from my colleague and chief tester, Marlene Newell. When I first made the eggs and served them at brunch, they were such a hit that I considered it a moral lapse not to include them here. All the ingredients go beautifully together. It's important to finely dice the bacon and chives so they're evenly distributed and don't take over the yolks.

6 eggs, hard-boiled (see facing page), halved or quartered, yolks and whites separated

2 to 3 tablespoons crumbled blue cheese

¼ cup/60 milliliters Mayonnaise (page 119)

2 tablespoons Dijon mustard

1 teaspoon dry mustard

Pinch of cayenne pepper (optional)

2 tablespoons minced fresh chives

3 ounces/85 grams bacon, finely diced and sautéed until crispy

In a small bowl, mash the egg yolks and blue cheese together with a fork or masher. Mix in the mayonnaise, both mustards, and the cayenne (if using). Add half of the chives and half of the bacon, and mix until well combined. Pipe or scoop the yolk mixture into the egg whites. Garnish with the remaining chives and bacon and serve.

CARAMEL-PECAN ICE CREAM

MAKES ABOUT 4 CUPS/960 MILLILITERS ICE CREAM

This ice cream takes the complexity of caramel and marries it with cream. As with many caramel preparations, salt is a critical counterpoint to the sweetness of the sugar. Simple toasted pecans can be used in the ice cream, but I think it is much better with sweet and salty nuts, so candying them is worth the trouble.

1 cup/200 grams sugar

4 tablespoons/55 grams butter

1 cup/240 milliliters heavy/double cream

2 cups/480 milliliters milk

8 large egg yolks

1 teaspoon vanilla

¾ teaspoon kosher salt

3 tablespoons bourbon (optional)

Candied pecans (recipe follows)

Put the sugar in a high-sided, heavy-bottomed saucepan over medium heat. When the sugar begins to melt around the edges, shake the pan to move the sugar around. Slowly stir the melted sugar into the center of the pan. Try not to stir too much, or the sugar may seize up (if it does, keep cooking it; it should eventually melt). Continue to cook until the sugar has dissolved and melted, and the caramel is a clear deep amber. It should read about 320°F/160°C on a candy thermometer. Add the butter and stir until melted. Add the cream and 1 cup/240 milliliters of the milk, and stir to combine. Raise the heat and bring the mixture to a simmer.

Put the egg yolks in a bowl. Whisk about ½ cup/120 milliliters of the hot cream mixture into the yolks, then pour the yolks and cream into the saucepan. Cook until the mixture thickens slightly, just before it returns to a boil. Remove from the heat and add the remaining 1 cup milk, the vanilla, salt, and bourbon (if using). Pour the mixture into a bowl set in ice to stop the cooking.

Thoroughly chill the caramel cream, then freeze it in an ice-cream maker. Transfer the ice cream to a 4-cup/960-milliliter container and stir in the candied pecans.

Candied Pecans/MAKES ABOUT 1½ CUPS/200 GRAMS PECANS

1½ cups/170 grams roughly chopped pecans

¼ cup/60 milliliters corn syrup

4 tablespoons/55 grams butter

2 tablespoons firmly packed brown sugar

Fleur de sel or Maldon salt

Cayenne pepper (optional)

Preheat the oven to 350°F/180°C/gas 4.

Put the pecans in a basket strainer and sift out any nut dust. Combine the corn syrup, butter, and brown sugar in a small saucepan over medium heat. When the butter has melted, add the pecans and stir to coat.

Spread the pecans on a baking sheet/tray and bake, stirring occasionally, for about 15 minutes. They will be very foamy looking at this point. Spread the nuts on parchment/baking paper and, while they are still warm, sprinkle with salt and with a little cayenne, if desired. Allow to cool completely.

Store in an airtight container at room temperature for up to 2 weeks.

GRAPEFRUIT GRANITA/SERVES 4 TO 6

Just because this recipe is so easy doesn't mean it isn't special. A version of grapefruit granita concluded one of the most expensive meals I've ever eaten, at a four-star Manhattan restaurant, and it was perfect. The granita makes a refreshing end to a meal and is especially appreciated in hot weather.

2 cups/480 milliliters freshly squeezed grapefruit juice

2 tablespoons sugar

¼ cup/60 milliliters white wine, preferably Sauvignon Blanc or Riesling (optional)

In a nonreactive, freezer-proof bowl, combine the juice, sugar, and wine (if using). Stir to dissolve the sugar. Put the bowl in the freezer and let the grapefruit juice mixture chill for 30 minutes. Remove the bowl from the freezer and stir the mixture to break up the ice crystals. Return to the freezer and chill for 30 minutes. Again remove the bowl and stir to break up the ice crystals. Repeat until the granita is fully crystallized. Depending on your freezer, the process should take 2 to 2½ hours. Cover, or transfer the granita to another container, cover, and freeze until serving.

EPILOGUE

NOT TOO LONG AGO I DEFENDED IN THE *Huffington Post* a popular television cook derided in food circles for her use of processed food in "from scratch" recipes, saying that when I began cooking, I used powdered mixes for the most basic preparations. I simply didn't know better, and it didn't hurt me. Over the decades, we have been trained by multinational food companies to buy already-cooked products instead of eating food we cook ourselves.

This is a danger: If young cooks only buy the powdered Alfredo sauce and the boxed brownie mix, they don't learn how to make the dishes themselves and may not even recognize that it's an option. But cooking powders out of packets may also be an opportunity for anyone who decides to keep cooking. The more you cook, the better you get, and the better you get, the better you want to become. If you're reading this, it's because you like to cook or you want to get better, or both. Getting better is one of the most enjoyable things about cooking. And one of the facts about cooking is that you can always get better, no matter what level of cook you are—beginner or four-star restaurant chef. So my young self, after using powdered Alfredo mix enough, inevitably wondered what the real version was like and how I could make it.

But how does one actively, rather than passively, get better?

You're already doing it by reading and thinking about cooking. You get better by asking and answering questions about food and cooking, and by comparing two recipes for the same preparation and seeing what ingredients and methods are the same and what ones are different.

You can also become better by following recipes, but not simply by rote. Recipes are not instruction manuals, like the instructions for making a LEGO helicopter. Recipes are like sheet music, the written descriptions of acts that are infinitely nuanced. If you are a cook who can only follow recipes, I recommend reading a recipe, understanding the steps involved, imagining moving through each step in your mind, gathering all your ingredients in their appropriate amounts, then closing the book and cooking the recipe that you've absorbed into your brain and fingers.

In your effort to be a better cook, buy the best food available. To do that, you have to know what good food is. Use your senses, chief among them being common sense. Evaluate the food: Does it look good? Does it smell good? Is it from a good source?

The often-used phrase in restaurant kitchens, "garbage in, garbage out," applies to the home kitchen. If you buy lettuce that's been sitting in a grocery store after spending a week on a truck, that salad is only going to be that good. If you buy lettuce handpicked at a local farm, you can be the best chef in the world simply by not doing too much to it. The best chef can't make a factory-raised pork chop taste as delectable as a chop from a thoughtfully raised and slaughtered pig that you yourself cook. But sources can be deceptive. Grocery stores can have exquisite products, and well-meaning farmers can grow mediocre livestock and plants, or treat them carelessly.

The first secret of great cooking that all chefs know and all home cooks ought to know is that great shopping is a skill to develop like any other.

If you are a beginner, I recommend that you master the fundamentals, the basic skills upon which all cooking rests. These fundamentals are primarily in technique #2 and techniques #14 through 20. Then proceed through the other sections more or less in order. Pastry chefs and bakers need to attend to flour first. Once you understand those fundamentals, work on performing them better.

If you already cook or bake intuitively and instinctively, you are teaching yourself as you go. This is the fastest way to get better: cook and watch what happens. If you know the fundamentals and why they work, you can create your own recipes without books, and you can use books the way chefs do, for ideas and inspiration, unusual pairings, and techniques that might be applied uncommonly.

As you work on fundamentals, go deep rather than broad. This means focusing on one new preparation or technique rather than several at the same time. If you've never made your own pizza or angel food cake, don't try both for the same dinner. Make the pizza, but for dessert choose Auntie Em's lemon bars, which you've made a thousand times and can do with your eyes closed.

Remember that you couldn't always make those lemon bars with your eyes closed. You perfected them over time. Why are chefs so good? They're good not because they're more gifted than you are, but because they've prepared their dishes over and over. They're not artistic geniuses—they just worked really hard. Dishes made by chefs almost never start out as good as what you are served at their restaurant. You, too, should make the same dishes over and over, and then you'll get better at them. Vary the dishes and pay attention to how the changes affect each one.

Pay attention. Pay attention. Pay attention. The best cooks get that way by being more aware than the cook at the next station. Everyone, in a kitchen, in life, is on a different level of awareness. Some people are oblivious, and others are so aware of their surroundings you'd think they have eyes in the back of their heads. Most of us are somewhere in between, but we can become increasingly aware as we pay closer and better attention to what is around us.

The final way to become a better cook, and it's a skill I rarely see acknowledged, is this: remember.

Remember what you just did. Remember how a custard looked and felt when you took it out of the oven; compare it to the one you remember from last month and last year. Remember how soft the steak was when you took it off the fire, how long you let it rest, and what it looked like when you cut into it, how juicy it was, or wasn't. Compare it to the last four or forty that you cooked.

I remember when the importance of remembering became clear to me. I was hanging out in the kitchen of Zuni Café, in San Francisco, one of my favorite restaurants. Its chef, Judy Rodgers, one of the best chef-writers I know, was talking about roasting a leg of lamb. She knew lamb. She knew that if lamb hit an internal temperature of 100°F/38°C within the first 45 minutes of cooking, she was doomed. There was no way it was going to cook properly; the outside would be done before the inside. "I know," she said. "I roasted a leg of lamb once a week for two years at The Union."

She paid attention to all those legs of lamb at that restaurant. She remembered what yesterday's looked like, and the one several months ago that was perfection itself, and the one a year ago that never seemed to finish cooking. She tried to figure out why the lamb behaved as it did. Was it cold when it went into the oven? Or had it sat out for an hour in the warm kitchen? When was it salted, and how was it tied? Judy had amassed years of days of cooking, and she remembered them and put them all to use each time she cooked.

You can, too. A cook is a lot like a physician in this respect. Physicians learn judgment by seeing a lot of different cases, developing a kind of Rolodex of cases in their minds, so that when they're evaluating a new case, they are informed by the patterns they've collected over years of practice. Cooks use experience in much the same way to inform and evaluate the present.

Cooking is easy when you understand the basics and cook with your senses. The world is better when we cook for ourselves.

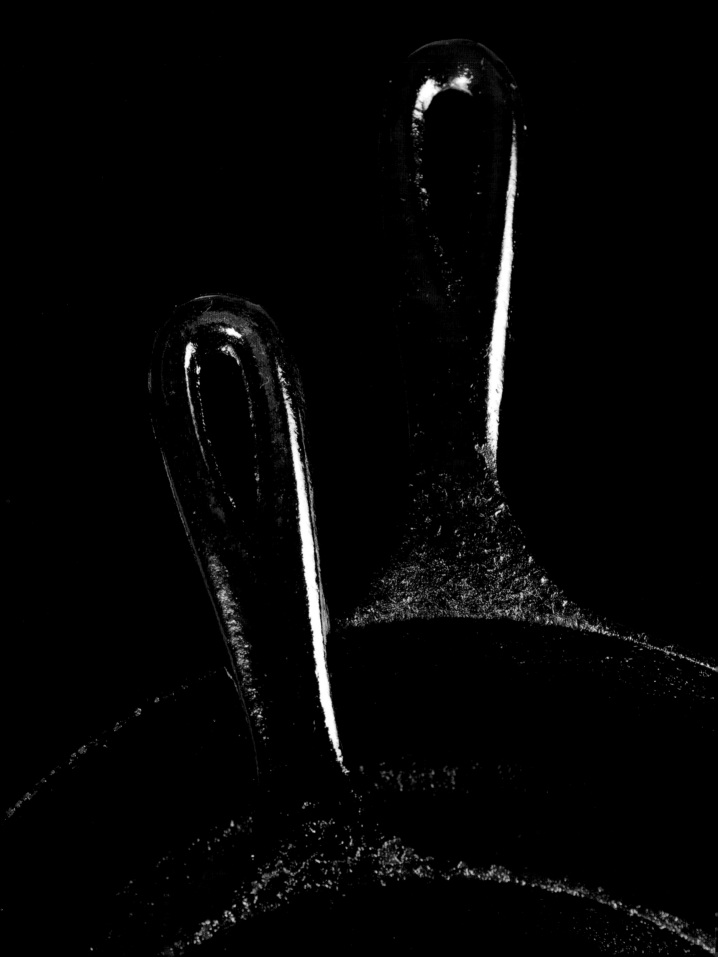

AFTERWORD

THIS BOOK BEGAN ON A PORCH AT THE Greenbrier Resort in White Sulphur Springs, West Virginia, at an annual food writer's symposium, where after a day of seminars I sat with Bill LeBlond, editorial director of food and wine for Chronicle Books, but, more important, a man who likes to cook. Sipping his mint julep, Bill lamented that he didn't feel he was improving as a cook, that he had plateaued. I said I got that sense from a lot of people who like to cook. It's almost inevitable if you cook only from recipes. That was the problem.

"Bill," I said, "there are about twenty techniques that you need to know in order to cook almost anything. If you know those twenty techniques, there's virtually nothing you can't do."

Bill's face lit up. He liked that idea. I'd used the number after only a moment's thought, but I knew it was the right order of magnitude. There weren't just five techniques and there weren't a hundred. There were about twenty.

"Now that's a book," he said, and before we headed off to dinner, he wrote down the title of this book on a piece of Greenbrier stationery, twice. He tore the paper in half, gave one piece to me, and kept one for himself.

The idea for a book on the twenty techniques took hold in my mind that May 2009, and grew over the summer, and by fall, I was ready to begin writing.

◆ ◆ ◆

I began my professional culinary career by accident, or at least not intending to pursue cooking as a profession but rather to pursue writing as a profession. But I fell into cooking by exercising the same muscles that propelled my writing—asking questions.

In my early thirties, I worked for a magazine in Cleveland, Ohio, and initiated a monthly column about cooking with chefs around the city. I'd begun to sense by then that recipes were not a beginning or a source, but the result of something else. That "something else" was what I needed to get at. And it didn't have anything to do with recipes. Recipes were like a ghost itch on an amputated limb. The real thing was somewhere else. And chefs, I figured, knew where that somewhere else was.

A chef I wrote about at the time, Parker Bosley, was one of the more notable chefs in the city, among the first to develop relationships with farmers and to become vocal about the importance of cooking seasonally and eating food grown nearby. When you did that, the simplest dishes were exquisite. A roast chicken for example.

"How do you roast a chicken?" I asked.

"You season it and put it on a bed of mirepoix and—"

"What's mirepoix?" I asked.

He paused to regard me, the writer, with my little notebook and pen. He paused long enough for me to get the point, before explaining that mirepoix was a mixture of onion, carrot, and celery, aromatic vegetables. His contempt for me was like heat coming off him. How can you possibly think you can write about food, he was clearly telling me with that pause, when you don't even know the most basic things about cooking?

That moment more than any other crystallized my recognition that chefs knew things that I didn't, things that weren't in recipes and books. So when I at last set about to write about what chefs knew that we didn't, I went where there were a lot of them. The Culinary Institute of America likely contained the greatest concentration of excellent chefs-per-square-foot anywhere.

I went to cooking school in order to write a book about what you need to know to become a chef. The United States had begun to appreciate the work of chefs as never before, and I hoped to tell a story about what being a chef meant: what you had to know and who you became when you became a chef. I also was looking forward to learning about cooking itself. I'd been an eager cook since I was nine years old and had worked my way through countless recipes. I'd never seen the word *mirepoix* in any of them and yet *not* knowing this word had resulted in withering contempt from a chef I respected. What else didn't I know? This I wanted to find out. I went to culinary school to ask *what* and *why* and *how*.

And I did. I was lucky to land in an intro kitchen with a young American chef who thrived on questions. I interviewed every chef I could. I spent time in their kitchens. I cooked their food. I kept asking questions. And I focused on the things that didn't change. Recipes changed; recipes were fashion, clothing. Some chefs' food was the equivalent of Hermes, others of Levi's and comfortable old T-shirts. One wasn't better than another; each was a matter of choice and disposition. I could study fashion later. What I needed first was the stuff that was bedrock, the stuff that remained fixed and immovable in the work of cooking.

These chefs always, always returned to the same thing: fundamentals.

From my notes:

Chef Rudy Smith, Intro to Hot Foods: "Culinary fundamentals are what it's all about. Everything else is fluff. These fundamentals will carry you through your entire culinary career. It's the fundamentals at every level."

Chef Uwe Hestnar, Skills Kitchens Team Leader, who before handing me a sheet of culinary ratios said, "The culinary fundamentals don't change."

Chef Dan Turgeon, American Bounty: "How to properly cook a green bean. That's what they really hammer into you here. It's really, really important. If you look at these master chefs, all they've really done is mastered those *basic cooking techniques*. They've mastered them. It's what they always do, it becomes habit—every time they cook a green bean, it's a *perfectly* cooked green bean."

Escoffier himself, who created the kitchen brigade and cataloged his preparations in *The Complete Guide to the Art of Modern Cooking*, opens his book with the basic preparations, the fundamentals, "without which," he wrote, "nothing of importance can be attempted."

I loved that line. Without the culinary fundamentals, nothing, *nothing*, of importance can be attempted. Classic chef arrogance and truth.

Those notions stayed with me, and I wrote about them as they played out at this prominent cooking school, but I wondered, Were the fundamentals just a school thing? Were they simply a teaching device? Did they apply to the real world of restaurant chefs? I'd spent plenty of time in restaurant kitchens by then, and I didn't hear people talking about the fundamentals. I saw stocks kept at raging boils and green beans cooked al dente, and no one chanted the culinary fundamentals mantra. Maybe that was just an in-an-ideal-world scenario.

By another accident of good fortune, shortly after I finished my cooking school book, I was invited to the French Laundry restaurant to work with Thomas Keller on his first cookbook. Among chefs, his reputation was peerless. He was born in California, grew up in Florida and Maryland, and had no formal training, and even the French guys were impressed with him. One told me, in a whisper, "He's the best *French* chef in America."

What I found when I arrived in Yountville, in California's Napa Valley, was that Keller hadn't achieved iconic status among cooks and chefs by abandoning culinary fundamentals for new and innovative techniques and dishes. Rather, he'd deepened the fundamentals and taken them to crazy extremes. When we talked about cooking, even *he* talked about green beans.

"How do you cook green beans?" he asked. "You've got a certain amount of water, a certain amount of salt in that water, and a certain amount of green beans relative to that salt and that water. All of it is important."

He wanted a vast kettle of water, salted like the Atlantic, at a raging boil, and so few beans that the water didn't lose its boil when you added them. And if those green beans were fava/broad beans, he didn't want you boiling them first, then peeling them (very easy to do). He wanted you to peel them first (a pain in the neck) and then boil them. One of his cooks spent all morning peeling raw beans. When the cook put them in heavily salted water, there were too many, and not enough water. The water stilled. Keller happened to be passing the stove and saw it. "Toss 'em. Do it again," he told the cook.

I do not recommend that cooks at home go to such lengths as discarding perfectly fine, if not perfect, beans. I tell the story to illustrate how one of the best and most respected chefs in the country got that way—not through innovation so much as through a deepening of the culinary fundamentals. ("How do you like your green beans cooked, Thomas?" I asked. He replied, "I like my green beans cooked through.")

In my last book, I explored the fundamental ratios, that is, how the proportions of basic ingredients create the finished product—what proportions of egg, milk, and flour make a pancake batter rather than a crêpe batter. As I wrote there, knowing a ratio and the base techniques frees you in the kitchen. A ratio is like a key. To turn that key, you need technique. If you understand a handful of basic methods, you can climb to new plateaus.

Moreover, only by reducing cooking to its core techniques can we begin to understand the infinite nuances that contribute to making something good, and what elevates the good to the great. Cooking can be broken down into these few parts, and doing so is enormously useful no matter what level you cook at—whether you're a beginning cook or an accomplished one.

APPENDIX

Mise en place begins with tools. Cooking is a craft, and having the right tools is critical. Regrettably, we've turned cooking tools into fetishes, and we like to fill up our kitchen drawers with gadgets and gewgaws that we use once, if ever, and then abandon. I recommend that no one buy unitaskers, those kitchen devices that serve only one function. There are exceptions, however. A coffee-maker only serves one function, but I use it every day. And I like my corn cutter, which I use only occasionally, and only for cutting corn for a specific dish. So while I have my convictions, tools are ultimately your own choice and deeply personal. I only ask you to think about them.

Here are the tools that, I believe, you must have, and other tools that are good to have if cooking is part of your routine.

Knives

Two good knives, a big one and a little one, are all you need. Brand is not important as long as the knives are good. I use Wüsthof because my cousin gave me a block of the knives for a wedding gift twenty years ago. Shun knives are popular as well. J. A. Henckels knives are good, too. I use an 8-inch/20-centimeter chef's knife and a 3-inch/7.5-centimeter paring knife, and they are going strong all these years later. If you're going to cook throughout your life, invest in these two good knives. Choosing quality is worth it.

A steel is worth buying and learning to use for bringing back the sharp edge on your knives. You should find a grinding service where you can get your knives sharpened once or twice a year.

A bread knife—a long blade with a serrated edge—is good to have. It is very difficult to cut bread or cake with a chef's knife without smashing it.

For using your knives, you need a cutting board. Invest in a big, heavy one. I prefer a wood board at least 1½ inches/4 centimeters thick and 18 by 24 inches/46 by 61 centimeters. You want a board that won't hurt your knives and that won't slide around on your work surface. If your space is confined, choose the biggest, thickest board that will fit. I like wood for its feel and look, and highly recommend it, but polyethelene boards are fine.

Sauté Pans and Frying Pans

Sauté pans, which have sloping sides, are what you'll use for most of your stove-top cooking. You need a small one for sautéing a small item or a small amount, and a big one for cooking larger quantities. Invest in high quality. I recommend All-Clad stainless-steel pans and, if you can afford them, the copper-lined ones, which control the heat very well.

Other manufacturers make good pans, so buy what you like, but be sure the pans are heavy. And just as important, the pans should have metal handles so that they can be used in a hot oven.

A nonstick pan comes in handy on occasion, for eggs or fish, but it should not be your go-to pan. Any nonstick pan you choose should be high quality, or the coating will come off, causing food to stick to the surface. Treat a quality nonstick pan well, and it will last forever.

If you want other pans and can afford them, get them. I wouldn't want to do without my cast-iron pans, for instance—all bought at the flea markets and antique stores. With minutes of work, I restored the rusted pans to their former glory. If you cook for a lot of people, multiple pans are necessary. But as a rule, all you need are two good pans, a big one and a little one.

Saucepans and Dutch Ovens

Once again, I recommend a big one and a little one. The large pot, 6 to 8 quarts/5.7 to 7.5 liters, is for pasta and green vegetables. The smaller pan, 1 to 2 quarts/960 milliliters to 2 liters, is for sauces, soups, rice, and small amounts of pasta and grains. Strictly speaking, that's all you need. If you do a lot of cooking or cook for more than one or two people, having multiple pans is useful.

If you make large quantities of stock, having a pot with a capacity of 16 or 20 quarts/15 or 19 liters comes in handy. It is also practical for blanching quantities of vegetables or cooking lobsters.

One of my all-time favorite cooking vessels is the enameled cast-iron Dutch oven. I couldn't do without mine. It holds heat well, can be used on the stove top or in the oven, and is stick resistant but still browns food well. There's no better vessel in which to braise foods.

The Important Countertop Appliances

STAND MIXER

Of all the countertop appliances, the stand mixer is among the most expensive but also the most important. I use my Kitchen-Aid stand mixer far more than I use a food processor. If you do a lot of cooking, I highly recommend it. Can you get by without it, say, by using a handheld electric mixer and a food processor? Yes, I suppose, but you're giving up some convenience and quality. Doughs are best prepared in a stand mixer fitted with a dough hook. Stand mixers have a lot of power, and the bowl—be sure to get a mixer with at least a 5-quart/4.7-liter bowl—has plenty of room for big batches. The mixer comes with other useful attachments, such as a whisk and grinder.

BLENDER

The blender, my second most-used countertop appliance, is invaluable for changing the texture of food. The Vita-Mix is the best blender made because of the power of its motor, the strength of its blades, and the variability of its speeds—but mainly for its power, which reduces solids to evenly textured purées. The Vita-Mix is expensive; if you have to make choices, put your money into the stand mixer first and purchase a less expensive blender. Regardless of quality, you should have a blender.

FOOD PROCESSOR

Food processors are good for pulverizing solids and semisolids. They are excellent for making bread crumbs, tapenade, bean purée, nut butter, aioli, pesto, and many other preparations. Frankly, though, if you have a stand mixer and a good blender, you'll use those more frequently than a food processor.

ASSORTED VESSELS AND TOOLS

I'm not going to offer an extensive list of all the tools a kitchen should have. Many are obvious or too personal to matter. The tools you have in your kitchen depend on the way you cook and what you feel comfortable using.

I like to have a variety of Pyrex mixing bowls at the ready. They have multiple uses beyond mixing. They can hold ingredients as part of your *mise en place*. Pyrex bowls are heatproof, so you can put one over simmering water to make a double boiler. You can also bake in the bowls.

I'm also a fan of Pyrex measuring cups and recommend having many in various sizes all the way up to 2 quarts/2 liters. The large size is useful not only for measuring but for mixing and storing food. I also end up storing food in the smaller measuring cups.

I use an instant-read thermometer for testing the doneness of meats and other foods, and I use a candy/deep-fry thermometer. I also use a cable thermometer, for keeping an eye on the temperature of something that's in the oven.

I buy three different sizes of deli cups—1 cup/240 milliliters, 2 cups/480 milliliters, and 4 cups/960 milliliters—for *mise en place* and storage. Their uniform sizes makes them easy to stack and store out of the way.

Tools that I wouldn't want to be without include a perforated spoon; a large soup spoon for basting and serving; a heavy, flexible rubber spatula; ¼-cup/60-milliliter and 1-cup/235-milliliter ladles; a good-quality sauce whisk; and a pepper grinder that grinds finely. I'd be cranky if someone took away my flat-edged wood spoon, one of the most-used tools in my kitchen. I keep near my work area a small mortar and pestle for quick grinding and crushing, and a Microplane grater for zesting citrus. I'm never without heavy-duty side towels near the stove for grabbing hot pans because I don't like clunky potholders. And, ever present beside my stove and cutting board are ramekins holding kosher salt.

SOURCES

We live in an extraordinary age for sourcing ingredients. I wonder if soon these pages will become obsolete, given that even the most out-there ingredient can be Googled, purchased over the Internet, and delivered to your door. For instance, when I looked for a source for Ras el Hanout for the braised lamb recipe, I not only found a source recommended by cooking authority Paula Wolfert, I was also able to find a link to a recipe for the spice blend from Wolfert herself.

Also, because of the Internet, I'm usually available for questions via **Ruhlman.com**. Check my site for answers to commonly asked questions, for more information about me, or to contact me by e-mail. To find sources for tools mentioned in this book, such as a scale, thermometers, and mandolins, as well as my own tools such as the All-Strain straining cloths, see **Ruhlman.com/shop**.

Of course, the Internet is so vast we do need some guidance in finding the best products. If you're looking for excellent grits to make shrimp and grits, or excellent polenta, heirloom and organic grains can be ordered from Anson Mills, **AnsonMills.com**.

For all my curing needs, I go to Butcher & Packer, **butcher-packer.com**, which carries an array of sausage-making products and sells sodium nitrite under the name DQ Cure #1, generically referred to as pink salt. It's tinted pink to avoid accidental ingestion, as too much can be very harmful. Sodium nitrite is an important curing salt and antimicrobial agent, and is responsible for the bacon and ham flavor in cured pork. As for foods that are overly charred on the grill/barbecue, bringing food cured with pink salt to very high temperatures has been found to create nitrosamines, which can be carcinogenic. Used as directed and in moderation, sodium nitrite should not present a health concern.

Specialty salts are invaluable for finishing many dishes. While Maldon salt and *fleur de sel* are now commonly available at many specialty stores, a great online source for these and many other salts is The Meadow, **AtTheMeadow.com**.

Yogurt cultures are available in many supermarkets and health food stores. A good online source for them, as well as for many other starters for all kinds of fermented products, is **Leeners.com**.

As one chef told me, one of the most incredible tools in the kitchen is the Internet. It can be a great asset for the home cook as well.

INDEX

Think

Salt

Water

Onion

Acid

Egg

Butter

Dough

Batter

Sugar

Sauce

Vinaigrette

Soup

Sauté

Roast

Braise

Poach

Grill

Fry

Chill